Scala for Java Developers

Build reactive, scalable applications and integrate Java
code with the power of Scala

Thomas Alexandre

[PACKT]
PUBLISHING

open source
community experience distilled

BIRMINGHAM - MUMBAI

Scala for Java Developers

First published: April 2014

Production Reference: 2230414

Published by Packt Publishing Ltd.
Livery Place
35 Livery Street
Birmingham B3 2PB, UK.

ISBN 978-1-78328-363-7

www.packtpub.com

Cover Image by Grégoire Alexandre (contact@gregoirealexandre.com)

Credits

Author
Thomas Alexandre

Reviewers
Carlos Estebes
Tomer Gabel
Eric Le Goff
Steve Perkins
Erik Wallin

Commissioning Editor
Kunal Parikh

Acquisition Editors
Rubal Kaur
Neha Nagwekar

Content Development Editors
Neil Alexander
Larissa Pinto

Technical Editors
Miloni Dutia
Kunal Anil Gaikwad
Kapil Hemnani
Mukul Pawar

Copy Editors
Roshni Banerjee
Deepa Nambiar
Alfida Paiva
Stuti Srivastava
Laxmi Subramanian
Sayanee Mukherjee

Project Coordinator
Akash Poojary

Proofreaders
Simran Bhogal
Paul Hindle
Maria Gould
Stephen Copestake

Indexer
Monica Ajmera Mehta

Graphics
Ronak Dhruv

Production Coordinator
Nilesh Bambardekar

Cover Work
Nilesh Bambardekar

Foreword

I wish this book had been available when I first started my own Scala journey.

As a Java developer, you must have heard a lot about Scala, even if you haven't yet written any Scala code. You must have noticed that Scala is becoming popular and heard vigorous debate about it. As I sat down to write this, I typed "scala is" into Google. The top completions included "scala is awesome", "scala is too complex", and "scala is hard." Understandably, you may be confused by such polarization. You may also have heard arcane, possibly off-putting details about obscure Scala idioms and advanced functional programming.

What you probably have *not* heard is a methodical, impartial attempt to answer questions such as "might Scala make me more productive in my daily work?", "will it be easy for me to pick up Scala?", and ultimately, "Should I switch from Java to Scala?".

Given the size of the Java community and the quality and ubiquity of the JVM, these are vital questions for many of us as developers and to our industry as a whole. Author Thomas Alexandre directly addresses them, presenting solid evidence in the form of working code. He shows that "Scala is awesome", if "awesome" means providing elegant solutions to common, real world problems. He shows that "Scala is *not* hard" by listing the straightforward steps to each of those solutions. He shows how Scala code is usually *less* complex than the familiar Java code to solve the same problem. He equips you to answer the question of whether you want to switch from Java to Scala.

The focus is on solving practical problem, and not on evangelizing language features for its own sake. Thomas explains core concept, such as functional programming, which may be relatively unfamiliar to Java developers, but his main emphasis is building on what the reader already knows. He does all this without a hint of the programming language chauvinism that often causes language debates to shed more heat than light.

The topics covered are all relevant to everyday Java development. Naturally, there is material that is purely Scala related, such as the coverage of REPL (the Scala interactive interpreter that has no Java equivalent). However throughout the book, the emphasis is on how to use Scala to provide better solutions to familiar problem, such as accessing relational data from Java. The coverage of Scala/Java integration is particularly welcome, as the topic seldom gets the attention it deserves. (In fact, Scala is so important partly because it does not force developers to abandon Java and the JVM). The material is up to date: for example, in its coverage of new but important technologies such as Typesafe Activator.

After reading this book, you will be ready to decide for yourself whether Scala is for you. Like Thomas and myself, you may well decide to program in Scala rather than Java when you have a choice. You will then be eager to learn more about functional programming and advanced Scala syntax, and you'll be ready for a more conceptual, reference-oriented book like Martin Odersky's *Programming in Scala*.

Thomas Alexandre provides the perfect starter to whet the appetite of Java developers for the rich main course that Scala has to offer. Bon appetit!

Rod Johnson

Creator of Spring framework

Co-founder of SpringSource

About the Author

Thomas Alexandre is a senior consultant at DevCode, specializing in Java and Scala software development. He is passionate about technology, enthusiastic about sharing knowledge, and is always looking for ways to code more effectively through the adoption of new open source software and standards. In addition to 15 years of Java development, he has focused these past few years on emerging languages and web frameworks such as Groovy and Scala. He also has a Ph.D. in Computer Science from the University of Lille, France, and has spent two years as a postdoc with Carnegie Mellon University in the fields of Security and E-commerce.

Thomas is a certified trainer by Typesafe, the creators of Scala.

Acknowledgments

There are many people who have contributed to this book in one form or another and I would like to thank them for their help.

First, I would like to thank Martin Odersky, the creator of Scala and co-founder of Typesafe for inspiring me through his fantastic lectures and two online courses to write this book. The online courses were written together with Erik Meijer and Roland Kuhn who are also to be thanked. I am also grateful to many Typesafe employees as well as Zengularity for creating and enhancing such amazing technologies. In particular, I would like to thank Viktor Klang and Jonas Bonér for their numerous tweets with links to great reading material and conference talks. Thanks to Heiko Seeberger and Trond Bjerkestrand for certifying me as a Typesafe Trainer for their *Fast Track to Scala* course.

A big thank you to the very active Scala Community for all their contributions in terms of open source projects, talks at user groups, and workshops. The meetups at the Stockholm Scala User Group have been a good source of inspiration as well, thanks.

The team at Packt Publishing has been very helpful and has done a great job at all levels in reviewing and producing this book. In particular, I would like to thank Akash Poojary, Neha Nagwekar, Neil Alexander, Miloni Dutia, Kunal Gaikwad, Mukul Pawar, Kunal Parikh, Rubal Kaur, Apeksha Chitnis, Larissa Pinto, Tomer Gabel, Steve Perkins, Eric Le Goff, and Sumeet Sawant for their extensive participation.

Thank you to my employer and awesome colleagues at DevCode for all the encouragement they have given me. Special thanks go to my colleague Erik Wallin for putting much effort into technical review and producing very useful feedback under a tight schedule. Thank you to all my great friends and ex-colleagues as well for their support.

Finally, I would like to thank my family. My parents have always supported me in everything I have been doing and I would like to thank them for that. I would like to thank my lovely wife Malin and awesome kids Valdemar (four years old) and Edvin (three years old) for their great patience and encouragement. Thank you to my parents-in-law for watching after the kids many a times during the writing of this book.

Also, a big thank you to my talented brother Grégoire for realizing this terrific cover picture.

I would like to express my sincere gratitude to Rod Johnson, creator of the Spring framework and co-founder of SpringSource, for his foreword.

About the Reviewers

Carlos Estebes is the founder of Ehxioz (`http://ehxioz.com/`), a Los Angeles-based software development startup that specializes in developing modern web applications and utilizing the latest web development technologies and methodologies. He has over 10 years of web development experience and holds a B.Sc. in Computer Science from California State University, Los Angeles.

Carlos previously collaborated with Packt Publishing as a technical reviewer in the third edition of *Learning jQuery* and in *jQuery Hotshot*.

Tomer Gabel is a programming junkie and computer history aficionado. He's been around the block a few times before settling at Wix (`http://www.wix.com`) as a system architect. In the last couple of years, he's developed a major crush on Scala, promoting it within the Israeli software industry as part of JJTV (Java & JVM Tel-Aviv user group) and Underscore (Israeli Scala user group), and finally organizing the Scalapeño conference in July 2013.

Eric Le Goff is a senior Java developer and an open source evangelist. Located in Sophia-Antipolis, France, he has more than 15 years of experience in large-scale system designs and server-side development in both startups to established corporate Banking / Trading software, and more recently in Mobile Financial Services. A former board member of the OW2 consortium (an international open source community for infrastructure), he is also a Scala enthusiast certified with the "Functional Programming Principles in Scala" online course delivered by Martin Odersky (École Polytechnique Fédérale de Lausanne).

I'd like to thank my wife Corine for all her support despite her own work constraints. I also want to thank all the contributors and the open source community at large who allow the delivery of reliable and innovative software.

Steve Perkins is the author of *Hibernate Search by Example, Packt Publishing (March 2013)* and has over 15 years of experience working with Enterprise Java. He lives in Atlanta, GA, USA with his wife Amanda and their son Andrew. Steve currently works as an architect at BetterCloud, where he writes software for the Google cloud ecosystem. When he is not writing code, Steve plays the violin in a local community orchestra and enjoys working with music production software.

I would like to thank my parents for all of their support over the years, and Martin Odersky, for opening up my mind to new ways of thinking about code.

Erik Wallin holds an M.Sc. degree in Electrical Engineering and has worked as a software engineer since 2005, mostly on the Java platform. Clean and maintainable code is a great passion for Erik. He likes to use DDD and an expressive language such as Scala to accomplish this.

Erik is employed as an IT consultant at DevCode. He has previously worked for IBM, Nanoradio, and ACE Interactive.

www.PacktPub.com

Support files, eBooks, discount offers, and more

You might want to visit www.PacktPub.com for support files and downloads related to your book.

Did you know that Packt offers eBook versions of every book published, with PDF and ePub files available? You can upgrade to the eBook version at www.PacktPub.com and as a print book customer, you are entitled to a discount on the eBook copy. Get in touch with us at service@packtpub.com for more details.

At www.PacktPub.com, you can also read a collection of free technical articles, sign up for a range of free newsletters and receive exclusive discounts and offers on Packt books and eBooks.

http://PacktLib.PacktPub.com

Do you need instant solutions to your IT questions? PacktLib is Packt's online digital book library. Here, you can access, read and search across Packt's entire library of books.

Why Subscribe?

- Fully searchable across every book published by Packt
- Copy and paste, print and bookmark content
- On demand and accessible via web browser

Free Access for Packt account holders

If you have an account with Packt at www.PacktPub.com, you can use this to access PacktLib today and view nine entirely free books. Simply use your login credentials for immediate access.

Table of Contents

Preface

When I tell people around me that I now program in Scala rather than Java, I often get the question, "So, in simple words, what is the main advantage of using Scala compared to Java?" I tend to respond with this: "<u>With Scala, you reason and program closer to the domain, closer to plain English</u>". **Raising the level of abstraction** is often the terminology employed to describe programs in a more readable and natural way for humans to understand rather than the zeros and ones understood by computers.

As computer systems that are encountered in telecom, manufacturing or financial applications mature and grow, different forms of complexity tend to emerge, which are as follows:

- Complexity due to the addition of supported features, for example, the variety of contract alternatives in an insurance system or the introduction of complicated algorithms to solve new challenges in our evolving society

- Complexity to offset the limitations of technologies; for instance, making a system distributed to handle larger loads or improve reliability and response time

- Accidental complexity, which is introduced because of factors other than the problem at stake, such as integration between legacy systems and not really compatible technologies, short-term workarounds to reach the consumer market in a quicker way, or misunderstanding how a large system is designed as a whole when many resources with different backgrounds and styles are contributing in a short period of time to a large code base

The third complexity is clearly unwanted and should be reduced to a minimum if not eliminated, whereas the other two should remain manageable. Scala tackles all of them, and the complexity of the business domain is something that will be manageable only if a system can be described in code as if it was described in well-written English.

In the past few years, the ability of many languages to express behaviors in a more concise way than the traditional object-oriented way is largely due to the increasing popularity of **functional programming (FP)**, a paradigm that has been around for a very long time but until recently thought of as a competitor to the so-called imperative programming languages such as C or Java. Michael Feathers nicely outlined the apparent duality between the two in the following statement:

> *"OO makes code understandable by encapsulating moving parts. FP makes code understandable by minimizing moving parts."*

The former focuses on breaking a large system into smaller, reusable parts. These parts are easy to reason about as they are modeled according to real-life objects. They use interfaces between them and are meant to encapsulate a mutating state. The latter emphasizes on the combination of functions that have ideally no side effects. It means that their result depends only on their input arguments, leading to minimizing or removing a mutating state in a program.

The declarative nature of FP, supported by Scala, aims at writing code to express "what is to be done" rather than "how to do it". Moreover, the FP approach tends to make algorithms more concise by composing (combining functions together), whereas the imperative approach tends to introduce side effects, that is, changes in the program state that will make it more difficult to see the algorithm, in its whole, in a concise way.

This book will show Java developers that Scala is a significant yet natural evolution from Java by reasoning at a higher level of abstraction. Making the transition should ultimately lead to a more robust, maintainable, and fun software.

The intent of this book is not so much about exploring the design or deep features of the language as well as its exhaustive syntax; there are already a number of excellent books about the Scala language, notably by the creator of the language himself, Martin Odersky, and people working with him at Typesafe.

Our aim is to concentrate on helping current Java developers to get started and feel comfortable using the language, and to make their daily job more productive and fun.

What this book covers

Chapter 1, Programming Interactively within Your Project, provides a short introduction about the **JVM (Java Virtual Machine)** and some of the key features that have made Java successful. We will then start getting our hands dirty and experiment with the Scala **REPL** (short for, **Read Eval Print Loop**), a powerful tool to program interactively. We will introduce some of the powerful constructs of Scala that make programming not only enjoyable but also intuitive and productive.

Chapter 2, Code Integration, is about making Scala and Java code collaborate under the same code base. Topics of interest in this chapter are interoperability between Java and Scala collections, and wrapping existing Java libraries with Scala. Moreover, we will touch on the topic of coding style, in particular, by comparing the well-established Java coding best practices to the more recent Scala guidelines.

Chapter 3, Understanding the Scala Ecosystem, helps you to know the Scala development ecosystem and its surrounding tools, most of which are being more or less inherited from Java. In particular, Java frameworks such as Maven, and IDEs such as Eclipse, cannot be overlooked. In addition to the essential elements of the development cycle, we will cover Scala-specific tools such as SBT, Scala Worksheets, and the introduction of Typesafe's Activator and its templates.

Chapter 4, Testing Tools, is a follow-up on the essential tools of a Scala developer, focusing on reviewing most of the useful tools for unit, integration, and functional testing of test data as well automated property-based testing.

Chapter 5, Getting Started with the Play Framework, will give you a concrete introduction to the Play Framework, where we will show you some of the cool features of Play that make one want to migrate from a more traditional servlet/J2EE model.

Chapter 6, Database Access and the Future of ORM, covers tackling the persistence of data in relational databases, whether you want to reuse well-established technologies such as JPA/Hibernate, or move to more innovative yet promising alternatives such as **SLICK (Scala Language-Integration Connection Kit)**, an interesting alternative to traditional ORM merely based on the power of the Scala language. Moreover, we will see how to reverse-engineer the existing relational databases into Play CRUD applications as a starting point in migrating Java projects.

Chapter 7, Working with Integration and Web Services, covers technologies that are found everywhere in today's Java development. In this chapter, we will explore how integrating with the external systems applies to the Scala world and what the benefits are. Topics included in this chapter relate to Web Services through SOAP XML, REST, and JSON.

Chapter 8, Essential Properties of Modern Applications – Asynchrony and Concurrency, refers to two aspects of scalable applications' development. To achieve better performance, software projects are often encouraged to introduce asynchronous invocations and concurrent code. Through this chapter, we will show that the more functional side of Scala can make this complexity more manageable and maintainable. We will also introduce the Akka framework, a toolkit to simplify the development of concurrent applications.

Chapter 9, Building Reactive Web Applications, takes the previous chapter one step further and introduces a new class of applications that has emerged in the market: reactive applications. They are characterized by their interactivity, the ability to push information to end users, elasticity to adapt to changes in load, and the ability to recover from failures. The aim of this chapter is to build such an app in Play using concepts learned throughout the book as well as emerging technologies such as WebSockets.

Chapter 10, Scala Goodies, concludes this book with some perspectives on the future of web development. For example, Java developers are more and more exposed to JavaScript on the client side, whether they like it or not. Another example is the emergence of **Domain Specific Languages (DSLs)**, a nontrivial task to achieve in Java.

What you need for this book

As Scala runs on the Java Platform **JVM** (short for Java Virtual Machine), you will be able to write and execute the code provided in the book on any computer that supports the Java standard edition. To set up the tools that you need, refer to *Chapter 1, Programming Interactively within Your Project* and *Chapter 3, Understanding the Scala Ecosystem*

Who this book is for

This book is obviously targeted mostly for developers. We want to help Java programmers to get started and feel comfortable with both the syntax of the language and the tools. We will achieve this by exploring progressively some of the new concepts brought by Scala, in particular, how to unify the best of Object-Oriented and functional programming without giving away any of the established and mature technologies built around Java for the past fifteen years.

Conventions

In this book, you will find a number of styles of text that distinguish between different kinds of information. Here are some examples of these styles, and an explanation of their meaning.

Code words in text, database table names, folder names, filenames, file extensions, pathnames, dummy URLs, user input, and Twitter handles are shown as follows: "We can include other contexts through the use of the `include` directive."

A block of code is set as follows:

```
import java.util.*;
public class ListFilteringSample {
    public static void main(String[] args) {
        List<Integer> elements = Arrays.asList(1, 2, 3, 4, 5);
        List<Integer> filteredElements = new ArrayList<Integer>();
        for (Integer element : elements)
            if (element < 4) filteredElements.add(element);
        System.out.println("filteredElements:" + filteredElements);
    }
}
```

When we wish to draw your attention to a particular part of a code block, the relevant lines or items are set in bold:

```
import java.util.*;
public class ListFilteringSample {
    public static void main(String[] args) {
        List<Integer> elements = Arrays.asList(1, 2, 3, 4, 5);
        List<Integer> filteredElements = new ArrayList<Integer>();
        for (Integer element : elements)
            if (element < 4) filteredElements.add(element);
        System.out.println("filteredElements:" + filteredElements);
    }
}
```

Any command-line input or output is written as follows:

```
> ./activator ui
```

New terms and **important words** are shown in bold. Words that you see on the screen, in menus or dialog boxes for example, appear in the text like this: "Out of curiosity, you may click on the **Code view & Open in IDE** tab and then on the **Run** tab."

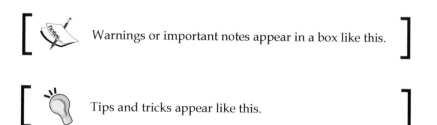

Warnings or important notes appear in a box like this.

Tips and tricks appear like this.

Reader feedback

Feedback from our readers is always welcome. Let us know what you think about this book—what you liked or may have disliked. Reader feedback is important for us to develop titles that you really get the most out of.

To send us general feedback, simply send an e-mail to feedback@packtpub.com, and mention the book title via the subject of your message.

If there is a topic that you have expertise in and you are interested in either writing or contributing to a book, see our author guide on www.packtpub.com/authors.

Customer support

Now that you are the proud owner of a Packt book, we have a number of things to help you to get the most from your purchase.

Downloading the example code

You can download the example code files for all Packt books you have purchased from your account at http://www.packtpub.com. If you purchased this book elsewhere, you can visit http://www.packtpub.com/support and register to have the files e-mailed directly to you.

Errata

Although we have taken every care to ensure the accuracy of our content, mistakes do happen. If you find a mistake in one of our books—maybe a mistake in the text or the code—we would be grateful if you would report this to us. By doing so, you can save other readers from frustration and help us improve subsequent versions of this book. If you find any errata, please report them by visiting http://www.packtpub.com/submit-errata, selecting your book, clicking on the **errata submission form** link, and entering the details of your errata. Once your errata are verified, your submission will be accepted and the errata will be uploaded on our website, or added to any list of existing errata, under the Errata section of that title. Any existing errata can be viewed by selecting your title from http://www.packtpub.com/support.

Piracy

Piracy of copyright material on the Internet is an ongoing problem across all media. At Packt, we take the protection of our copyright and licenses very seriously. If you come across any illegal copies of our works, in any form, on the Internet, please provide us with the location address or website name immediately so that we can pursue a remedy.

Please contact us at copyright@packtpub.com with a link to the suspected pirated material.

We appreciate your help in protecting our authors, and our ability to bring you valuable content.

Questions

You can contact us at questions@packtpub.com if you are having a problem with any aspect of the book, and we will do our best to address it.

1
Programming Interactively within Your Project

Moving away from a well established and mature language such as Java requires some pretty good reasons. Before pragmatically trying out some of the apparent differences between Java and Scala in order to get acquainted with the Scala syntax, we are going to clarify what makes Scala so attractive.

In this chapter, we will cover the following topics:

- The advantages of using Scala for Java projects
- Getting familiar with the syntax of the language through a crash course following an interactive session, including case classes, operations on collections, and a glimpse of some useful features such as options, tuples, maps, pattern matching, and string interpolation

Advantages of using Scala for Java projects

The order of appearance and importance that we propose here only reflects our personal experience since every project and group of programmers usually have their own agenda when it comes to priorities.

More concise and expressive

The ultimate reason why you should adopt Scala is readability: code that is similar to plain English will make it easier for anyone (including yourself) to understand, maintain, and refactor it. Scala is unique in that it unifies the object-oriented side that Java has in order to make code modular with the power of functional languages to express transformations concisely. To illustrate how to achieve conciseness by the introduction of anonymous functions (also called **lambdas**) into the language, take a look at the following line of code:

```
List(1,2,3,4,5) filter (element => element < 4)
```

As a Java programmer, the line might look awkward at first since it does not follow the usual pattern of invoking method signatures on classes. A possible Java translation of the previous code could be as follows:

```
import java.util.*;

public class ListFilteringSample {

  public static void main(String[] args) {

    List<Integer> elements = Arrays.asList(1, 2, 3, 4, 5);

    List<Integer> filteredElements = new ArrayList<Integer>();

    for (Integer element : elements)
      if (element < 4) filteredElements.add(element);

    System.out.println("filteredElements:" + filteredElements);

  }
}
```

We first create a `List` with five integers, then create an empty `List` that will hold the result of the filtering and then loop over the elements of the `List` to retain only the ones that match the `if` predicate (`element < 4`) and finally print out the result. Even if this is straightforward to write, it requires a few lines of code, whereas the Scala line could just be read like the following:

"From the given `List`, filter each element such that this element is lower than 4".

The fact that the code becomes really concise but expressive makes it easier for the programmer to comprehend at once a difficult or lengthy algorithm.

Increased productivity

Having a compiler that performs a lot of type checking and works as a personal assistant, is in our opinion, a significant advantage over languages that check types dynamically at runtime, and the fact that Java is a statically-typed language is probably one of the main reasons that made it so popular in the first place. The Scala compiler belongs to this category as well and goes even further by finding out many of the types automatically, often relieving the programmer from specifying these types explicitly in the code. Moreover, the compiler in your IDE gives instant feedback, and therefore, increases your productivity.

Natural evolution from Java

Scala integrates seamlessly with Java, which is a very attractive feature, to avoid reinventing the wheel. You can start running Scala today in a production environment. Large corporations such as Twitter, LinkedIn, or Foursquare (to name a few) have done that on large-scale deployments for many years now, followed recently by other big players such as Intel or Amazon. Scala compiles to Java bytecode, which means that performance will be comparable. Most of the code that you are running while executing Scala programs is probably Java code, the major difference being what programmers see and the advanced type checking while compiling code.

Better fit for asynchronous and concurrent code

To achieve better performance and handle more load, modern Java frameworks and libraries for web development are now tackling difficult problems that are tied to multi-core architectures and the integration with unpredictable external systems. Scala's incentive to use immutable data structures and functional programming constructs as well as its support for parallel collections has a better chance to succeed in writing concurrent code that will behave correctly. Moreover, Scala's superior type system and macro support enable DSLs for trivially safe asynchronous constructs, for example, composable futures and asynchronous language extensions.

In summary, Scala is the only language that has it all. It is statically typed, runs on the JVM and is totally Java compatible, is both object-oriented and functional, and is not verbose, thereby leading to better productivity, less maintenance, and therefore more fun.

If you are now getting impatient to start experimenting with the promising features of Scala that were briefly described previously, this is a good time to open a browser, access the Typesafe page URL at `http://www.typesafe.com/platform/getstarted`, and download the Typesafe Activator.

The intent of the rest of the chapter is to incrementally introduce some of the basic concepts of Scala by typing commands in an interactive shell and get direct feedback from the compiler. This method of learning by experimentation should feel like a breath of fresh air and has already proven to be a very effective way of learning the syntax and useful constructs of the language. While Scala continues to evolve at École Polytechnique Fédérale de Lausanne (EPFL), many large and small corporations are now taking advantage of the features of the Typesafe platform.

As stated on their website, the Typesafe Activator is "a local web and command-line tool that helps developers get started with the Typesafe platform". We will cover the Activator in more detail in a later chapter dedicated to programming tools, but for now, we will only take the shortest path in getting up and running and get familiar with some of the syntax of the language.

You should now be able to extract the downloaded zip archive to your system in a directory of your choice.

Locate the activator script within the extracted archive and either right-click on it and select **Open** if you are running Windows or enter the following command in a terminal window if you are on Linux/Mac:

```
> ./activator ui
```

In both cases, this will start the Activator UI in a browser window.

In the **New application** section of the HTML page of the Activator, click on the `[Basics] Hello-Scala!` template.

Notice the **Location** field of the HTML form in the following screenshot. It indicates where your project will be created:

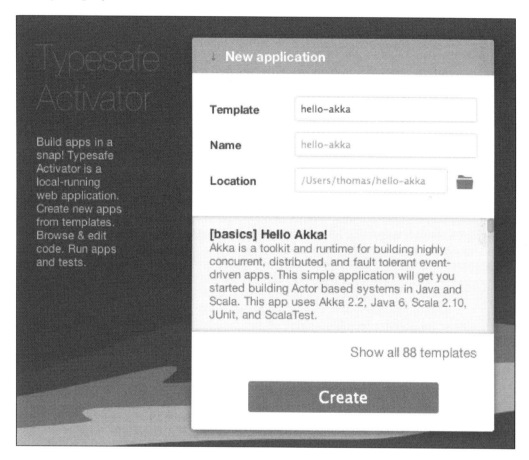

At present, you don't need to pay too much attention to all of the things that happen in the background nor to the generated structure of the project. Out of curiosity, you may click on the **Code view & Open in IDE** tab and then on the **Run** tab to execute this Hello World Scala project, which should print, well, **"Hello, world !"**.

...l window and navigate to the root directory of the *hello-scala* project
...eated, by entering the following command on the command line
... project is under `C:\Users\Thomas\hello-scala`):

```
\Thomas\hello-scala
as\hello-scala> activator console
```

...... will start the Scala interpreter, also known as Scala **REPL**
(**Read-Eval-Print-Loop**), a simple command-line tool to program interactively.

Learning Scala through the REPL

As a Java developer, an REPL may be new to you since there is no such thing for
the Java language. It used to refer to the Lisp language interactive environment,
and today, equivalent tools are available for many programming languages such
as JavaScript, Clojure, Ruby, and Scala. It consists of a command-line shell where
you can enter one or more expressions rather than complete files and get immediate
feedback by evaluating the result. The REPL is a fantastic tool that helps us to learn
all the Scala syntax because it compiles and executes every statement that you write
using the full power of the compiler. In such an interactive environment, you get
instant feedback on every line of code you write.

If you are new to Scala, we recommend that you carefully follow this REPL session
as it will give you a lot of useful knowledge for programming with Scala.

Let's dive into some of the most apparent differences between Java and Scala in
order to get acquainted with the Scala syntax.

Declaring val/var variables

In Java, you would declare a new variable by putting in order its type, followed by
the name, and then the optional value:

```
String yourPast = "Good Java Programmer";
```

In Scala, the order of declaring the variable name and type is inverted, with the name
appearing before its type. Let's enter the following line into the REPL:

```
scala> val yourPast : String = "Good Java Programmer"  [Hit Enter]
yourPast : String = "Good Java Programmer"
```

Inverting the order of declaring the variables, type, and name as compared to Java
might at first seem a strange idea if you want to make it as easy as possible for a Java
developer to grab the Scala syntax. However, it makes sense for several reasons:

- The Scala compiler, in this case, is able to deduct the type automatically. You could (and probably should, for conciseness) omit this type by entering the equivalent but shorter line of code instead:

```
scala> val yourPast = "Good Java Programmer"
yourPast : String = "Good Java Programmer"
```

This is the most basic illustration of what is called **Type Inference**, and you will see that the Scala compiler will try to deduct types whenever it can. If we had omitted this optional type but followed the Java syntax, the parsing done by the compiler would have been more difficult to implement.

- In our opinion, it is more important to know a variable name than its type in order to understand the flow of a program (and therefore make it appear first); for instance, if you deal with a variable representing a **social security number (ssn)**, we think the term ssn is more valuable than knowing if it is represented as a string or an integer or any other type.

You probably noticed the `val` variable in front of the declaration; it means that we explicitly declare the variable as immutable. We can try to modify it as shown in the following code snippet:

```
scala> yourPast = "Great Scala Programmer"
<console>:8: error: reassignment to val
  yourPast = "Great Scala Programmer"
           ^
```

The preceding code will not only give you a clear explanation of what was wrong but also the exact place where the parser did not agree (notice the ^ character precisely showing where the error lies in the line).

If we want to create a mutable variable instead, we should declare it with `var` as shown in the following code snippet:

```
scala> var yourFuture = "Good Java Programmer"
yourFuture: String = "Good Java Programmer"
scala> yourFuture = "Great Scala Programmer"
yourFuture: String = "Great Scala Programmer"
```

In summary, you cannot change `yourPast` but you can change `yourFuture`!

The semicolon at the end of the lines is optional in Scala; a small but pleasant feature of the language.

Let's move on to an important difference. In Java, you have primitive types such as int, char, or boolean (eight in total), as well as operators to manipulate data such as + or >. In Scala, there are only classes and objects, making Scala more "object-oriented" than Java in some way. For instance, enter the following value into the REPL:

```
scala> 3
res1: Int = 3
```

By default, the compiler created an immutable Int (integer) variable with the res1 name (that is, result 1) in case you need to reuse it later on.

Now, enter the following line in REPL:

```
scala> 3 + 2
res2: Int = 5
```

The preceding code resembles the usage of an operator (as in Java) but is in fact the invocation of a method named + called on object 3 with the input parameter 2, equivalent to the slightly less clear statement:

```
scala> (3).+(2)
res3: Int = 5
```

Syntactic sugar (that is, syntax designed to make things easier to read or express) was added here by removing the necessity to specify the parenthesis. This also means that we can now implement similar methods on our own defined types to express code elegantly. For example, we can express the addition of two Money objects of different currencies (note that the Money type does not exist in the default Scala library) by simply stating Money(10,"EUR") + Money(15,"USD"). Let's try to do that in the REPL.

Defining classes

First, we can define a new class Money that has a constructor parameter named amount of type Int as follows:

```
scala> class Money(amount:Int)
defined class Money
```

 Scala has a special syntax for declaring constructor parameters that will be explored in more depth later.

Now, we can create a Money instance as shown in the following code snippet:

```
scala> val notMuch = new Money(2)
notMuch : Money = Money@76eb235
```

You get back an object with its displayed reference. The REPL provides you with **TAB completion**, so type notMuch. and hit the *Tab* key:

```
scala> notMuch. [Tab]
asInstanceOf isInstanceOf toString
```

By using the preceding autocompletion, you will get suggestions of the available methods for that class, as you will get with most Java IDEs.

As shown previously, you can construct new instances of Money by invoking the constructor, but you do not have access to the amount variable since it is not a field. To make it a field of the Money class, you have to add a 'val' or 'var' declaration in front of it, as shown in the following code snippet:

```
scala> class Money(val amount:Int)
defined class Money
```

This time, instead of again typing the line that created an instance, we will use the up arrow (the shortcut to display previous expressions: the history of the console) and navigate to it:

```
scala> val notMuch = new Money(2)
notMuch : Money = Money@73cd15da
```

 The *Tab* key can be pressed at any time in the REPL and provides autocompletion.

Invoking autocompletion on this new instance will display the following:

```
scala> notMuch. [Tab ]
amount asInstanceOf isInstanceOf toString
```

So, we can simply read the value of the getter for this amount field by referring to it:

```
scala> notMuch.amount
res4: Int = 2
```

Similarly, if we had declared the amount to be a var variable instead of val, we would also have access to the setter method:

```
scala> class Money(var amount:Int)
defined class Money
scala> val notMuch = new Money(2)
notMuch: Money = Money@6517ff0
scala> notMuch. [ Tab ]
amount    amount_=    asInstanceOf    isInstanceOf    toString
```

The setter method is invoked when we use the following code snippet:

```
scala> notMuch.amount=3
notMuch.amount: Int = 3
```

Explaining case classes

As Java developers, we are accustomed to the JavaBean style domain classes that not only include fields with getters and setters but also constructors as well as hashCode, equals, and toString methods, as shown in the following code snippet:

```
public class Money {

    private Integer amount;
    private String currency;

    public Money(Integer amount, String currency) {

        this.amount = amount;
        this.currency = currency;

    }

    public Integer getAmount() {
        return amount;
    }

    public void setAmount(Integer amount) {
        this.amount = amount;
    }

    public String getCurrency() {
        return currency;
    }
```

```java
    public void setCurrency(String currency) {
        this.currency = currency;
    }


    @Override
    public int hashCode() {
        int hash = 5;
        hash = 29 * hash + (this.amount != null ? this.amount.
hashCode() : 0);
        hash = 29 * hash + (this.currency != null ? this.currency.
hashCode() : 0);
        return hash;
    }


    @Override
    public boolean equals(Object obj) {

        if (obj == null) {
            return false;
        }

        if (getClass() != obj.getClass()) {
            return false;
        }

        final Money other = (Money) obj;
        return true;
    }


    @Override
    public String toString() {
        return "Money{" + "amount=" + amount + ", currency=" +
currency + '}';

    }
}
```

Achieving this in Scala is very straightforward and only requires the addition of the `case` word in front of the class declaration:

```scala
scala> case class Money(amount:Int=1, currency:String="USD")
defined class Money
```

We have just defined a class Money with two immutable fields named amount and currency with default values.

Without going too much into the details of the case classes, we can say that in addition to the preceding features of a traditional JavaBean style domain class, they have a powerful mechanism for pattern matching. The case word is analogous to the switch statement in Java, though it is more flexible, as we will see later on. The case classes contain additional features among which one is a factory method to create instances (no need to use the new keyword to create one).

By default, the fields declared in Scala classes are public, unlike Java, where they have a package-private scope, defined between private and protected. We could have written case class Money(private val amount: Int, private val currency: String) to make them private instead, or used var instead of val to make the fields mutable.

The shortest way to create an instance of Money is very straightforward:

```
scala> val defaultAmount = Money()

defaultAmount: Money = Money(1,USD)

scala> val fifteenDollars = Money(15,"USD")

fifteenDollars: Money = Money(15,USD)

scala> val fifteenDollars = Money(15)

fifteenDollars: Money = Money(15,USD)
```

In the previous instance declaration, since only one parameter is given instead of two, the compiler matched it against the first declared field, that is, amount. Since the value 15 is of the same type as amount (that is, Integer), the compiler was able to populate the instance with this amount, using the default value "USD" as the currency.

Unlike the amount variable, invoking the Money constructor with the sole currency parameter will fail, as seen in the following statement:

```
scala> val someEuros = Money("EUR")

<console>:9: error: type mismatch;

  found    : String("EUR")

  required: Int

        val someEuros = Money("EUR")
                              ^
```

The preceding code does not work because the compiler could not guess which parameter we were referring to, and therefore tried to match them in order of declaration. To be able to use the default value for amount with the given "EUR" string, we need to include the parameter name explicitly, as shown in the following code snippet:

```
scala> val someEuros = Money(currency="EUR")
someEuros: Money = Money(1,EUR)
```

We could therefore also mark all parameters explicitly, which can be recommended when there are many parameters as shown in the following code snippet:

```
scala> val twentyEuros = Money(amount=20,currency="EUR")
twentyEuros: Money = Money(20,EUR)
```

An additional useful method when constructing instances is the copy method, which creates a new instance out of the original and eventually replaces given parameters:

```
scala> val tenEuros = twentyEuros.copy(10)
tenEuros: Money = Money(10,EUR)
```

We can use the copy method with explicitly named parameters, as follows:

```
scala> val twentyDollars = twentyEuros.copy(currency="USD")
twentyDollars: Money = Money(20,USD)
```

The copy method can be very useful when writing test fixtures, in particular, when the mockup instances to be initialized have constructors with many fields that are similar.

Let's move on by creating an addition operation of our Money class. For simplicity, we will pretend for a moment that we only deal with amounts of the same currency, the default USD.

In Java, we would probably add such a method with the following signature and simple content:

```
public class Money {

    Integer amount;
    String currency;

    public Money(Integer amount, String currency) {
        this.amount = amount;
        this.currency = currency;
    }

    public Money add(Money other) {
        return new Money(this.amount +
        other.amount, this.currency);
    }
    ...
}
```

In Scala, we use the def keyword to define a class method or a function. In the REPL, we can have multiline expressions. The following case class declaration, containing the implementation of a summing method + is an example of such features:

```
scala> case class Money(val amount:Int=1, val currency:String="USD"){
     |    def +(other: Money) : Money = Money(amount + other.amount)
     | }
defined class Money
```

Notice that we can use + as a method name. We have also included the return type Money in the signature declaration, which is only optional since the type inference of Scala will deduct it, but including it explicitly is a good documentation practice for public methods (and methods are public by default if no other scope is specified). Moreover, in Scala, since the return word at the end of the method is optional, the last statement is always the one that is returned to the caller of the method. Furthermore, it is generally considered a good practice to omit the return keyword since it is not mandatory.

We can now write the addition of two Money instances with the following simple expression:

```
scala> Money(12) + Money(34)
res5: Money = Money(46,USD)
```

Things start becoming exciting once we start manipulating collections of objects, and the functional programming part of Scala helps very much for that matter. Since generics are part of the language (Java 5 onwards), Java can, for example, iterate over a list of integers by writing the following code snippet:

```
List<Integer> numbers = new ArrayList<Integer>();
numbers.add(1);
numbers.add(2);
numbers.add(5);
for(Integer n: numbers) {
    System.out.println("Number "+n);
}
```

The preceding code produces the following output:

```
Number 1
Number 2
Number 5
```

In Scala, the declaration of a list can be written as follows:

```
scala> val numbers = List(1,2,5)
numbers: List[Int] = List(1,2,5)
```

Scala collections systematically distinguish between immutable and mutable collections, but encourage immutability by constructing immutable collections by default. They simulate additions, updates, or removals by returning new collections from such operations instead of modifying them.

One way to print out the numbers is that we can follow Java's imperative style of programming and iterate over the collection by creating a `for` loop:

```
scala> for (n <- numbers) println("Number "+n)
Number 1
Number 2
Number 5
```

Another way to write the code in Scala (as well as many other languages on the JVM, such as Groovy, JRuby, or Jython) involves a more functional style, using lambda expressions (sometimes referred to as closures). In brief, lambdas are just functions that you can pass around as parameters. These functions take input parameters (in our case, the n integer) and return the last statement/line of their body. They are in the following form:

```
functionName { input =>
            body
        }
```

A typical example of lambda to iterate over the elements of the numbers list we have defined earlier, is given as follows:

```
scala> numbers.foreach { n:Int =>
    | println("Number "+n)
    | }
Number 1
Number 2
Number 5
```

In that case, the body consists of only one statement (`println...`), and therefore returns `Unit`, that is, an empty result roughly equivalent to `void` in Java, except that `void` does not return anything.

As the time of writing this book, lambda expressions in Java are around the corner and will be introduced very soon as part of the JDK8 release, adopting a Scala-like style. Some of the functional constructs will therefore soon be available to Java developers.

It should become possible to write our tiny example in the following way:

```
numbers.forEach(n -> { System.out.println("Numbers "+n);});
```

As we stated previously, Scala collections are, by default, immutable. This is a very important aspect for making them behave as expected when dealing with multiprocessor architectures. One unique feature of the Scala collections compared to Java is that they include support for running operations in parallel.

Operations on collections

In this section, we are going to illustrate how the manipulation of collections in Scala can be expressed in a concise and expressive way.

Transforming collections containing primitive types

The REPL is a great tool to try out the powerful operations that we can apply to the collection elements. Let's go back to our interpreter prompt:

```
scala> val numbers = List(1,2,3,4,5,6)
numbers: List[Int] = List(1,2,3,4,5,6)
scala> val reversedList = numbers.reverse
reversedList: List[Int] = List(6,5,4,3,2,1)
scala> val onlyAFew = numbers drop 2 take 3
onlyAFew: List[Int] = List(3, 4, 5)
```

The `drop` method indicates that we get rid of the first two elements of the list, and the `take` method indicates that we keep only three elements from the result obtained after the `drop` method.

This last command is interesting for two reasons:

- Since every method call is evaluated to an expression, we can chain several method calls at once (here, `take` is invoked on the result of `drop`)
- As already stated before, the syntactic sugar added to the Scala syntax makes it equivalent to write `numbers drop 2` instead of the more traditional Java `numbers.drop(2)`

Another way of writing elements in a given list is by using the `::` method, generally referred to in Scala documentation as the "cons operator". This alternative syntax looks like the following expression:

```
scala> val numbers = 1 :: 2 :: 3 :: 4 :: 5 :: 6 :: Nil
numbers: List[Int] = List(1, 2, 3, 4, 5, 6)
```

If you are wondering why there is a `Nil` value at the end of this expression, this is because there is a simple rule in Scala that says that a method whose last character is `:` (that is, a colon) is applied on its right side rather than the left side (such a method is called as right-associative). So, the evaluation of `6 :: Nil` is not equivalent to `6.::(Nil)` in that case, but rather `Nil.::(6)`. We can exhibit that into the REPL as follows:

```
scala> val simpleList = Nil.::(6)
simpleList: List[Int] = List(6)
```

The evaluation of `5 :: 6 :: Nil` is therefore done by applying the `::` method on the `simpleList` that we saw earlier, which is `List(6)`:

```
scala> val twoElementsList = List(6).::(5)
twoElementsList: List[Int] = List(5, 6)
```

In this case, 5 was appended before 6. Repeating this operation several times will give you the final `List(1,2,3,4,5,6)`.

This convenient way of expressing lists is not just for simple values such as integers but can be applied to any type. Moreover, we can concatenate two `List` instances by using the `:::` method in a similar way:

```
scala> val concatenatedList = simpleList ::: twoElementsList
concatenatedList: List[Int] = List(6, 5, 6)
```

We can even mix elements of various types in the same `List`, for example, integers and Booleans, as shown in the following code snippet:

```
scala> val things = List(0,1,true)
things: List[AnyVal] = List(0, 1, true)
```

However, as you probably noticed, the result type `AnyVal` chosen by the compiler in that case is the first common type between integers and Booleans encountered in their hierarchy. For instance, retrieving only the Boolean element (at index two in the list) will return an element of type `AnyVal` rather than a `Boolean` value:

```
scala> things(2)
res6: AnyVal = true
```

Now, if we put an element of type `String` within the list as well, we will get a different common type:

```
scala> val things = List(0,1,true,"false")
things: List[Any] = List(0, 1, true, false)
```

The reason for that can be directly visualized by looking at the hierarchy of Scala types. Classes representing primitive types such as `Int`, `Byte`, `Boolean`, or `Char` belong to value types of `scala.AnyVal`, whereas `String`, `Vector`, `List`, or `Set` belong to reference types of `scala.AnyRef`, both being subclasses of the common type `Any`, as shown in the following diagram:

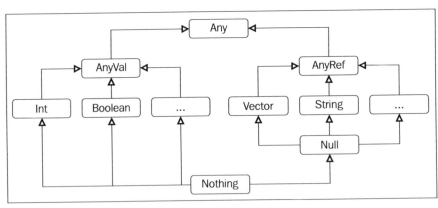

The full hierarchy of Scala types is given in the official Scala documentation at `http://docs.scala-lang.org/tutorials/tour/unified-types.html`.

Collections of more complex objects

Let's manipulate objects that are more complex than integers. We can, for instance, create some collections of `Money` instances that we made earlier and experiment with them:

```
scala> val amounts = List(Money(10,"USD"),Money(2,"EUR"),Money(20,"GBP"),
Money(75,"EUR"),Money(100,"USD"),Money(50,"USD"))
amounts: List[Money] = List(Money(10,USD), Money(2,EUR), Money(20,GBP),
Money(75,EUR), Money(100,USD), Money(50,USD))

scala> val first = amounts.head
first: Money = Money(10,USD)

scala> val amountsWithoutFirst = amounts.tail
amountsWithoutFirst: List[Money] = List(Money(2,EUR), Money(20,GBP),
Money(75,EUR), Money(100,USD), Money(50,USD))
```

Filter and partition

Filtering elements of a collection is one of the most common operations and can be written as follows:

```
scala> val euros = amounts.filter(money => money.currency=="EUR")
euros: List[Money] = List(Money(2,EUR), Money(75,EUR))
```

The parameter given to the `filter` method is a function that takes a `Money` item as the input and returns a `Boolean` value (that is, a predicate), which is the result of evaluating `money.currency=="EUR"`.

The `filter` method iterates over the collection items and applies the function to each element, keeping only the elements for which the function returns `True`. Lambda expressions are also referred to as **anonymous functions** because we could give any name we want to the input argument, for example, x instead of the `money` used previously, and still get the same output:

```
scala> val euros = amounts.filter(x => x.currency=="EUR")
euros: List[Money] = List(Money(2,EUR),Money(75,EUR))
```

A slightly shorter way of writing this one-liner can be done using an _ sign, a character that one encounters often when reading Scala code and that might seem awkward for a Java developer at first sight. It simply means "that thing", or "the current element". It can be thought of as the blank space or gap used to fill paper-based inquiries or passport registration forms, in the olden days. Other languages that deal with anonymous functions reserve other keywords, such as `it` in Groovy, or `self` in Python. The previous lambda example can be rewritten with the short underscore notation as the following:

```
scala> val euros = amounts.filter(_.currency=="EUR")
euros: List[Money] = List(Money(2,EUR),Money(75,EUR))
```

A `filterNot` method also exists to keep elements for which the evaluation of the function returns `False`. Moreover, a `partition` method is available to combine both the `filter` and `filterNot` methods into one single call that returns two collections, one evaluating to `True` and the other to its complement, as shown in the following code snippet:

```
scala> val allAmounts = amounts.partition(amt =>
     |    amt.currency=="EUR")
allAmounts: (List[Money], List[Money]) = (List(Money(2,EUR), Money(75,EUR
)),List(Money(10,USD), Money(20,GBP), Money(100,USD), Money(50,USD)))
```

Dealing with tuples

Notice the return type of the partition result, (List[Money],List[Money]).
Scala supports the concept of tuples. The preceding parenthesis notation denotes
a Tuple type, which is a part of the standard Scala library and useful to manipulate
several elements at once without having to create a more complex type for
encapsulating them. In our case, allAmounts is a Tuple2 pair containing two
lists of Money. To access only one of the two collections, we just need to type the
following expressions:

```
scala> val euros = allAmounts._1
euros: List[Money] = List(Money(2,EUR),Money(75,EUR))
scala> val everythingButEuros= allAmounts._2
everythingButEuros: List[Money] = List(Money(10,USD),Money(20,GBP),Money(
100,USD),Money(50,USD))
```

A cleaner and more natural syntax to achieve this as a one-liner, is the one that
expresses the partition method without referring to ._1 and ._2, as shown in the
following code snippet:

```
scala> val (euros,everythingButEuros) = amounts.partition(amt =>
     |    amt.currency=="EUR")
euros: List[Money] = List(Money(2,EUR), Money(75,EUR))
everythingButEuros: List[Money] = List(Money(10,USD), Money(20,GBP),
Money(100,USD), Money(50,USD))
```

This time, as a result, we get two variables, euros and everythingButEuros, which
we can reuse individually:

```
scala> euros
res2: List[Money] = List(Money(2,EUR), Money(75,EUR))
```

Introducing Map

Another elegant usage of tuples is related to the definition of a Map collection,
another structure that is part of the Scala collections. Similar to Java, the Map
collection stores key-value pairs. In Java, a trivial HashMap definition that populates
and retrieves elements of a Map collection with a couple of values can be written with
a few lines of code:

```
    import java.util.HashMap;
    import java.util.Map;

    public class MapSample {
```

```java
public static void main(String[] args) {
    Map amounts = new HashMap<String,Integer>();
    amounts.put("USD", 10);
    amounts.put("EUR", 2);

    Integer euros = (Integer)amounts.get("EUR");
    Integer pounds = (Integer)amounts.get("GBP");

    System.out.println("Euros: "+euros);
    System.out.println("Pounds: "+pounds);
    }
}
```

Since no amount of GBP currency has been inserted into the Map collection, running this sample will return a null value for the Pounds variable:

```
Euros: 2
Pounds: null
```

Populating a Map collection in Scala can be elegantly written as follows:

```
scala> val wallet = Map( "USD" -> 10, "EUR" -> 2 )
wallet: scala.collection.immutable.Map[String,Int] = Map(USD -> 10, EUR
-> 2)
```

The "USD" -> 10 expression is a convenient way of specifying a key-value pair and is equivalent to the definition of a Tuple2[String,Integer] object in this case, as illustrated directly in the REPL (which could infer the type automatically):

```
scala> val tenDollars = "USD"-> 10
tenDollars : (String, Int) = (USD,10)
scala> val tenDollars = ("USD",10)
tenDollars : (String, Int) = (USD,10)
```

The process of adding and retrieving an element is very straightforward:

```
scala> val updatedWallet = wallet + ("GBP" -> 20)
wallet: scala.collection.immutable.Map[String,Int] = Map(USD -> 10, EUR
-> 2, GBP -> 20)
scala> val someEuros = wallet("EUR")
someEuros: Int = 2
```

However, accessing an element that is not included in the Map collection will throw an exception, as follows:

```
scala> val somePounds = wallet("GBP")

java.util.NoSuchElementException: key not found: GBP    (followed by a full
stacktrace)
```

Introducing the Option construct

A safer way to retrieve an element from the Map collection that was introduced in the previous section is to invoke its .get() method, which will instead return an object of type Option, a feature that is not currently available in Java. Basically, an Option type wraps a value into an object that can either return the type None if the value is null, or Some(value) otherwise. Let's enter this in the REPL:

```
scala> val mayBeSomeEuros = wallet.get("EUR")

mayBeSomeEuros: Option[Int] = Some(2)

scala> val mayBeSomePounds = wallet.get("GBP")

mayBeSomePounds: Option[Int] = None
```

A glimpse at pattern matching

Avoiding the throwing of an exception makes it convenient to continue handling the flow of an algorithm as an evaluated expression. It not only gives the programmer the freedom of sophisticated chaining of the Option values without having to check for the existence of a value, but also enables one to handle the two different cases via **pattern matching**:

```
scala> val status = mayBeSomeEuros match {
     |    case None => "Nothing of that currency"
     |    case Some(value) => "I have "+value+" Euros"
     | }
status: String = I have 2 Euros
```

Pattern matching is an essential and powerful feature of the Scala language. We will look at more examples of it later on.

The filter and partition methods were just two examples of the so-called "higher-order" functions on lists, since they operate on containers of collection types (such as lists, sets, and so on) rather than the types themselves.

The map method

Among the collections' methods that cannot be overlooked lies the map method (not to be confused with the Map object). Basically, it applies a function to every element of a collection, but instead of returning Unit for the foreach method, it returns a collection of a similar container type (for example, a List will return a List of the same size) that contains the result of transforming each element through the function. A very simple example is shown in the following code snippet:

```
scala> List(1,2,3,4).map(x => x+1)
res6: List[Int] = List(2,3,4,5)
```

In Scala, you may define standalone functions as follows:

```
scala> def increment = (x:Int) => x + 1
increment: Int => Int
```

We have declared an increment function that takes an Int value as the input (denoted by x) and returns another Int value (x+1).

The previous List transformation can be rewritten slightly in a different manner as shown in the following code snippet:

```
scala> List(1,2,3,4).map(increment)
res7: List[Int] = List(2,3,4,5)
```

Using a bit of syntactic sugar, the . sign in the method call, as well as the parenthesis on the function parameter can be omitted for readability, which leads to the following concise one-liner:

```
scala> List(1,2,3,4) map increment
res8: List[Int] = List(2, 3, 4, 5)
```

Going back to our initial list of the Money amounts, we can, for example, transform them into strings as follows:

```
scala> val printedAmounts =
     |    amounts map(m=> ""+  m.amount + " " + m.currency)
printedAmounts: List[String] = List(10 USD, 2 EUR, 20 GBP, 75 EUR, 100 USD, 50 USD)
```

Looking at String Interpolation

In Java, concatenating strings using a + operator, as we did in the previous line, is a very common operation. In Scala, a more elegant and efficient way to deal with the presentation of strings is a feature named **String Interpolation**. Available since Scala Version 2.10, the new syntax involves prepending a s character to the string literal as shown in the following code snippet:

```scala
scala> val many = 10000.2345
many: Double = 10000.2345
scala> val amount = s"$many euros"
amount: String = 10000.2345 euros
```

Any variable in scope can be processed and embedded in a string. Formatting can even be more precise by using an f interpolator instead of s. In that case, the syntax follows the same style as that of the printf method of other languages, where, for instance, %4d means a four-digit formatting or %12.2f means a floating point notation with exactly twelve digits before the comma and two afterwards:

```scala
scala> val amount = f"$many%12.2f euros"
amount: String = "    10000.23 euros"
```

Moreover, the String Interpolation syntax enables us to embed the full evaluation of an expression, that is, a full block of code performing a calculation. The following is an example, where we want to display the value of our many variable twice:

```scala
scala> val amount = s"${many*2} euros"
amount: String = 20000.469 euros
```

The preceding block of code obeys the same rules as any method or function evaluation, meaning that the last statement in the block is the result. Although here we have a very simple computation, it is perfectly valid to include a multiline algorithm if needed.

Knowing the interpolation syntax, we can rewrite our previous amounts as follows:

```scala
scala> val printedAmounts =
     |    amounts map(m=> s"${m.amount} ${m.currency}")
printedAmounts: List[String] = List(10 USD, 2 EUR, 20 GBP, 75 EUR, 100
USD, 50 USD)
```

The groupBy method

Another convenient operation is the `groupBy` method that transforms a collection into a `Map` collection:

```
scala> val sortedAmounts = amounts groupBy(_.currency)

sortedAmounts: scala.collection.immutable.Map[String,List[Money]] =
Map(EUR -> List(Money(2,EUR), Money(75,EUR)), GBP -> List(Money(20,GBP)),
USD -> List(Money(10,USD), Money(100,USD), Money(50,USD)))
```

The foldLeft method

One last method that we would like to introduce here is the `foldLeft` method, which propagates some state from one element to the next. For instance, to sum elements in a list, you need to accumulate them and keep track of the intermediate counter from one element to the next:

```
scala> val sumOfNumbers = numbers.foldLeft(0) { (total,element) =>
     |    total + element
     | }
sumOfNumbers: Int = 21
```

The value `0` given as the first argument to `foldLeft` is the initial value (which means `total=0` when applying the function for the first `List` element). The `(total,element)` notation represents a `Tuple2` pair. Note, however, that for summation, the Scala API provides a `sum` method, so the last statement could have been written as follows:

```
scala> val sumOfNumbers = numbers.sum
sumOfNumbers: Int = 21
```

Summary

This interactive chapter that introduced some of the commonly used operations on objects and collections was only a glimpse to demonstrate some of the expressiveness and powerful constructs of Scala.

In the next chapter, we are going to increasingly blend Scala with an existing standard Java web application. Since there are so many ways by which one can create a standard web application, combining some of the many frameworks and database technologies available, irrespective of whether they involve Spring, Hibernate, JPA, SQL, or NoSQL, we will take the straightforward path of some of the well-established JavaEE tutorials.

2
Code Integration

Being able to make Java and Scala cooperate on the same code base is a prerequisite to guarantee a smooth transition between the two languages.

In this chapter, we are going to quickly create a small Java web application in which we will show you how to add Scala code to it. Then, we will cover some of the most common integration points between Java and Scala and how programming styles differ so that programmers who want to refactor and extend their Java application can do it according to some guidelines.

To avoid spending too much time on creating, understanding, and documenting a sample Java project, we are going to use a small database that is already available as part of the Oracle's NetBeans IDE distribution and create a JPA persistence layer as well as a REST API from it using the code generation features of the IDE.

Download the sample Java project

If you are impatient to directly jump into the Scala code integration features of this chapter, you may skip the following section and download the ready-to-use maven Java project instead from Packt's website at www.packtpub.com.

Creating a REST API from an existing database

The sample database bundled with the NetBeans IDE can be downloaded from the www.netbeans.org website. Just click on the **Download** button on this website and pick the JavaEE version of the IDE.

Once you have run the installation wizard, seen the **The installation was successful!** message, and started the IDE (Version 8.0 in our case), we are ready to create a fully functional web app in five minutes. The first time you use it, just click on the upper-left corner of the NetBeans IDE to close the startup screen and you should see the three tabs: **Projects**, **Files**, and **Services** on the left-hand side of the IDE.

The sample database

Our reference database can be seen from the IDE by clicking on the **Services** panel. Under the **Databases** menu that is part of the **Services** tab, double-click on the `jdbc:derby://localhost:1527/sample [app on APP] Database Connection` link to connect to the sample database on port 1527 (the default port for Derby databases) with the `app` user on the `APP` schema. Under the `APP` schema, you should find seven tables including `CUSTOMER` and `PRODUCT`. By right-clicking on the `CUSTOMER` table and choosing **View Data...**, you should be able to browse the content of the table.

The following diagram depicts the whole database schema so that you can visualize the dependencies or foreign keys between the different tables:

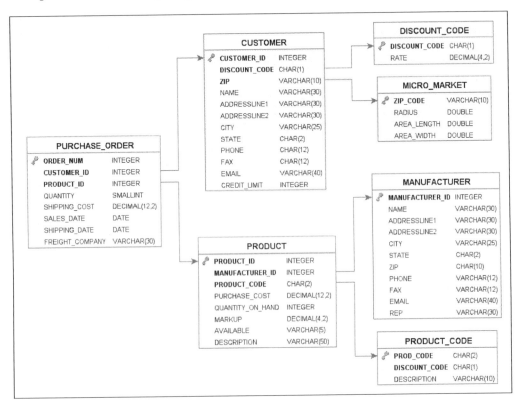

Setting up a Maven project

To quickly set up our sample Java project, you may either import it directly in your favorite IDE from the downloaded code (and skip creating JPA entities and the REST web service) or perform the following simple steps on the NetBeans IDE:

1. Right-click anywhere within the **Projects** tab in the IDE, select **New Project...**, and then choose the **Maven** category and the **Web Application** project type.

2. Enter `Sample` as **Project Name** and `com.demo` as **Group Id**, and then click on the **Next >** button.

3. Make sure a **Server** container is selected for deployment (we use the default GlassFish 4.0 as part of the NetBeans distribution) as well as **Java EE 7 Web** as the Java EE version.

4. Click on the **Finish** button and you should see the structure of the created project under the **Projects** tab.

Creating JPA entities and REST web services

Right-click on the **Sample** project root we just created and navigate to **New | RESTful Web Services from Databases...**. Selecting the `derby sample` database connection from the drop-down list in the newly opened window should bring up the database tables into the **Available Tables** section. Mark only the CUSTOMER table and select **Add>**, both CUSTOMER and DISCOUNT_CODE (which are dependent on CUSTOMER) should be listed as **Selected Tables**, as shown in the following screenshot:

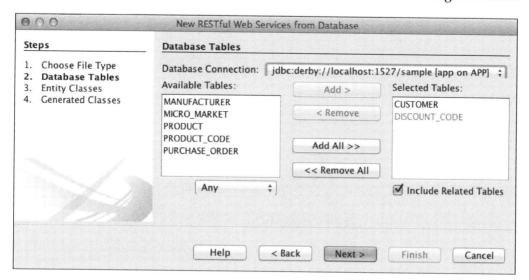

Clicking on the **Next** button and again on **Next** on the next page, and finally clicking on **Finish** will generate both the persistence JPA entities for `Customer` and `DiscountCode` and the service facade classes, `CustomerFacadeREST` and `DiscountCodeFacadeREST`. Note that since Java EE6, the `EntityManager` class is instantiated in each service class, which avoids the need for JPA controller classes that were generated in the previous versions.

A more detailed version of how to generate a RESTful web service from a database is available under the NetBeans tutorial at www.netbeans.org.

Running and testing the project

Before we start introducing Scala code into our Java project, we may launch our application and test REST invocations in a browser. Right-click on the **Sample** root node of the project and select **Run** to deploy the application. Once the console displays that the GlassFish server is running, and that the message **Hello World!** appears in your browser to show that everything is deployed correctly, right-click on the `RESTful Web Services` folder under the project root, and select **Test RESTful Web Services**. The opening dialog lets you choose between generating a test client as part of the same project or externally, as shown in the following screenshot:

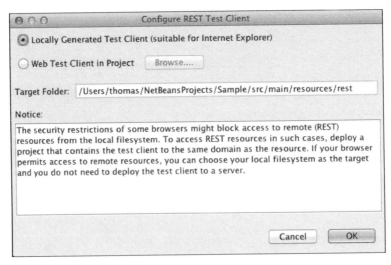

Select **Locally Generated Test Client (suitable for Internet Explorer)** and click on **OK**.

Once deployment completes, the browser will display a test page where we can invoke REST methods on our `customer` and `discountcode` entities. If we expand the `com.demo.sample.customer` folder, additional parameters will be shown. Clicking on the `{id}` parameter, we will get an input field on the right pane where we can enter a particular customer `id` value. For instance, we can enter `409`. In the drop-down list that shows **MIME** types, select **application/json** and `GET` as the method to test, and then click on **Test**, as shown in the following screenshot:

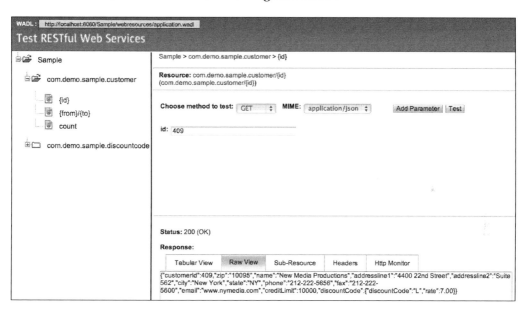

The bottom part of the page will now display the response to the REST query. It consists of a **Status: 200 (OK)** message and a **Response** content where the **Raw View** tab will display the body of the response as JSON, as shown in the previous screenshot.

Adding a unit test in Java

Finally, we can generate a very simple unit test for the `Customer` class by selecting the `Customer.java` source file from the **Projects** pane, and then right-clicking on it and navigating to **Tools | Create Tests**. Simply click on the **OK** button in the dialog and eventually allow the installation of the **JUnit 4.xx** if required. The resulting generated file appears within **Test Packages** under the same Java package structure as the original class under test, in our case `com.demo.sample.CustomerTest.java`, which is a common convention when dealing with unit testing in Java. Right-clicking on the `CustomerTest` class and choosing **Test File** will make all the test methods run with **JUnit** and fail as a `fail` clause is present by default at the end of each tested method. For now, just comment out the `fail` statement of `testGetCustomerId` and remove all the other test methods. Then, rerun the test to see it in green in the IDE. Alternatively, if you have set up the Maven project with another IDE or a plain text editor, from the root of the project in the filesystem (where the `pom.xml` file is located), you may enter the following Maven command, which you probably are familiar with, in a terminal window:

```
> mvn test
-------------------------------------------------------
 T E S T S
-------------------------------------------------------
Running com.demo.sample.CustomerTest
getCustomerId
Tests run: 1, Failures: 0, Errors: 0, Skipped: 0, Time elapsed: 0.034 sec
Results :
Tests run: 1, Failures: 0, Errors: 0, Skipped: 0
```

Adding a test in Scala

For now, we have only Java code in the small sample Maven project. We are ready to introduce a few lines of Scala to the same codebase in order to show how both languages seamlessly interoperate. Let's create a `src/test/scala` directory, next to the existing `java/` directory, where we will put our following new `CustomerScalaTest.scala` class, which is a similar test to the one we already have under `src/test/java`:

```
package com.demo.sample

import org.junit._
import Assert._
```

```scala
class CustomerScalaTest {

  @Before
  def setUp: Unit = {
  }

  @After
  def tearDown: Unit = {
  }

  @Test
  def testGetCustomerId = {
    System.out.println("getCustomerId")
    val instance = new Customer()
    val expResult: Integer = null
    val result: Integer = instance.getCustomerId()
    assertEquals(expResult, result)
  }
}
```

If we run the tests again, that is, type >mvn clean test again, the class will just be ignored as it is not a .java source file.

Setting up Scala within a Java Maven project

In order to be able to start writing a Scala unit test and compile Scala code into our Java project, we need to add a few dependencies and the scala-maven-plugin to the pom.xml file. The dependencies are as follows:

* Dependency for the core scala-library:

```xml
<dependency>
  <groupId>org.scala-lang</groupId>
  <artifactId>scala-library</artifactId>
  <version>2.10.0</version>
</dependency>
```

- Dependency for scalatest (a framework for testing in Scala that supports JUnit and other styles; we will cover it in detail in *Chapter 4, Testing Tools*):

```xml
<dependency>
  <groupId>org.scalatest</groupId>
  <artifactId>scalatest_2.10</artifactId>
  <version>2.0/version>
  <scope>test</scope>
</dependency>
```

- Dependency for JUnit to use Java `Assert` statements in our test case:

```xml
<dependency>
  <groupId>junit</groupId>
  <artifactId>junit</artifactId>
  <version>4.11</version>
  <scope>test</scope>
</dependency>
```

Concerning the `scala-maven-plugin`, just add something similar to the following XML block to the `<plugins>` section of your `pom.xml` build file:

```xml
<plugin>
  <groupId>net.alchim31.maven</groupId>
  <artifactId>scala-maven-plugin</artifactId>
  <executions>
    <execution>
      <id>scala-compile-first</id>
      <phase>process-resources</phase>
      <goals>
        <goal>add-source</goal>
        <goal>compile</goal>
      </goals>
    </execution>
    <execution>
      <id>scala-test-compile</id>
      <phase>process-test-resources</phase>
      <goals>
        <goal>testCompile</goal>
      </goals>
    </execution>
  </executions>
</plugin>
```

If we try to rerun the tests, this time our newly created Scala test will be picked up and executed, as shown in the following code snippet:

```
> mvn clean test
-------------------------------------------------------
 T E S T S
-------------------------------------------------------
Running com.demo.sample.CustomerScalaTest
getCustomerId
Tests run: 1, Failures: 0, Errors: 0, Skipped: 0, Time elapsed: 0.035 sec
Running com.demo.sample.CustomerTest
getCustomerId
Tests run: 1, Failures: 0, Errors: 0, Skipped: 0, Time elapsed: 0.004 sec


Results :


Tests run: 2, Failures: 0, Errors: 0, Skipped: 0
```

A couple of observations are worth mentioning about the `CustomerScalaTest.scala` class. They are as follows:

- The package declaration at the top of the file is similar to package declarations in Java. However, having a package declaration in Scala mirroring the path of directories in the filesystem is not a requirement unlike Java, but is still recommended.

- Import statements in Scala are similar to Java except that the * wildcard is replaced by the underscore, _.

> You probably noticed that we suddenly have the enormous power to use any Java library in our Scala code, which means that we will never be stuck and can always invoke methods in the existing Java classes if we need a piece of functionality that is not directly available in Scala.

With very few additions to the `pom.xml` build file, we now have made a regular Java project Scala aware, which means that we can freely add Scala classes and invoke any Java library within them. This also means that as Java developers, we are now able to migrate or refactor only small parts of a project if it makes sense and progressively improve our codebase as we get more acquainted with the Scala constructs.

This approach of dealing with an existing Maven project is only one way of proceeding. In the next chapter, we will see some other approaches with a more radical change that involves the Scala's **Simple Build Tool** (**SBT**), an alternative to Maven builds.

Scala and Java collaboration

Going back to the REPL, we are going to experiment further with mixing Scala and Java to explore some common integration needs, and in particular, testing and manipulating the Java REST API that we have built at the beginning of the chapter.

As a reminder on how to restart the REPL from the *hello-scala* project introduced in *Chapter 1*, *Programming Interactively within Your Project*, if you closed it in the meantime, just start a new terminal window, navigate to the root of the *hello-scala* project, and enter the following command in the command prompt:

```
> ./activator console
```

Converting between collection types

Let's start by comparing Java and Scala collection classes and see how we can go from one to the other. For instance, a Scala `List` (from the `scala.collection.immutable` package) is different from `java.util.List`, and sometimes, it can be useful to convert from one to the other. A convenient way in Java to create `java.util.List` is to use the `java.util.Arrays` utility method, `asList`, whose exact signature is `public static<T> List<T> asList(T... a)`, where `T` refers to a generic type. Let's import it in the REPL as follows:

```
scala> import java.util.Arrays
import java.util.Arrays
```

As the JDK classes are in the class path, they can be directly accessed into the REPL as shown in the following code snippet:

```
scala> val javaList = Arrays.asList(1,2,3,4)
javaList: java.util.List[Int] = [1, 2, 3, 4]
```

Now that we have instantiated a Java list of integers, we want to convert it to its Scala equivalent and need to import the `JavaConverters` classes for that using the following lines of command:

```
scala> import scala.collection.JavaConverters._
import scala.collection.JavaConverters._
```

Looking at the documentation of `JavaConverters` in Scaladoc (which is similar to Javadoc, used to document Scala APIs, and available online at `www.scala-lang.org/api/current/index.html`), we can see, for example, that the equivalent of `java.util.List` is `scala.collection.mutable.Buffer`. So, if we invoke the `asScala` method on `java.util.List`, we will get exactly that:

```
scala> val scalaList = javaList.asScala
scalaList: scala.collection.mutable.Buffer[Int] = Buffer(1, 2, 3, 4)
```

Now, by invoking the `asJava` method on `scalaList`, we will get back our original `java.util.List` collection:

```
scala> val javaListAgain = scalaList.asJava
javaListAgain: java.util.List[Int] = [1, 2, 3, 4]
```

A good test to verify that we get back the original object after converting it to a target type and back again is to use an `assert` statement, as shown in the following command:

```
scala> assert( javaList eq javaListAgain)
[no output]
```

Having no output from `assert` means that it evaluated to `True`; otherwise, we would get a stack trace that shows why they are not equal. You might wonder where this `assert` method comes from; `assert` is a method of the `Predef` class, a Scala class imported by default containing useful aliases for commonly used types, assertions like the one we have used, and simple functions for console's I/O and implicit conversions.

JavaBean-style properties

To ensure compatibility with Java frameworks such as Hibernate or JMX, you may sometimes need Java-style getters and setters on the fields of your class. For example, if we declare a `Company` class in the REPL as follows:

```
scala> class Company(var name:String)
defined class Company
```

We have seen in *Chapter 1, Programming Interactively within Your Project*, that Scala accessor methods to read and mutate the `name` field are `name` and `name_=`, respectively, as shown in the following commands:

```
scala> val sun = new Company("Sun Microsystems")
sun: Company = Company@55385db5
scala> sun.name
```

```
res33: String = Sun Microsystems
scala> sun.name_=("Oracle")
[no output is returned]
scala> sun.name
res35: String = Oracle
```

A straightforward way to have Java-style getters and setters is to annotate the field with scala.beans.BeanProperty as shown in the following lines of command:

```
scala> import scala.beans.BeanProperty
import scala.beans.BeanProperty
scala> class Company(@BeanProperty var name:String)
defined class Company
scala> val sun = new Company("Sun Microsystems")
sun: Company = Company@42540cca
scala> sun.getName()
res36: String = Sun Microsystems
scala> sun.setName("Oracle")
[no output is returned]
scala> sun.name    (alternatively sun.getName)
res38: String = Oracle
```

Scala and Java object orientation

The interoperability between Scala and Java classes makes it very straightforward to replace or extend an existing Java class with a Scala class. Compiling a Scala class produces bytecode that is pretty similar to what Java produces. For example, let's take a shorter version of the Customer Java class we generated earlier:

```java
public class Customer {

    private Integer customerId;
    private String zip;

    public Customer(Integer customerId) {
        this.customerId = customerId;
    }

    public Customer(Integer customerId, String zip) {
        this.customerId = customerId;
        this.zip = zip;
```

```
        }
        public Integer getCustomerId() {
            return customerId;
        }

        public void setCustomerId(Integer customerId) {
            this.customerId = customerId;
        }

        public String getZip() {
            return zip;
        }

        public void setZip(String zip) {
            this.zip = zip;
        }
    }
```

If we refactor it into a Scala class with class parameters and create an instance, we get the following in the REPL:

```
scala> class Customer ( var customerId: Int, var zip: String) {
        def getCustomerId() = customerId
        def setCustomerId(cust: Int): Unit = {
          customerId = cust
        }
      }
defined class Customer
scala> val customer = new Customer(1, "123 45")
customer: Customer = Customer@13425838
scala> customer.zip
res5: String = 123 45
```

However, a constructor that takes only a single `zip` parameter does not exist in this definition:

```
scala> val otherCustomer = new Customer("543 21")
<console>:8: error: not enough arguments for constructor Customer:
(customerId: Int, zip: String)Customer.
Unspecified value parameter zip.
        val otherCustomer = new Customer("543 21")
                            ^
```

To complete our refactoring of the Java class, we need an extra constructor as follows:

```scala
scala> class Customer ( var customerId: Int, var zip: String) {
     |    def this( zip: String) = this(0,zip)
     |    def getCustomerId() = customerId
     |    def setCustomerId(cust: Int): Unit = {
     |      customerId = cust
     |    }
     | }
defined class Customer
scala> val customer = new Customer("123 45")
customer: Customer = Customer@7944cdbd
```

This time, we were able to create an instance with the auxiliary constructor, which obeys to a couple of rules. They are as follows:

- Any auxiliary constructor must immediately call another this(...) constructor
- The primary constructor has to be called in the end to make sure all the parameters are initialized

Scala traits as enhanced Java interfaces

Software interfaces are useful mechanisms to make a piece of code interact via a contract to other external software systems, isolating the specification of what it does from its implementation. Although Java classes on the JVM have the limitation to only extend one single class, they can have multiple types by implementing several interfaces. However, Java interfaces are purely abstract, that is, they contain only constants, method signatures, and nested types, but no method bodies; for example, see the following code snippet:

```java
interface VIPCustomer {
   Integer discounts();
}
```

In contrast, Scala traits are more powerful by allowing partial implementation of method bodies and therefore, more reusable. One can use a trait to mix in behavior into a class. Let's take an example in the REPL:

```scala
scala> class Customer(val name:String, val discountCode:String="N" ){
     |    def discounts() : List[Int] = List(5)
     |    override def toString() = "Applied discounts: " +
```

```
|      discounts.mkString(" ","%, ","% ")
| }
```
defined class Customer

This class declares two fields, `name` and `discountCode` (initialized to `"N"` for normal), as well as two methods, `discounts()` and `toString()`, where `discounts()` accumulates discounts for a customer into `List` of integers (initialized to a `5` percent discount) and `toString()` displays it.

We can define a couple of traits that extends the class we just created:

```
scala> trait VIPCustomer extends Customer {
|      override def discounts = super.discounts ::: List(10)
| }
```
defined trait VIPCustomer

A `VIPCustomer` class is a customer who gets an extra `10` percent discount concatenated to the list of all of the already available discounts he/she has. The second trait is given as follows:

```
scala> trait GoldCustomer extends Customer {
|      override def discounts =
|        if (discountCode.equals("H"))
|           super.discounts ::: List(20)
|        else super.discounts ::: List(15)
   }
```
defined trait GoldCustomer

A `GoldCustomer` class is a customer who gets an additional `15` percent discount or even `20` percent if her rating, that is, `discountCode` is `"H"` (high).

Let's now write a `Main` class to show the addition of stackable traits when instantiating the `Customer` class. We use the `with` keyword to mix in these additional behaviors into the class as shown in the following lines of command:

```
scala> object Main {
|      def main(args: Array[String]) {
|        val myDiscounts = new Customer("Thomas","H") with
|          VIPCustomer with GoldCustomer
|        println(myDiscounts)
|      }
| }
```
defined module Main

We can now simply execute the main method and get the expected result as follows:

```
scala> Main.main(Array.empty)
Applied discounts:  5%, 10%, 20%
```

Note that the order in which traits are stacked is important. They are calling each other from right to left. `GoldCustomer` is, therefore, the first one to be called.

Traits lie between interfaces and abstract classes. However, you can only extend one abstract class whereas you can extend several traits.

Declaring objects

Java code often refers to the `static` keyword to refer to singleton methods and constants. Scala does not support the `static` identifier, but instead provides the notion of `object` in place of the `class` declaration. If you need to refactor Java code into Scala, by simply using the `object` declaration instead of `class`, you get singleton instances and you're done, having the extra advantage that such Scala objects can also extend interfaces and traits. A simple example of `object` is the declaration of the `Main` program we exhibited earlier in the usage of stackable traits, or the following simple `hello world` application:

```
scala> object Main {
     |    def main(args: Array[String]) {
     |      println("Hello Scala World !")
     |    }
     | }

defined module Main
```

In addition to the notion of object, Scala provides the notion of companion object, which consists of an object that cohabits with a class of the same name in the same package and file. This is why it is called **companion**.

Introducing companion objects

The companion object enables storing of static methods and from this, you have full access to the classes' members, including private ones. It is, for example, a good place to declare static factory methods, and **case classes** overload the `apply` factory method so that you are not required to use the `new` keyword when creating case class instances:

```
scala> case class Customer(val name:String)
defined class Customer
scala> val thomas = Customer("Thomas")
thomas: Customer = Customer(Thomas)
```

However, you can still use the new keyword if you want to, shown as follows:

```
scala> val thomas = new Customer("Thomas")
thomas: Customer = Customer(Thomas)
```

Under the hood, the case class is constructed as a regular class that has, among other things, a companion object similar to the following (although simplified) code snippet:

```
object Customer {
  def apply()= new Customer("default name")
}
class Customer(name:String) {
...
}
```

Handling exceptions

We conclude this section about how to migrate code from Java to Scala with exceptions, a notion that appears everywhere in Java. In a quite similar way to Java, you can write the try { } catch { } blocks to capture method invocations that might fail. In Java, you would write something similar to the following code snippet:

```
package com.demo.sample;

public class ConversionSample {

   static Integer parse(String numberAsString) {
     Integer number = null;
     try {
       number = Integer.parseInt(numberAsString);
     } catch (NumberFormatExceptionnfe) {
       System.err.println("Wrong format for "+numberAsString);
     } catch (Exception ex) {
       System.err.println("An unknown Error has occurred");
     }
     System.out.println("Parsed Number: "+number);
     return number;
   }
```

```
    public static void main(String[] args) {
      parse("2345");
      parse("23ab");
    }
  }
```

The preceding code produces the following output:

```
run:
Parsed Number: 2345
Wrong format for number 23ab
Parsed Number: null
BUILD SUCCESSFUL (total time: 0 seconds)
```

In Scala, you could translate it directly to the equivalent code:

```
scala> def parse(numberAsString: String) =
         try {
           Integer.parseInt(numberAsString)
         } catch {
           case nfe: NumberFormatException =>
             println("Wrong format for number "+numberAsString)
           case e: Exception => println("Error when parsing number"+
             numberAsString)
         }
parse: (numberAsString:String)AnyVal
scala> parse("2345")
res10: AnyVal = "2345"
scala> parse("23ab")
Wrong format for number 23ab
res11: AnyVal = ()
```

However, in this case, the return value inferred by the compiler is not only empty but also of the wrong type, AnyVal, which is the common type found between an Int value and whatever is returned by the exception. To make sure we get an integer as the output, we need to return an Int value from all the possible cases found in the catch block:

```
scala> def parse(numberAsString: String) =
         try {
           Integer.parseInt(numberAsString)
```

```
        } catch {
            case nfe: NumberFormatException =>
                println("Wrong format for number "+numberAsString); -1
            case _: Throwable =>
                println("Error when parsing number "+numberAsString)
                -1
        }
parse: (numberAsString:String)Int
```

This time we can capture the correct return type from the parsing invocation as follows:

```
scala> val number = parse("23ab")
Wrong format for number 23ab
number: Int= -1
```

In all cases, we return an `Int` value, `-1` in case of failure. This solution is still only partly satisfying as the caller does not really know the reason of failure unless we display/log it. A better way is to use, for example, an `Either` class that represents a value of one of the two possible types, where its instances are either of the `scala.util.Left` or `scala.util.Right` type. In this case, we can use the `Left` part to handle the failure and the `Right` part to handle a successful result as shown in the following code snippet:

```
scala> case class Failure(val reason: String)
defined class Failure
scala> def parse(numberAsString: String) : Either[Failure,Int] =
        try {
            val result = Integer.parseInt(numberAsString)
            Right(result)
        } catch {
            case _ : Throwable => Left(Failure("Error when parsing
number"))
        }
parse: (numberAsString:String)Either[Failure,Int]
scala> val number = parse("23ab")
number: Either[Failure,Int] = Left(Failure(Error when parsing number))
scala> val number = parse("2345")
number: Either[Failure,Int] = Right(2345)
```

Writing explicitly the return type will cause a compilation error on these types of errors, and therefore, is highly recommended.

Finally, without going into too much detail, there is an even more appropriate way of handling the `try` and `catch` blocks that are derived from `Either` using the `scala.util.Try` class. Instead of handling the exception as `Left` and `Right`, it returns `Failure[Throwable]` or `Success[T]`, `T` being a generic type. The advantage of this approach is that it can be used in for comprehensions (but we have not covered them yet, examples will come in *Chapter 5, Getting Started with the Play Framework*). Moreover, the semantics of `Try` for error handling is better than `Either` as it describes `Success` or `Failure` rather than the less meaningful and more generic terms `Left` and `Right`.

Differences in style between Java and Scala code

If you are going to refactor or rewrite Java code into Scala code, there are a number of style differences that are useful to be aware of. Obviously, programming style is largely a matter of taste; however, a few guidelines generally acknowledged by the Scala community can help someone new to Scala to write easier-to-read and more maintainable code. This section is dedicated to showing some of the most common differences.

Writing an algorithm in Java follows an imperative style, that is, a sequence of statements that change a program state. Scala, focusing primarily on functional programming, adopts a more declarative approach, where everything is an expression rather than a statement. Let's illustrate this in an example.

In Java, you would commonly find the following code snippet:

```
...
String customerLevel = null;
if(amountBought > 3000) {
    customerLevel = "Gold";
} else {
    customerLevel = "Silver";
}
...
```

The Scala equivalent consists of the following code snippet:

```
scala> val amountBought = 5000
amountBought: Int = 5000
scala> val customerLevel =
        if (amountBought> 3000) "Gold" else "Silver"
customerLevel: String = Gold
```

Note that unlike the Java statements, `if` is now embedded as part of the resulting evaluated expression.

In general, working where everything is evaluated as an expression (and here an immutable expression) will make it much easier for reuse as well as composition.

Being able to chain the result of one expression to the next will give you a concise way of expressing fairly complicated transformations that would require much more code in Java.

Adjusting the code layout

As the intent of functional programming is to minimize state behavior, it often consists of short lambda expressions so that you can visualize a fairly complicated transformation in an elegant and concise way, in many cases even as one-liners. For this reason, general formatting in Scala recommends that you use only two-space indentations instead of the four-space indentation that is generally admitted in Java code, as shown in the following code snippet:

```
scala> class Customer(
        val firstName: String,
        val lastName: String,
        val age: Int,
        val address: String,
        val country: String,
        valhasAGoodRating: Boolean
        ) {

        override def toString() =
          s" $firstName $lastName"
      }
defined class Customer
```

If you have many constructor/method parameters, having them aligned as previously illustrated makes it easier to change them without the need to reformat the whole indentation. It is also the case if you want to refactor the class with a longer name, for example, `VeryImportantCustomer` instead of `Customer`; it will make smaller and more precise differences against your version control management system (Git, subversion, and so on).

Naming conventions

Conventions for naming packages, classes, fields, and methods in the camel case generally follow the Java conventions. Note that you should avoid the underscore (_) in variable names (such as `first_name` or `_first_name`) as the underscore has a special meaning in Scala (`self` or `this` in anonymous functions).

However, constants, most likely declared as `private static final myConstant` in Java, are normally declared in Scala in the upper camel case, such as in the following enclosing object:

```
scala> object Constants {
     |     val MyNeverChangingAge = 20
     | }
defined module Constants
```

Choosing a meaningful name for variables and methods should always be a priority in Java, and it is often recommended to use rather long variable names to precisely describe what a variable or method represents. In Scala, things are a little bit different; meaningful names are, of course, a good way to make code more readable. However, as we are at the same time aiming at making behavior transformations concise through the use of functions and lambda expressions, short variable names can be an advantage if you can capture a whole piece of functionality in a short block of code. For example, incrementing a list of integers in Scala can simply be expressed as follows:

```
scala> val amounts = List(3,6,7,10) map ( x => x +1 )
amounts: List[Int] = List(4, 7, 8, 11)
```

Although using x as a variable name is often discouraged in Java, here it does not matter that much as the variable is not reused and we can capture the transformation it does at once. There are many short or long alternatives to the previous lambda syntax that will produce the same result. So, which one to choose? Some of the alternatives are as follows:

```
scala> val amounts = List(3,6,7,10) map ( myCurrentAmount =>
         myCurrentAmount +1 )
amounts: List[Int] = List(4, 7, 8, 11)
```

In this case, a long variable name breaks a clear and concise one-liner into two lines of code, thereby, making it difficult to understand. Meaningful names make more sense here if we start expressing logic on several lines as shown in the following code snippet:

```
scala> val amounts = List(3,6,7,10) map { myCurrentAmount  =>
         val result = myCurrentAmount + 1
         println("Result: " + result)
         result
       }
Result: 4
Result: 7
Result: 8
Result: 11
amounts: List[Int] = List(4, 7, 8, 11)
```

A shorter but still expressive name is sometimes a good compromise to indicate to the reader that this is an amount we are currently manipulating in our lambda expression, as follows:

```
scala> val amounts = List(3,6,7,10) map( amt => amt + 1 )
amounts: List[Int] = List(4, 7, 8, 11)
```

Finally, the shortest syntax of all that is well accepted by fluent Scala programmers for such a simple increment function is as follows:

```
scala> val amounts = List(3,6,7,10) map( _ + 1 )
amounts: List[Int] = List(4, 7, 8, 11)
```

Underscores are also encountered in Scala for expressing more complicated operations in an elegant but more awkward way, as is the following *sum* operation using the foldLeft method that accumulates the state from one element to the other (and is covered in the previous chapter):

```
scala> val sumOfAmounts = List(3,6,7,10).foldLeft(0)( _ + _ )
sumOfAmounts: Int = 26
```

Instead of explicitly having 0 as the initial value for the sum, we can write this summation a bit more elegantly by using the `reduce` method that is similar to `foldLeft`. However, we take the first element of the collection as the initial value (here, 3 will be the initial value), as shown in the following command:

```scala
scala> val sumOfAmounts = List(3,6,7,10) reduce ( _ + _ )
sumOfAmounts: Int = 26
```

As far as style is concerned, fluent Scala programmers will not have any problem reading this code. However, if the state accumulation operation is more complicated than just a simple + operation, it might be wise to write it more explicitly as shown in the following command:

```scala
scala> val sumOfAmounts =
          List(3,6,7,10) reduce ( (total,element) => total + element )
sumOfAmounts: Int = 26
```

Summary

In this chapter, we have covered how to start integrating Scala code into a Java codebase as well as how to refactor some of the most common Java constructs into Scala by following some style guidelines. A much more exhaustive list of style recommendations is available at http://docs.scala-lang.org/style/ if you are interested in learning more.

So far we have been mostly addressing the Scala language and syntax. In the next chapter, we are going to introduce the tools that complement it and that are necessary to make our Scala programming both productive and enjoyable.

3
Understanding the Scala Ecosystem

Learning a new language also means getting acquainted with a new ecosystem of frameworks and tools. The good news is, in Scala, we can largely inherit the very rich and mature set of available tools and libraries from Java. In this chapter, we are going to cover the major novelties and additions to the existing ecosystem that we, as Java developers, are already familiar with.

In this chapter, we will cover the following topics:

- Code editing environments—also known as IDEs
- SBT—a tool specific to Scala to build, test, and execute code
- Utilities as plugins to SBT to integrate with the Java ecosystem
- Scala Worksheets—a novel approach to interactive programming
- Working with HTTP and interacting with external web-based services, including the introduction of "for comprehensions"—a useful Scala construct
- Typesafe Activator—a convenient tool to bootstrap projects quickly
- Using Scala for scripting

Inheriting Java Integrated Development Environments (IDEs)

Scala is supported on all the three major Java IDEs: Eclipse-based (including all the different versions of Eclipse, Typesafe's own bundled version known as Scala IDE as well as more commercial IDEs such as SpringSourceSTS), IntelliJ IDEA, and NetBeans. This means that you can just keep working as you used to with Java, for instance, running Scala JUnit tests inside the IDE, directly debugging or remote debugging. The extended Scala support on all of these platforms will provide you with the very useful autocompletion feature and instant feedback on the various types that are inferred by the compiler. In *Chapter 2, Code Integration*, we used NetBeans mostly because it had a convenient, small, and ready-to-use database and embedded tools to reverse engineer this database into a RESTful API in Java. As the usage of Eclipse targets a larger audience and is also the reference IDE that Typesafe provides support to, we are going to use it for the following chapters as our main development environment.

From the `scala-ide.org` website, you can download and install the Scala IDE for Eclipse either as the bundled version that supports Scala or the Scala plugin through the use of update sites (as you would do in Java for installing any other Eclipse plugin into an existing environment). All instructions to install either the bundled or the plugin versions are very well explained on this site, so we won't spend much time here repeating this process. Instructions to install IDEA and NetBeans are available from `http://www.jetbrains.com/` and `http://www.netbeans.org/`, respectively.

Building with Simple Build Tool (SBT)

A major addition to the Java ecosystem when dealing with Scala is **Simple Build Tool (SBT)**, a flexible build system written in Scala that also powers both Typesafe Activator, which we used in the previous chapters, and the Play framework that we will cover later on in this book. In contrast to the existing XML formats used by Ant and Maven in Java environments, SBT build definitions are written in Scala in the form of a **Domain Specific Language (DSL)**, having the benefit of compile-time checking. As we will see in this section, SBT provides a number of additional convenient features. In addition to its dependency management ability based on Ivy and supporting Maven-format repositories, SBT offers both incremental compilation and an interactive shell (that is, the REPL we were using earlier). It also supports continuous testing and deployment, and integrates with many Scala test frameworks, making it the de facto build tool for the Scala community.

Getting started with SBT

SBT consists of a single `.jar` archive as well as a very small start script. Therefore, it can be installed and run on any platform that supports JVM. Installation instructions are available at `http://www.scala-sbt.org/`.

Creating a sample project

Once SBT is in your path (we used Version 0.13.0 at the time of writing this book), create a directory called `SampleProject` anywhere in your filesystem by entering the following commands in a terminal window:

```
> cd <your_filesystem_dir> (e.g. /Users/Thomas/projects/)
> mkdir SampleProject
> cd SampleProject
> sbt
[info] Set current project to sampleproject
> set name := "SampleProject"
[info] Defining *:name
[info] ...
> session save
```

To end the SBT session, enter the following command:

```
> exit (or press CTRL-D)
```

This will create a `build.sbt` file under the project root. This file gathers information about the project, that is, the equivalent of the Maven's `.pom` file in the Java world except that `build.sbt` compiles to Scala rather than being XML. The whole file structure of the project is illustrated in a diagram later on, once we have added some library dependencies.

Open and edit `build.sbt` to fill out the basic information as follows:

```
name := "SampleProject"

version := "1.0"

scalaVersion := "2.10.3"
```

Note that the extra line between each statement is important. The `.sbt` files are not Scala programs; they are a list of Scala expressions, where a blank line is the delimiter between these expressions.

We are now going to import our empty project into our IDE before we start writing some code.

Importing the project in Eclipse, IntelliJ IDEA, and NetBeans

The `sbteclipse` plugin is available to adapt a pure SBT project to an Eclipse project. You just need to create a `plugins.sbt` file under the `project/` directory and type the following line into it to import the `sbteclipse` plugin:

```
addSbtPlugin("com.typesafe.sbteclipse" % "sbteclipse-plugin" % "2.4.0")
```

The preceding given string is a way in SBT to express a dependency to a Maven library; it is the equivalent to what you would normally write into a pom file:

```
<groupId>com.typesafe.sbteclipse</groupId>
<artifactId>sbteclipse-plugin</artifactId>
<version>2.4.0</version>
```

You see, downloading libraries and their dependencies in SBT is pretty much the same as working with Maven; they will be fetched from Maven repositories (Maven central and some other common repositories are already referenced by default in SBT; this is why you do not have to write them explicitly).

Note that eventually you should use a different version number as this plugin evolves from time to time. The current version is available together with the plugin documentation at `https://github.com/typesafehub/sbteclipse`.

Once `SampleProject/project/plugins.sbt` is present in your project, you can simply execute the following command to generate an Eclipse compliant project (still from the root of the project):

```
> sbt eclipse

...

[info] Successfully created Eclipse project files for project(s):

[info] SampleProject
```

Now just start your Eclipse IDE if you haven't already done so, then select **File |Import...**. Navigate to **General | Existing Projects into Workspace**. Browse to the root directory of your project as you would do in Java and click on **OK**. Then, click on **Finish** to complete the import of the project, which will appear in the **Project Explorer** window.

IntelliJ also has its plugin, which is available at `https://github.com/mpeltonen/sbt-idea`.

Note that for the various IDEs, there are two plugin concepts: **SBT plugins** for particular IDEs and **IDE plugins** for SBT.

The sbteclipse, sbt-idea, and nbsbt (`https://github.com/dcaoyuan/nbscala/wiki/SbtIntegrationInNetBeans`) plugins are all SBT plugins that require modifications to your `plugins.sbt` file. When you run the appropriate SBT command, they generate project files to be used by Eclipse, IntelliJ, or NetBeans. When you update your SBT files, you may need to rerun the plugin in order to update your IDE configuration.

However, if an IntelliJ user browses the available IntelliJ plugins, then they will see a different Scala plugin there (`http://confluence.jetbrains.com/display/SCA/Scala+Plugin+for+IntelliJ+IDEA`). This is an add-on for IntelliJ, rather than an add-on for SBT. It helps IntelliJ to configure itself around an SBT project automatically, without the need for any modification to your SBT files or extra commands. This approach is arguably more popular in the IntelliJ community.

If you use Maven and Eclipse in the Java world, then this is pretty much the same story as the m2eclipse Eclipse plugin versus the eclipse: eclipse Maven plugin.

Similar to Eclipse, you should edit a `plugins.sbt` file under `project/` and place the dependency to the `sbt-idea` plugin as follows:

```
addSbtPlugin("com.github.mpeltonen" % "sbt-idea" % "1.5.2")
```

The command to create an IntelliJ-compliant project is as follows:

```
> sbt gen-idea
```

It is worth noting that as of IntelliJ IDEA 13, the IDEA Scala plugin natively supports SBT and doesn't require the external plugin to work. Refer to the IntelliJ documentation on how to import an SBT project into the IDE.

Sometimes newer versions of the plugin that are not present (yet) in the default Maven repositories exist. In this case, you have to add such a repository for SBT to be able to upload the plugin/library. You can do this by having an extra line as follows:

```
resolvers += "Sonatype snapshots" at "http://oss.sonatype.org/content/
repositories/snapshots/"

addSbtPlugin("com.github.mpeltonen" % "sbt-idea" % "1.6.0-SNAPSHOT")
```

Since Scala Version 2.10+, NetBeans also has its plugin:

```
addSbtPlugin("org.netbeans.nbsbt" % "nbsbt-plugin" % "1.0.2")
```

The plugin itself can be downloaded and built from a GitHub repository as follows:

```
> git clone git@github.com:dcaoyuan/nbsbt.git
> cd nbsbt
> sbt clean compile publish-local
```

The `publish-local` command will deploy it locally on your filesystem.
Then, creating the files for your project is done using the following command:

```
> sbt netbeans
```

We are going to continue the chapter adopting Eclipse as our IDE, but most of the tools should also work under the other IDEs. Moreover, if you need additional integration with other editors such as ENSIME and Sublime Text, browse the documentation at `http://www.scala-sbt.org`.

Once the project is imported into Eclipse, you will notice that the file structure is the same as for Maven projects; source files have the default directories `src/main/scala` and `src/test/scala`, and this is the same structure for Java too.

Creating a web application that runs on a servlet container

Among the growing list of available SBT plugins is the xsbt-web-plugin (available at `https://github.com/JamesEarlDouglas/xsbt-web-plugin`), a useful plugin to create traditional web apps that runs on a servlet container (such as Jetty).
As for the plugins we've previously seen, installation consists of adding single line to the `plugins.sbt` file as follows:

```
addSbtPlugin("com.earldouglas" % "xsbt-web-plugin" % "0.4.2")
```

Then, add the following line to the `build.sbt` file:

```
seq(webSettings :_*)
```

We also need to include Jetty in the container classpath as follows:

```
libraryDependencies += "org.mortbay.jetty" % "jetty" % "6.1.22" %
"container"
```

The whole minimal `build.sbt` file is given as a summary, as follows:

```
name := "SampleProject"

organization := "com.samples"

version := "1.0"

scalaVersion := "2.10.3"

seq(webSettings :_*)

libraryDependencies += "org.mortbay.jetty" % "jetty" % "6.1.22" %
"container"

libraryDependencies += "javax.servlet" % "servlet-api" % "2.5" %
"provided"
```

As we have updated our build file with new dependencies, we need to rerun
`sbteclipse` to update the Eclipse files for our project. This operation can be
achieved by re-entering from the SBT command prompt:

```
> eclipse
```

Let's now write a tiny servlet in Scala in the IDE to exhibit our small sample logic,
which mimics the Java syntax. Right-click on the root of the project in the **Package
Explorer** window, and select **Refresh** to make sure the new dependencies are picked
up. The whole structure of the project is shown in the following screenshot:

We can now start editing a new Scala file under `src/main/scala` (in a new `com.samples` package) as follows:

```scala
package com.samples
import scala.xml.NodeSeq
import javax.servlet.http._

class SimpleServlet extends HttpServlet {
  override def doGet(request: HttpServletRequest, response:
HttpServletResponse) {

    response.setContentType("text/html")
    response.setCharacterEncoding("UTF-8")

    val responseBody: NodeSeq =
      <html><body><h1>Hello, world!</h1></body></html>

    response.getWriter.write(responseBody.toString)
  }
}
```

Finally, we need to add a `web.xml` file as we would normally do in Java to configure the servlet deployment (to be put under the `src/main/webapp/WEB-INF` directory) as follows:

```xml
<?xml version="1.0" encoding="UTF-8"?>
<web-app
xmlns="http://java.sun.com/xml/ns/javaee"
xmlns:xsi="http://www.w3.org/2001/XMLSchema-instance"
xsi:schemaLocation="http://java.sun.com/xml/ns/javaee http://java.sun.
com/xml/ns/javaee/web-app_2_5.xsd"
version="2.5">
  <servlet>
    <servlet-name>simpleservlet</servlet-name>
    <servlet-class>com.samples.SimpleServlet</servlet-class>
  </servlet>
  <servlet-mapping>
    <servlet-name>simpleservlet</servlet-name>
    <url-pattern>/*</url-pattern>
  </servlet-mapping>
</web-app>
```

From the root of the project, in our command prompt, we are now ready to deploy and execute our little example in the Jetty container by invoking `sbt` as follows:

```
> sbt
> container:start
2014-03-15 14:33:18.880:INFO::Logging to STDERR via org.mortbay.log.
StdErrLog
[info] jetty-6.1.22
[info] NO JSP Support for /, did not find org.apache.jasper.servlet.
JspServlet
[info] Started SelectChannelConnector@0.0.0.0:8080
[success] Total time: 20 s, completed Mar 15, 2014 2:33:19 PM
>
```

By default, the container will listen on localhost at port 8080.

You can now open `http://localhost:8080/` on a web browser and verify whether we get the Hello, world! message as shown in the following screenshot:

You may also run the `package` command from SBT that will assemble a `.war` archive and put it under `target/scala-2.10/sampleproject_2.10-1.0.war` as follows:

```
> package
```

Using sbt-assembly to build a single .jar archive

The sbt-assembly plugin can gather all your project code and its dependencies into a single `.jar` file that can be published into a repository or deployed on other environments.

Installing the plugin consists of adding sbt-assembly as a dependency in `project/assembly.sbt` (from SBT 0.13), as follows:

```
addSbtPlugin("com.eed3si9n" % "sbt-assembly" % "0.11.2")
```

To be able to run the assembly command within SBT, you just need to create an `assembly.sbt` file in the project root directory as shown in the following code snippet:

```
import AssemblyKeys._ // put this at the top of the file

assemblySettings
// your assembly settings here
```

Assembly settings are documented at `https://github.com/sbt/sbt-assembly`. They enable you to modify, for example, the `jarName` or the `outputPath`, variables as well as skipping tests during the assembly phase or setting a main class explicitly if you wish to create a runnable `.jar` file.

Formatting code with Scalariform

Automatic code formatting is a useful feature not only for its ability to apply the same formatting rules to code written by various individuals but also to make the differences appear more consistently in a source management tool.

The Scala IDE for Eclipse uses Scalariform as its code formatter, which is also available as an sbt-plugin that can be added to the `plugins.sbt` file as follows:

```
addSbtPlugin("com.typesafe.sbt" % "sbt-scalariform" % "1.2.0")
```

Once you have it in place, Scalariform will format your source code automatically whenever you run `compile` or `test:compile` in SBT.

In Eclipse, formatting code is performed the same way as with Java, that is, right-clicking in the editor and then navigating to **Source** | **Format** (or *Ctrl + Shift + F*).

Experimenting with Scala Worksheets

In the previous chapters, we had run the REPL as an interactive environment to experiment and get immediate feedback when entering the Scala syntax. This allowed us to very quickly write some small algorithms and get the right syntax to make things work. Although the SBT console provides programmers with a `:replay` command to rerun what has already been written in the session, wouldn't it be nice to be able to save our experiments for later use, as part of our project ? This is exactly what **Scala Worksheets** are all about.

Scala Worksheet is an innovative feature of the Scala support for Eclipse that brings an interactive environment, that is, a REPL in the context of a project. This feature is also now available on the Scala support for IntelliJ.

Let's go to our small servlet sample in Eclipse to try it out.

To start a worksheet, right-click on any package or source file and navigate to **New | Scala Worksheet** (or if not present in the drop-down list, navigate to **Other... | Scala Wizards | Scala Worksheet**), as shown in the following screenshot:

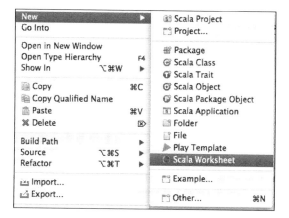

We will choose, for example, the current `com.samples` package. Click on **Next** and enter a name for your worksheet: `experiment`.

This will create a file named `experiment.sc` that is saved within the source code but as it is not a `.scala` file, it will not be in conflict with the rest of our current code base nor be present in the deployed `.jar` archive.

The default page looks like the following code snippet:

```
packagecom.samples

object experiment {
  println("Welcome to the Scala worksheet")       > Welcome to the
Scala worksheet
}
```

Everything after the > sign on each statement is the result of the evaluation that gets (re)evaluated as soon as you save the Worksheet file. You may try out a few statements, for instance, by replacing the `println` statement with a few lines, as follows:

```
object experiment {

  val number = 1 + 2

  List(1,2,3,3,3,4) filter (x => x < 4) distinct

  case class Customer(name:String)

  Customer("Helen")

  new SimpleServlet()
}
```

As soon as you save it (*Ctrl + S*), the style sheet will display statement evaluations on the right-hand side as shown in the following screenshot:

```
package com.samples

object experiment {

  val number = 1 + 2                            > number  : Int = 3

  List(1,2,3,3,4) filter (x => x < 4) distinct  > res0: List[Int] = List(1, 2, 3)

  case class Customer(name:String)

  Customer("Helen")                             > res1: com.samples.experiment.Customer = Customer(Helen)

  new SimpleServlet()                           > res2: com.samples.SimpleServlet = com.samples.SimpleServlet@55da4057
}
```

Working with HTTP

As Scala can import and invoke Java classes as well as extend them, many of the Scala libraries available as part of the Scala ecosystem are only a thin layer on top of robust and mature Java libraries, to either provide additional features or simplify their usage by adding some syntactic sugar.

One such example is the Scala dispatch library (available at `http://dispatch.databinder.net/Dispatch.html`), a useful library to achieve HTTP interaction based on Apache's robust HttpClient. Let's run a little dispatch session in the REPL.

As dispatch is an external library; we first need to import it into our SBT project to be able to use it from the REPL console. Add the dispatch dependency to the `build.sbt` file of the `SampleProject` so that it looks like the following code snippet (make sure to have a blank line between statements in `build.sbt`):

```
name := "SampleProject"
...

libraryDependencies += "net.databinder.dispatch" %% "dispatch-core" %
"0.11.0"
```

Restart the REPL to make the libraries available, and import them into the session as follows:

```
scala> import dispatch._ , Defaults._
import dispatch._
import Defaults._
```

Let's make a basic request to an online geolocation service, where the REST API is a simple GET request to the `freegeoip.net/{format}/{ip_or_hostname}` URL as follows:

```
scala> val request = url("http://freegeoip.net/xml/www.google.com")
request: dispatch.Req = Req(<function1>)
```

Now, we will send the GET request through HTTP and take the response as a string (wrapping XML as this is what we ask as response format from the service):

```
scala> val result = Http( request OK as.String)
result: dispatch.Future[String] = scala.concurrent.impl.
Promise$DefaultPromise@22aeb07c
```

Notice the result type of `dispatch.Future[String]` returned by the interpreter. The previous versions of dispatch were synchronous (and still available under the library name, `dispatch-classic`) but the latest versions such as the one we are using cope with modern development practices, namely asynchrony. We will study the asynchronous Scala code later in *Chapter 8, Essential Properties of Modern Applications – Asynchrony and Concurrency*, but similar to Java, `Future` acts as a placeholder for a computation that does not block. This means that we can continue the flow of the program without waiting for the variable to be populated, which is convenient when invoking potentially long-running method calls (such as a REST service). Note, however, that here `dispatch.Future` is a different implementation than `java.util.concurrent.Future`, which is found in the standard Java library.

To read and display the result of our HTTP request, we can just type the following command lines:

```
scala> val resultAsString = result()
resultAsString: String =
"<?xml version="1.0" encoding="UTF-8"?>
```

```
<Response>

<Ip>74.125.225.114</Ip>

<CountryCode>US</CountryCode>

<CountryName>United States</CountryName>

<RegionCode>CA</RegionCode>

<RegionName>California</RegionName>

<City>Mountain View</City>

<ZipCode>94043</ZipCode>

<Latitude>37.4192</Latitude>

<Longitude>-122.0574</Longitude>

<MetroCode>807</MetroCode>

<AreaCode>650</AreaCode>

</Response>

"
```

Calling `result()` here is the syntactic sugar for actually calling the `result.apply()` method, a convenient way to make code look elegant in many situations.

Dispatch provides a lot of ways to handle both the request, such as adding headers and parameters, and the processing of the response such as handling the response as XML or JSON, splitting into two different handlers or dealing with streams. To exhibit these behaviors, we are going to call another online service as an example, the **Groupon** service. Groupon is a service that offers discount coupons when you buy a product or service such as holidays, beauty products, and so on in a variety of categories. The Groupon API can be queried to gather offerings within a geographic location determined by either city or coordinates (latitude and longitude).

To be able to experiment with the API, upon registration to the `http://www.groupon.com/pages/api` URL, you should obtain a unique `client_id` key that authenticates you and that you have to pass along whenever you call the API. Let's illustrate this in the REPL:

```
scala> val grouponCitiesURL = url("http://api.groupon.com/v2/divisions.
xml?client_id=<your own client_key>")

grouponCitiesURL: dispatch.Req = Req(<function1>)

scala> val citiesAsText = Http(grouponCitiesURL OK as.String)

citiesAsText: dispatch.Future[String] = scala.concurrent.impl.
Promise$DefaultPromise@4ad28057

scala> citiesAsText()
```

```
res0: String = <response><divisions><division><id>abbotsford</
id><name>Abbotsford</name><country>Canada</country><timezone>Pacific Time
(US &amp; Canada)</timezone>...
```

The REPL limits the amount of output for better readability. Instead of getting the response as a string, let's handle it as XML:

```
scala> val citiesAsXML = Http(grouponCitiesURL OK as.xml.Elem)
```

```
citiesAsXML: dispatch.Future[scala.xml.Elem] = scala.concurrent.impl.
Promise$DefaultPromise@27ac41a3
```

```
scala> citiesAsXML()
```

```
res1: scala.xml.Elem = <response><divisions><division><id>abbotsford</
id><name>Abbotsford</name><country>Canada</country><timezone>Pacific Time
(US &amp; Canada)</timezone>...
```

This time our result is more structured as it is represented as an XML tree. We can print it in a better format by applying a `PrettyPrinter` object that will make the output fit within a width of 90 characters with an indentation of 2:

```
scala> def printer = new scala.xml.PrettyPrinter(90, 2)
printer: scala.xml.PrettyPrinter
scala> for (xml <- citiesAsXML)
          println(printer.format(xml))
scala> <response>
  <divisions>
    <division>
      <id>abbotsford</id>
      <name>Abbotsford</name>
      <country>Canada</country>
      <timezone>Pacific Time (US &amp; Canada)</timezone>
      <timezoneOffsetInSeconds>-25200</timezoneOffsetInSeconds>
      <timezoneIdentifier>America/Los_Angeles</timezoneIdentifier>
      <lat>49.0568</lat>
      <lng>-122.285</lng>
      ...
    </division>
    <division>
      <id>abilene</id>
      <name>Abilene, TX</name>
      <country>USA</country>
      <timezone>Central Time (US &amp; Canada)</timezone>...
```

Extracting partial information from our XML structure can be achieved by applying the `map` transformations including XPath expressions. XPath expressions are useful to navigate through XML elements to retain only the relevant parts. We can progressively extract pieces of XML and return them as collections such as `Lists` or `Seqs` (sequences), as shown in the following code snippet:

```
scala> val cityDivisions = citiesAsXML() map ( city => city \\
"division")
cityDivisions: scala.collection.immutable.Seq[scala.xml.NodeSeq]
= List(NodeSeq(<division><id>abbotsford</id><name>Abbotsford</
name><country>Canada</country>...

scala> val cityNames =
        cityDivisions map ( div => (div \ "name").text)
cityNames: scala.collection.immutable.Seq[String] =
List(AbbotsfordAbilene, TXAkron / CantonAlbany / Capital
RegionAlbuquerqueAllentown...
```

Here, we got back a sequence of city names for which there are coupons available.

Scala's for comprehension

Instead of applying successive `map` transformations to extract XML, in Scala, we can use a powerful construct that represents the silver bullet of iterations called `for comprehension` or `for expression`. Unlike the `for` loops found in Java and used for iterating, `for comprehension` returns a result. They are specified as follows:

```
for (sequence) yield expression
```

In the preceding code, `sequence` can contain the following components:

- **Generators**: They drive the iteration and are written in the following form:

  ```
  element <- collection
  ```

  As for Java loops, `element` represents a local variable bound to the current element of the iteration whereas `collection` represents the data to be iterated. Moreover, the first generator (there needs to be at least one) determines the type of the result. For example, if the input collection is a `List` or a `Vector`, the `for comprehension` will yield a `List` or a `Vector`, respectively.

- **Filters**: They control the iteration and are written in the following form:

  ```
  if expression
  ```

  The preceding expression must evaluate to a Boolean value. Filters can be defined either on the same line as generators or separately.

- **Definitions**: They are local variable definitions and are written in the following form:

```
variable = expression
```

   They are intermediate values that can contribute to compute the result.

A `for comprehension` construct is much easier to visualize with a few concrete examples:

```
scala> for {
        elem <- List(1,2,3,4,5)
      } yield "T" + elem
res3: List[String] = List(T1, T2, T3, T4, T5)
```

We have transformed `List[Int]` into `List[String]` using only one generator. Using two generators is illustrated in the following code:

```
scala> for {
        word <- List("Hello","Scala")
        char <- word
      } yield char.isLower
res4: List[Boolean] = List(false, true, true, true, true, false, true,
true, true, true)
```

We can add a filter on any generator. For instance, if we want to retain only the uppercase characters of every word, we can write as follows:

```
scala> for {
        word <- List("Hello","Scala")
        char <- word if char.isUpper
      } yield char
res5: List[Char] = List(H, S)
```

In the following example, we illustrate how to add a local variable definition:

```
scala> for {
        word <- List("Hello","Scala")
        char <- word
        lowerChar = char.toLower
      } yield lowerChar
res6: List[Char] = List(h, e, l, l, o, s, c, a, l, a)
```

Going back to our HTTP Groupon service, we can now extract names of cities using `for comprehension` as follows:

```
scala> def extractCityNames(xml: scala.xml.Elem) =
        for {
          elem <- xml \\ "division"
          name <- elem \ "name"
        } yield name.text
extractCityNames: (xml: scala.xml.Elem)scala.collection.immutable.
Seq[String]
scala> val cityNames = extractCityNames(citiesAsXML())

cityNames: scala.collection.immutable.Seq[String] = List(Abbotsford,
Abilene, TX, Akron / Canton, Albany / Capital Region, Albuquerque,
Allentown / Reading, Amarillo, Anchorage...
```

To be able to query the second part of the API to retrieve special discount deals for a specific area, we also need the latitude and longitude information from the queried cities. Let's do that by returning a tuple including three elements, the first one being the name, the second being the latitude, and the third being the longitude:

```
scala> def extractCityLocations(xml: scala.xml.Elem) =
        for {
          elem<- xml \\ "division"
          name <- elem \ "name"
          latitude <- elem \ "lat"
          longitude <- elem \ "lng"
        } yield (name.text,latitude.text,longitude.text)
extractCityLocations: (xml: scala.xml.Elem)scala.collection.immutable.
Seq[(String, String, String)]
scala> val cityLocations = extractCityLocations(citiesAsXML())

cityLocations: scala.collection.immutable.Seq[(String, String,
String)] = List((Abbotsford,49.0568,-122.285), (Abilene, TX,32.4487,-
99.7331), (Akron / Canton,41.0814,-81.519), (Albany / Capital
Region,42.6526,-73.7562)...
```

Out of the list of returned cities, we might be interested in just one for now. Let's retrieve only the location for Honolulu using the following command:

```
scala> val (honolulu,lat,lng) = cityLocations find (_._1 == "Honolulu")
getOrElse("Honolulu","21","-157")
honolulu: String = Honolulu

lat: String = 21.3069

lng: String = -157.858
```

The `find` method in the preceding code takes a predicate as a parameter. As its return type is an `Option` value, we can retrieve its content by invoking `getOrElse` where we can write a default value in case the `find` method does not return any match.

An alternative representation could be done using pattern matching, briefly described in *Chapter 1, Programming Interactively within Your Project*, as follows:

```
scala> val honolulu =
          cityLocations find { case( city, _, _ ) =>
            city == "Honolulu"
          }
honolulu: Option[(String, String, String)] = Some((Honolu
lu,21.3069,-157.858))
```

The regular syntax of pattern matching normally uses the `match` keyword before all the `case` alternatives, so here it is a simplified notation where the `match` keyword is implicit. The underscore (_) as well as the `city` variable given in `case` are wildcards in the pattern matching. We could have given these underscores variable names but it is not necessary as we are not using them in the predicate (that is, `city == "Honolulu"`).

Let's now create a request to query for all the deals that match a particular geographic area:

```
scala> val dealsByGeoArea =   url("http://api.groupon.com/v2/deals.
xml?client_id=<your client_id>")
dealsByGeoArea: dispatch.Req = Req(<function1>)
```

An alternative to handle data as tuples is to define case classes to encapsulate elements in a convenient and reusable way. We can, therefore, define a `Deal` class and rewrite our previous `for comprehension` statement returning the `Deal` instances instead of tuples:

```
scala> case class Deal(title:String = "",dealUrl:String = "", tag:String
= "")
defined class Deal

scala> def extractDeals(xml: scala.xml.Elem) =
          for {
            deal <- xml \\ "deal"
            title = (deal \\ "title").text
            dealUrl = (deal \\ "dealUrl").text
```

```
        tag = (deal \\ "tag" \ "name").text
    } yield Deal(title, dealUrl, tag)
extractDeals: (xml: scala.xml.Elem)scala.collection.immutable.Seq[Deal]
```

As we did previously for retrieving cities, we can now retrieve deals via HTTP GET and parse XML this time for the particular city of Honolulu, knowing its latitude and longitude, as follows:

```
scala> val dealsInHonolulu =
  Http(dealsByGeoArea <<? Map("lat"->lat,"lng"->lng) OK as.xml.Elem)
dealsInHonolulu: dispatch.Future[scala.xml.Elem] = scala.concurrent.impl.
Promise$DefaultPromise@a1f0cb1
```

The `<<?` operator means that we attach input parameters of a GET method to the `dealsByGeoArea` request. The `Map` object contains the parameters. It is equivalent to the normal representation of HTTP GET where we put the input parameters as key/value pairs in the URL (that is, `request_url?param1=value1;param2=value2`). This is in contrast with the `<<` operator, which would have specified a POST request. Creating a structured sequence of `Deal` instances out of the raw XML produced by the `dealsInHonolulu()` service call can be written as follows:

```
scala> val deals = extractDeals(dealsInHonolulu())
```

```
deals: scala.collection.immutable.Seq[Deal] = List(Deal(Laundry
Folding StylesExam with Posture Analysis and One or Three
Adjustments at Cassandra Peterson Chiropractic (Up to 85% Off)
One initial consultation, one exam, one posture analysis, and one
adjustmentOne initial consultation, one exam, one posture analysis,
and three adjustments,http://www.groupon.com/deals/cassandra-peterson-
chiropractic,Beauty & Spas), Deal(Laundry Folding Styles1.5-Hour Whale-
Watching SunsetÂ ï»¿Tour for an Adult or Child from Island Water Sports
Hawaii (50% Off) A 1.5-hour whale watching sunset tour for one childA
1.5-hour whale watching sunset tour for one adult,http://www.groupon.
com/deals/island-water-sports-hawaii-18,Arts and EntertainmentOutdoor
Pursuits), Deal(Dog or Horse?$25 for Take-Home Teeth-Whit...
```

Sorting the list of deals by their category is only a matter of applying a `groupBy` method on the collection as follows:

```
scala> val sortedDeals = deals groupBy(_.tag)
```

```
sortedDeals: scala.collection.immutable.Map[String,scala.collection.
immutable.Seq[Deal]] = Map("" -> List(Deal(SkeleCopSix Bottles of 3
Wine Men 2009 Merlot with Shipping Included6 Bottles of Premium Red
Wine,http://www.groupon.com/deals/gg-3-wine-men-2009-merlot-package,),
Deal(Famous...
```

Notice how the `groupBy` method is a very convenient way of applying the `Map` part of a **MapReduce** job operating on a collection, in our case creating a `Map` object where keys are the tags or categories of the Groupon deals and values are a list of the deals that belong to the specific category. A possible tiny `Reduce` operation on the `Map` object can, for example, consist of counting the number of deals for each category, using the `mapValues` method that transforms the values of this (key,value) store:

```
scala> val nbOfDealsPerTag = sortedDeals mapValues(_.size)

nbOfDealsPerTag: scala.collection.immutable.Map[String,Int] = Map("" ->
2, Arts and EntertainmentOutdoor Pursuits -> 1, Beauty & Spas ->3, Food
& DrinkCandy Stores -> 1, ShoppingGifts & Giving -> 1, ShoppingFraming
-> 1, EducationSpecialty Schools -> 1, Tickets -> 1, Services -> 1,
TravelTravel AgenciesEurope, Asia, Africa, & Oceania -> 1)
```

The example we went through only explores the surface of what we can do with HTTP tools such as dispatch and much more is described in their documentation. The direct interaction with the REPL greatly enhances the learning curve of such APIs.

There are several excellent alternatives of lightweight frameworks for dealing with HTTP interaction, and in the case of dispatch, we have only looked at the client side of things. Lightweight REST APIs can, therefore, be constructed by frameworks such as Unfiltered, Finagle, Scalatra, or Spray to name a few. Spray is currently being architected again to become the HTTP layer of the Play framework (on top of Akka); technologies we are going to cover later on in this book.

Taking advantage of Typesafe Activator

To be able to run an interactive programming session in the previous chapters, we have downloaded and installed a tool named **Typesafe Activator**. Running either as a command-line tool or through a web browser, the activator lets us create and execute a sample project out of a template, in this case, a minimal `hello-scala` project. From it, we have accessed the SBT console, which acts as a REPL.

Typesafe Activator can be seen as a lightweight IDE powered by SBT. It provides many project templates that programmers can reuse as a starting point in their new development project.

Creating an application based on activator templates

Open a command terminal window and go to the directory where you extracted the activator, then enter the following command:

```
> ./activator new
Enter an application name
>
```

You need to enter a name for your new project as follows:

```
> javasample
Fetching the latest list of templates...
Enter a template name, or hit tab to see a list of possible templates
> [Hit TAB]
activator-akka-cassandra                    activator-akka-spray
activator-play-autosource-reactivemongo     activator-scalding
activator-spray-twitter                      akka-callcenter
akka-cluster-sharding-scalaakka-clustering
akka-distributed-workers     akka-distributed-workers-java
akka-java-spring                             akka-sample-camel-java
akka-sample-camel-scalaakka-sample-cluster-java
akka-sample-cluster-scalaakka-sample-fsm-java-lambda
akka-sample-fsm-scalaakka-sample-main-java
akka-sample-main-scalaakka-sample-multi-node-scala
akka-sample-persistence-java     akka-sample-persistence-scala
akka-sample-remote-java                      akka-sample-remote-scala
akka-scala-spring                            akka-supervision
angular-seed-play                            atomic-scala-examples
dart-akka-spray                              eventual
hello-akka                                   hello-play
hello-play-backbone                          hello-play-java
hello-play-scala                             hello-sbt
hello-scala                                  hello-scala-eclipse
hello-scaloid                                hello-slick
just-play-scalamacwire-activator
matthiasn-sse-chat-template                  modern-web-template
```

play-akka-angular-websocket	play-angularjs-webapp-seed
play-cake	play-example-form
play-guice	play-hbase
play-java-spring	play-mongo-knockout
play-scalatest-subcut	play-slick
play-slick-advanced	play-spring-data-jpa
play-sqlite	play-with-angular-requirejs
play-yeoman	play2-crud-activator
reactive-maps	reactive-stocks
realtime-search	scala-phantom-types
scaldi-play-example	scalikejdbc-activator-template
six-minute-apps	slick-android-example
slick-codegen-customization-example	slick-codegen-example
slick-plainsql	spray-actor-per-request
tcp-async	template-template
test-patterns-scala	tweetmap-workshop

Version 1.0.13 that we are using already contains 76 templates combining diverse technologies and frameworks together to make some interesting demo projects, but this list is increasing quickly (from 38 to 76 between Version 1.0.0 and 1.0.13, which are only a few months apart).

For now, let's take a look at the `play-java-spring` template, a project sample in Java, so that we can feel comfortable with the code it contains. Therefore, enter its name when prompted for the name of the template to be used:

```
> play-java-spring
```

```
OK, application "javasample" is being created using the "play-java-
spring" template.
```

```
To run "javasample" from the command-line, run:
/Users/thomas/scala/activator-1.0.13/javasample/activator run
```

```
To run the test for "javasample" from the command-line, run:
/Users/thomas/scala/activator-1.0.13/javasample/activator test
```

```
To run the Activator UI for "javasample" from the command-line, run:
/Users/thomas/scala/activator-1.0.13/javasample/activator ui
```

The activator creates a SBT project, meaning you can edit `build.sbt` or `plugins.sbt` to add dependencies, repositories (that is, resolvers) as well as SBT plugins. We can, for example, reuse the `addSbtPlugin("com.typesafe.sbteclipse" % "sbteclipse-plugin" % "2.4.0")` line in `plugins.sbt` that we stated earlier to be able to create Eclipse project files and import the project into our Scala IDE.

First, let's execute the program to see what it does:

```
> cd javasample
> ./activator run
```

As the sample is based on the Play framework (that we will cover in later chapters), the following is displayed to indicate that the web application is deployed on localhost at port 9000:

```
--- (Running the application from SBT, auto-reloading is enabled) ---
[info] play - Listening for HTTP on /0:0:0:0:0:0:0:0:9000
(Server started, use CTRL +D to stop and go back to the console...)
```

Open a browser at localhost:9000 to visualize the very basic web form of the sample and submit a couple of entries to be stored in the tiny database, as shown in the following screenshot:

This web application takes an input from a simple HTML form and saves `Bar` objects into a small database through JPA.

To take a look at the code that is part of this template; we can run it through the activator by first pressing *Ctrl + D* in the command window to interrupt the current execution, and then, enter the following command:

```
> ./activator ui
```

After a few seconds, a browser page should open at `http://localhost:8888/app/javasample/` displaying the activator user interface specifically targeted to this application. Click on the **Code view & Open in IDE** item and navigate to the `app/models/Bar.java` file by double-clicking on the items on the left-hand side panel, as shown in the following screenshot:

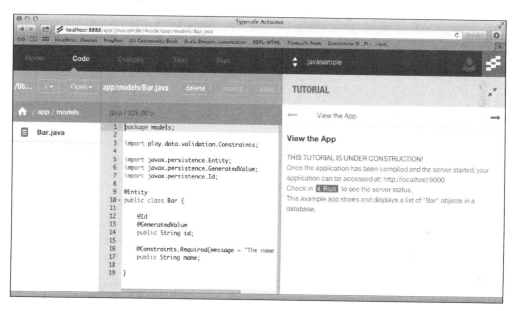

The browser displays a JPA-annotated entity as we are used to working with typically in the Eclipse IDE with colored and formatted syntax. The panel on the right-hand side leaves room for a tutorial, a precious feature to quickly understand the code and start modifying it. The top menu enables you to compile, run, or test the application from within the browser. You can open some of the other source files to identify the structure of the code, although we will cover play web applications in detail later on.

In summary, Typesafe Activator is a way to get you started in just minutes and is very flexible as you can run activator projects directly as SBT projects, therefore, having the possibility to generate IDE-specific files to continue working in Eclipse, IDEA, or NetBeans if you wish to.

The REPL as a scripting engine

To deal with interoperability with programs written in scripting languages, the Java community process has defined *JSR-223*, *Scripting for the JavaTM Platform*, a Java specification request that makes it possible to execute scripts written in other languages (such as Groovy, JavaScript, Ruby, or Jython to name of few) from within a Java program. For instance, we can write a Java program embedding a basic JavaScript snippet as follows:

```
package com.demo;
import javax.script.*;

public class JSR223Sample {

   public static void main(String[] args) throws Exception {
     ScriptEngineManager manager = new ScriptEngineManager();
     ScriptEngine engine = manager.getEngineByName("JavaScript");

     // expose object as variable to script
     engine.put("n", 5);

     // evaluate a script string.
     engine.eval("for(i=1; i<= n; i++) println(i)");
   }
}
```

We will get the following output from the IDE:

```
run:
1
2
3
4
5
BUILD SUCCESSFUL (total time: 0 seconds)
```

Starting from Scala's upcoming Version 2.11, this very convenient functionality will let you interpret scripts written in Scala as well. The following is an example that we can just run directly in the REPL (taken from the `scala-lang.org` documentation):

```
scala> import javax.script.ScriptEngineManager
importjavax.script.ScriptEngineManager
scala> val engine =
       new ScriptEngineManager().getEngineByName("scala")
```

```
engine: javax.script.ScriptEngine = scala.tools.nsc.interpreter.
IMain@7debe95d
scala> engine.put("n", 5)
n: Object = 5
scala> engine.eval("1 to n.asInstanceOf[Int] foreachprintln")
1

2

3

4

5

res4: Object = null
```

The engine context can bind the n variable to the integer value 5, which can be invoked in the one-liner script which consists of a `foreach` lambda expression. The script, in this case, is only a side effect and does not return any interesting value.

Summary

In this chapter, we have covered some of the major differences between the Java and Scala ecosystems, and it is noticed that apart from SBT and REPL, which are not found in the Java world, we are able to reuse all the Java libraries, tools, and frameworks. We have seen that this `group % artifact % version` format used to load dependencies in SBT is the same as that of Java's Maven, and in fact, SBT, by default, is similar to most of the Maven repositories (for example, Maven Central). We can, therefore, feel confident that the vast majority of our Java skills are reusable, and they make the transition easier at least as long as the ecosystem is concerned. We voluntarily omitted talking about the testing ecosystem as this is the main topic of our next chapter.

4
Testing Tools

No matter which language you are programming in, testing should be performed with great care, as it will not only document your code in a consistent way but will also be of great help for refactoring and maintenance activities, such as fixing bugs.

The Scala ecosystem largely follows Java trends towards testing at all levels, but with some differences. At many places, we will see that Scala is using **DSLs** (**Domain Specific Languages**), which makes the testing code very clear to read and understand. As a matter of fact, testing can be a good area to start with when introducing Scala, migrating progressively from an existing Java project.

In this chapter, we are going to cover some of the major testing tools and their usage through a number of code examples. We have already written a tiny JUnit-like test in Scala in *Chapter 3, Understanding the Scala Ecosystem*, so we will go from here and focus on BDD-style tests that belong to **Behavior Driven Development (BDD)**. Agnostic to which technology stack is used, BDD has emerged in these past few years as a compliant choice for writing clear specifications in the Gherkin language (which is part of the cucumber framework and is explained at `http://cukes.info/gherkin.html`) on how code should behave. Already used in Java and many other languages, tests written in that style are often easier to understand and maintain as they are closer to plain English. They are one step closer to the true adoption of BDD that aims at making the business analysts write the test specifications in a structured way, which the programs can understand and implement. They often represent the sole documentation; it is therefore very important to keep them up to date and close to the domain.

Scala primarily offers two frameworks to write tests, **ScalaTest** (`www.scalatest.org`) and **Specs2** (`etorreborre.github.io/specs2/`). As they are quite similar to each other, we are only going to cover ScalaTest, and interested readers can look through the Specs2 documentation to understand their differences. Moreover, we will take a look at automated property-based testing using the **ScalaCheck** framework (`www.scalacheck.org`).

Writing tests with ScalaTest

To be able to quickly start visualizing some of the tests that can be written with ScalaTest, we can take advantage of the `test-patterns-scala` template from the Typesafe Activator that we introduced in the previous chapter. It consists of a number of examples that essentially target the ScalaTest framework.

Setting up the `test-patterns-scala` activator project only requires you to go to the directory where you installed the Typesafe Activator, as we did earlier, and then, either start the GUI through the `> activator ui` command, or type `> activator new` to create a new project and select the appropriate template when prompted.

The template project already contains the `sbteclipse` plugin; therefore, you can generate eclipse-related files by simply entering from a command prompt in the root directory of the project, as follows:

```
> activator eclipse
```

Once the eclipse project is successfully created, you may import it into your IDE workspace by selecting **File | Import... | General | Existing Projects**. As a reminder from the previous chapter, you can also create project files for IntelliJ or other IDEs since the Typesafe Activator is just a customized version of SBT.

You can look into the various test cases in `src/test/scala`. As some of the tests use frameworks such as Akka, Spray, or Slick, which we haven't covered yet, we will skip these for now to concentrate on the most straightforward ones.

In its simplest form, a `ScalaTest` class (which, by the way, might also test Java code and not just Scala code) can be declared by extending `org.scalatest.FunSuite`. Each test is represented as a function value, and this is implemented in the `Test01.scala` class, as shown in the following code:

```scala
package scalatest
import org.scalatest.FunSuite

class Test01 extends FunSuite {
  test("Very Basic") {
    assert(1 == 1)
  }
  test("Another Very Basic") {
    assert("Hello World" == "Hello World")
  }
}
```

To execute only this single test class, you should enter the following command in the command prompt:

```
> activator

> test-only <full name of the class to execute>
```

In our case, this command will be as follows:

```
> test-only scalatest.Test01    (or scalatest.Test01.scala)
[info] Test01:
[info] - Very Basic (38 milliseconds)
[info] - Another Very Basic (0 milliseconds)
[info] ScalaTest
[info] Run completed in 912 milliseconds.
[info] Total number of tests run: 2
[info] Suites: completed 1, aborted 0
[info] Tests: succeeded 2, failed 0, canceled 0, ignored 0, pending 0
[info] All tests passed.
[info] Passed: Total 2, Failed 0, Errors 0, Passed 2
[success] Total time: 9 s, completed Nov 11, 2013 6:12:14 PM
```

The example given under `src/test/scala/scalatest/Test02.scala` within the `test-patterns-scala` project is very similar, but the extra `===` instead of `==` will give you additional info when the test fails. This is shown as follows:

```
class Test02 extends FunSuite {
  test("pass") {
    assert("abc" === "abc")
  }
  test("fail and show diff") {
    assert("abc" === "abcd") // provide reporting info
  }
}
```

Once again running the test can be done by entering the following command:

```
> test-only scalatest.Test02
[info] Test02:
[info] - pass (15 milliseconds)
[info] - fail and show diff *** FAILED *** (6 milliseconds)
[info]    "abc[]" did not equal "abc[d]" (Test02.scala:10)
[info] …
[info] *** 1 TEST FAILED ***
[error] Failed: Total 2, Failed 1, Errors 0, Passed 1
```

Before fixing the failing test, this time, we can execute the test in the continuous mode, using the ~ character in front of `test-only` (from the activator prompt), as follows:

```
>~test-only scalatest.Test02
```

The continuous mode will make SBT rerun the `test-only` command each time the `Test02` class is edited and saved. This feature of SBT can make you save a significant amount of time by running in the background tests or just programs without having to explicitly write the command. On the first execution of `Test02`, you can see some red text indicating `"abc[]"` did not equal `"abc[d]"` (`Test02.scala:10`).

As soon as you correct the `abdc` string and save the file, SBT will automatically re-execute the test in the background, and you can see the text turning green.

The continuous mode works for the other SBT commands as well, such as `~run` or `~test`.

`Test03` shows you how to expect or catch exceptions:

```scala
class Test03 extends FunSuite {
  test("Exception expected, does not fire, FAIL") {
    val msg = "hello"
    intercept[IndexOutOfBoundsException] {
      msg.charAt(0)
    }
  }
  test("Exception expected, fires, PASS") {
    val msg = "hello"
    intercept[IndexOutOfBoundsException] {
      msg.charAt(-1)
    }
  }
}
```

The first scenario fails as it was expecting an `IndexOutOfBoundsException`, but the code is indeed returning a valid h, the character at index 0 of the `hello` string.

To be able to run ScalaTest test suites as JUnit test suites (for example, to run them within the IDE or when extending an existing JUnit-based project that is already built in Maven, or when reporting to a build server), we can use the available `JUnitRunner` class along with the `@RunWith` annotation, as shown in the following sample:

```scala
import org.junit.runner.RunWith
import org.scalatest.junit.JUnitRunner
import org.scalatest.FunSuite
@RunWith(classOf[JUnitRunner])
```

```
class MyTestSuite extends FunSuite {
  // ...
}
```

BDD-style testing

Test06 is an example of a test written in a different style, namely BDD. In short, you specify some kind of a user story in almost plain English that describes the behavior of the scenario you want to test. This can be seen in the following code:

```
class Test06 extends FeatureSpec with GivenWhenThen {
  feature("The user can pop an element off the top of the stack")
  {
info("As a programmer")
  info("I want to be able to pop items off the stack")
  info("So that I can get them in last-in-first-out order")
  scenario("pop is invoked on a non-empty stack") {
    given("a non-empty stack")
    val stack = new Stack[Int]
    stack.push(1)
    stack.push(2)
    val oldSize = stack.size

  when("when pop is invoked on the stack")
  val result = stack.pop()

  then("the most recently pushed element should be returned")
  assert(result === 2)

  and("the stack should have one less item than before")
  assert(stack.size === oldSize - 1)
  }
  scenario("pop is invoked on an empty stack") {
    given("an empty stack")
    val emptyStack = new Stack[Int]

    when("when pop is invoked on the stack")
    then("NoSuchElementException should be thrown")
    intercept[NoSuchElementException] {
    emptyStack.pop()
    }
  and("the stack should still be empty")
  assert(emptyStack.isEmpty)
  }
}
}
```

BDD-style tests represent a higher level of abstraction than JUnit tests, and are more suitable for integration and acceptance testing as well as documentation, for people knowledgeable about the domain. You just need to extend the `FeatureSpec` class, optionally with a `GivenWhenThen` trait, to describe acceptance requirements. More details about BDD-style tests can be found at http://en.wikipedia.org/wiki/ Behavior-driven_development. We just want to illustrate here that it is possible to write the BDD-style tests in Scala, but we won't go further into their details as they are already largely documented for Java and other programming languages.

ScalaTest provides a convenient DSL to write assertions in a way close to plain English. The `org.scalatest.matchers.Matchers` trait contains many possible assertions and you should look at its ScalaDoc documentation to see many usage examples. `Test07.scala` expresses a very simple matcher, as shown in the following code:

```
package scalatest

import org.scalatest._
import org.scalatest.Matchers

class Test07 extends FlatSpec with Matchers {
"This test" should "pass" in {
    true should be === true
  }
}
```

Although built with Version 2.0 of ScalaTest, the original sample given in the activator project uses the now deprecated `org.scalatest.matchers.ShouldMatchers` trait; the preceding code sample achieves the same behavior but is more up to date.

Let's write a few more assertions using a Scala Worksheet. Right-click on the `scalatest` package that contains all the test files that were previously reviewed and then select **new | Scala Worksheet**. We will name this worksheet as `ShouldWork`. We can then write and evaluate matchers by extending a `FlatSpec` specification with the `Matchers` trait, as shown in the following code:

```
package scalatest
import org.scalatest._
object ShouldWork extends FlatSpec with Matchers {

  true should be === true

}
```

Saving this worksheet will not produce any output as the matcher passes the test. However, try to make it fail by changing one `true` to `false`. This is shown in the following code:

```
package scalatest
import org.scalatest._

object ShouldWork extends FlatSpec with Matchers {

  true should be === false

}
```

This time, we get a full stack trace as part of the evaluation, as shown in the following screenshot:

We can start evaluating many more `should` matchers, as shown in the following code:

```
package scalatest
import org.scalatest._

object ShouldMatchers extends FlatSpec with Matchers {

  true should be === true

  List(1,2,3,4) should have length(4)

  List.empty should be (Nil)

  Map(1->"Value 1", 2->"Value 2") should contain key (2)
```

```
    Map(1->"Java", 2->"Scala") should contain value ("Scala")

    Map(1->"Java", 2->"Scala") get 1 should be (Some("Java"))

    Map(1->"Java", 2->"Scala") should (contain key (2) and not contain
value ("Clojure"))

    3 should (be > (0) and be <= (5))

    new java.io.File(".") should (exist)
}
```

The evaluation of the worksheet stops whenever we encounter a test failure. Therefore, we have to fix it in order to be able to progress in the test. This is identical to running the whole testsuite with the SBT `test` command, as we did previously, and as shown in the following code:

```
object ShouldMatchers extends FlatSpec with Matchers {

"Hello" should be ("Hello")

"Hello" should (equal ("Hej")
                or equal ("Hell")) //> org.scalatest.exceptions.
TestFailedException:

"Hello" should not be ("Hello")
}
```

In the previous example, the last statement (which is the opposite of the first one) should fail; instead, it is not evaluated.

Functional testing

ScalaTest is well integrated with Selenium (it is a tool for automating testing in browsers and is available at www.seleniumhq.org) by providing a complete DSL, making it straightforward to write functional tests. Test08 is a clear example of this integration:

```
class Test08 extends FlatSpec with Matchers with WebBrowser {

  implicit val webDriver: WebDriver = new HtmlUnitDriver
go to "http://www.amazon.com"
click on "twotabsearchtextbox"
```

```
textField("twotabsearchtextbox").value = "Scala"
submit()
pageTitle should be ("Amazon.com: Scala")
pageSource should include("Scala Cookbook: Recipes")
}
```

Let's try to run a similar invocation directly into a worksheet. As worksheets give feedback on every statement evaluation, they are very convenient to directly identify what the problem is, for instance, if a link, a button, or content is not found as expected.

Just create another worksheet called **Functional** next to the **ShouldWork** worksheet that is already present. Right-click on the `scalatest` package and select **New | Scala Worksheet**.

The worksheet can be filled as follows:

```
package scalatest
import org.scalatest._
import org.scalatest.selenium.WebBrowser
import org.openqa.selenium.htmlunit.HtmlUnitDriver
import org.openqa.selenium.firefox.FirefoxDriver
import org.openqa.selenium.WebDriver
object Functional extends FlatSpec with Matchers with WebBrowser {
implicit val webDriver: WebDriver = new HtmlUnitDriver
  go to "http://www.packtpub.com/"
  textField("keys").value = "Scala"
  submit()
  pageTitle should be ("Search | Packt Publishing")
  pageSource should include("Akka")
}
```

Upon the save operation (*Ctrl + S*), the worksheet will be evaluated and should probably display some output information for every statement, except for the last two lines with `should` matchers, as they should evaluate to `true`.

Try to change (`"Search | Packt Publishing"`) to a different value, such as `Results` or just `Packt Publishing`, and notice how the console output provides handy information on what does not match. This is shown in the following screenshot:

```
package scalatest
import org.scalatest._
import org.scalatest.selenium.WebBrowser
import org.openqa.selenium.htmlunit.HtmlUnitDriver
import org.openqa.selenium.firefox.FirefoxDriver
import org.openqa.selenium.WebDriver
object Functional extends FlatSpec with Matchers with WebBrowser {
implicit val webDriver: WebDriver = new HtmlUnitDriver
                                      > webDriver  : org.openqa.selenium.WebDriver = org.openqa.selenium.htmlunit.Ht
                                      | mlUnitDriver@3b82fb2d

  go to "http://www.packtpub.com/"
  textField("keys").value = "Scala"
                                      > HtmlTextInput[<input type="text" name="keys" id="edit-keys" size="49" value=
                                      | "" placeholder="Search..." class="form-text form-autocomplete">] -> HtmlHtml
                                      | [<html xmlns="http://www.w3.org/1999/xhtml" lang="en" xml:lang="en">]
                                      | HtmlTextInput[<input type="text" name="keys" id="edit-keys" size="49" value=
                                      | "" placeholder="Search..." class="form-text form-autocomplete">] -> HtmlHtml
                                      | ...
                                      | Output exceeds cutoff limit.
  submit()                            > HtmlTextInput[<input type="text" name="keys" id="edit-keys" size="49" value=
                                      | "Scala" placeholder="Search..." class="form-text form-autocomplete">] -> Htm
                                      | lHtml[<html xmlns="http://www.w3.org/1999/xhtml" lang="en" xml:lang="en">]
                                      | ...
                                      | Output exceeds cutoff limit.
  pageTitle should be ("Packt Publishing")
                                      > org.scalatest.exceptions.TestFailedException: "[Search | ]Packt Publishing"
                                      | was not equal to "[]Packt Publishing"
                                      |     at org.scalatest.MatchersHelper$.newTestFailedException(MatchersHelper.s
                                      | cala:160)

  pageSource should include("Akka")
}
```

This functional test just scratches the surface of what's possible. As we are using the Java Selenium library, in Scala, you can inherit the power of the Selenium framework that is available in Java.

Mocking with ScalaMock

Mocking is a technique by which you can test code without requiring all of its dependencies in place. Java offers several frameworks for mocking objects when writing tests. The most well known are JMock, EasyMock, and Mockito. As the Scala language introduces new elements such as traits and functions, the Java-based mocking frameworks are not enough, and this is where ScalaMock (`www.scalamock.org`) comes into play.

ScalaMock is a native Scala-mocking framework that is typically used within ScalaTest (or Specs2), by importing the following dependencies into the SBT (`build.sbt`) file:

```
libraryDependencies +="org.scalamock" %% "scalamock-scalatest-support"
% "3.0.1" % "test"
```

Within Specs2, the following dependencies need to be imported:

```
libraryDependencies +=
"org.scalamock" %% "scalamock-specs2-support" % "3.0.1" % "test"
```

Since the release of the Scala Version 2.10, ScalaMock has been rewritten, and the ScalaMock Version 3.*x* is the version that we are going to cover briefly by going through an example of mocking a trait.

Let's first define the code that we are going to test. It consists of a tiny currency converter (available at http://www.luketebbs.com/?p=58) that fetches currency rates from the European Central Bank. Retrieving and parsing the XML file of currency rates is only a matter of a few lines of code, as follows:

```
trait Currency {
  lazy val rates : Map[String,BigDecimal] = {
  val exchangeRates =
    "http://www.ecb.europa.eu/stats/eurofxref/eurofxref-daily.xml"
  for (
    elem <- xml.XML.load(exchangeRates)\"Cube"\"Cube"\"Cube")
  yield
    (elem\"@currency").text -> BigDecimal((elem\"@rate").text)
  }.toMap ++ Map[String,BigDecimal]("EUR" -> 1)

  def convert(amount:BigDecimal,from:String,to:String) =
    amount / rates(from) * rates(to)
}
```

In this example, the currency rates are fetched from a URL using the xml.XML.load method. As XML is part of the Scala standard library, there is no need for imports here. The load method parses and returns the XML rates as an immutable structure of type Elem, which is a case class that represents XML elements. This is shown in the following code:

```
<gesmes:Envelope xmlns:gesmes="http://www.gesmes.org/xml/2002-08-01"
xmlns="http://www.ecb.int/vocabulary/2002-08-01/eurofxref">
  <gesmes:subject>Reference rates</gesmes:subject>
    <gesmes:Sender>
      <gesmes:name>European Central Bank</gesmes:name>
    </gesmes:Sender>
    <Cube>
      <Cube time="2013-11-15">
      <Cube currency="USD" rate="1.3460"/>
      <Cube currency="JPY" rate="134.99"/>
      <Cube currency="BGN" rate="1.9558"/>
      <Cube currency="CZK" rate="27.155"/>
      <Cube currency="DKK" rate="7.4588"/>
      <Cube currency="GBP" rate="0.83770"/>
            . . .
        . . .
      </Cube>
    </Cube>
</gesmes:Envelope>
```

Accessing the list of currency rates from this XML document is done through an XPath expression by navigating inside the Cube nodes, hence the `xml.XML. load(exchangeRates) \ "Cube" \ "Cube" \ "Cube"` expression. A single for comprehension (the `for (...) yield (...)` construct that we introduced in the previous chapter) is required to loop over the currency rates and return a collection of `key -> value` pairs where, in our case, a key will be a string that represents the currency name, and `value` will be a BigDecimal value that represents the rate. Notice how the information is extracted from `<Cube currency="USD" rate="1.3460"/>` by writing `(elem \ "@currency").text` to capture the currency attribute and `(elem \ "@rate").text` to capture the rate respectively. The latter will be further processed by creating a new `BigDecimal` value from the given string.

In the end, we get a `Map[String, BigDecimal]` that contains all our currencies with their rates. To this value, we add the mapping for the currency EUR (Euros) that will represent the reference rate one; this is why we use the `++` operator to merge two maps, that is, the one we just created together with a new map containing only one `key -> value` element, `Map[String,BigDecimal]("EUR"-> 1)`.

Before mocking, let's write a regular test using ScalaTest with `FlatSpec` and `Matchers`. We will make use of our `Converter` trait, by integrating it into the following `MoneyService` class:

```
package se.chap4

class MoneyService(converter:Converter ) {

  def sendMoneyToSweden(amount:BigDecimal,from:String): BigDecimal = {
    val convertedAmount = converter.convert(amount,from,"SEK")
    println(s" $convertedAmount SEK are on their way...")
    convertedAmount
  }

  def sendMoneyToSwedenViaEngland(amount:BigDecimal,from:String):
BigDecimal = {
    val englishAmount = converter.convert(amount,from,"GBP")
    println(s" $englishAmount GBP are on their way...")
    val swedishAmount = converter.convert(englishAmount,"GBP","SEK")
    println(s" $swedishAmount SEK are on their way...")
    swedishAmount
  }
}
```

A possible test specification derived from the `MoneyService` class is as follows:

```
package se.chap4

import org.scalatest._
import org.junit.runner.RunWith
import org.scalatest.junit.JUnitRunner

@RunWith(classOf[JUnitRunner])
class MoneyServiceTest extends FlatSpec with Matchers {

"Sending money to Sweden" should "convert into SEK" in {
    val moneyService =
      new MoneyService(new ECBConverter)
    val amount = 200
    val from = "EUR"
    val result = moneyService.sendMoneyToSweden(amount, from)
    result.toInt should (be > (1700) and be <= (1800))
  }

"Sending money to Sweden via England" should "convert into GBP then
SEK" in {
    val moneyService =
      new MoneyService(new ECBConverter)
    val amount = 200
    val from = "EUR"
    val result = moneyService.sendMoneyToSwedenViaEngland(amount,
from)
    result.toInt should (be > (1700) and be <= (1800))
  }
}
```

To be able to instantiate the `Converter` trait, we use an `ECBConverter` class defined in the `Converter.scala` file as follows:

```
class ECBConverter extends Converter
```

If we execute the test from the SBT command prompt or directly within Eclipse (as a JUnit), we get the following output:

```
> test
[info] Compiling 1 Scala source to /Users/thomas/projects/internal/
HttpSamples/target/scala-2.10/test-classes...
 1792.2600 SEK are on their way...
 167.70000 GBP are on their way...
```

```
1792.2600 SEK are on their way...
[info] MoneyServiceTest:
[info] Sending money to Sweden
[info] - should convert into SEK
[info] Sending money to Sweden via England
[info] - should convert into GBP then SEK
[info] Passed: : Total 2, Failed 0, Errors 0, Passed 2, Skipped 0
[success] Total time: 1 s, completed
```

If the URL from which we are retrieving the currency rates is not always available, or if the currency rates have changed a lot on one particular day and the resulting amount of the conversion is not in the given interval of the assertion should (be > (1700) and be <= (1800)), then our test might fail. In that case, mocking the converter in our test seems appropriate, and can be done as follows:

```
package se.chap4

import org.scalatest._
import org.junit.runner.RunWith
import org.scalatest.junit.JUnitRunner
import org.scalamock.scalatest.MockFactory

@RunWith(classOf[JUnitRunner])
class MockMoneyServiceTest extends FlatSpec with MockFactory with
Matchers {

"Sending money to Sweden" should "convert into SEK" in {

    val converter = mock[Converter]
    val moneyService = new MoneyService(converter)

    (converter.convert _).expects(BigDecimal("200"),"EUR","SEK").
returning(BigDecimal(1750))

    val amount = 200
    val from = "EUR"
    val result = moneyService.sendMoneyToSweden(amount, from)
    result.toInt should be (1750)
  }
}
```

The `expects` method contains the arguments that we expect when our code should invoke the `convert` method, and the returning method contains our expected output in place of the real return result.

ScalaMock has many variations on how to apply the mocking code, and is planning to enhance the mocking syntax using the **Macros** in future releases. In short, Macros are functions that are called by the compiler during compilation. It is an experimental feature added in Scala from Version 2.10 that makes it possible for the developer to access the compiler APIs and apply transformations to the **AST** (**Abstract Syntax Tree**), that is, the tree representation of a program. Macros are out of the scope of this book, but among other things, they are useful for the Code Generation and DSLs. Their usage will improve the ScalaMock syntax; for instance, you can apply your mock expectations within `inSequence {... }` or the `inAnyOrder {... }` blocks of code or in nested combinations of these blocks, as illustrated in their documentation, which is available at `scalamock.org`. ScalaMock also supports a more Mockito-like style with a **Record-then-Verify** cycle rather than the **Expectations-First** style, which we have been using.

Testing with ScalaCheck

Having a complete and consistent test suite that consists of unit, integration, or functional tests is essential in ensuring a good overall quality of your software development. However, sometimes, such a suite is not enough. While testing for example-specific data structures, it often happens that there are too many possible values to test with, which means that there is a very large amount of mocking or production of test data. Automated property-based testing is the aim of ScalaCheck, a Scala library inspired by Haskell that allows generating, more or less randomly, the test data to verify some properties about the code you are testing. This library can be applied to Scala as well as to Java projects.

To get up and running quickly with ScalaCheck, you can include the appropriate library in the `build.sbt` file, as we have often done till now. This is shown as follows:

```
resolver += Resolver.sonatypeRepo("releases")


libraryDependencies ++= Seq(
"org.scalacheck" %% "scalacheck" % "1.11.0" % "test")
```

From the SBT prompt, you may type `reload` instead of exiting and relaunching SBT, to get a fresh version of the build file, and then type `update` to fetch the new dependency. Once this is done, you may also type `eclipse` to update your project with the dependency so that it will be a part of your classpath, and the editor will recognize the ScalaCheck classes.

Let's first run the `StringSpecification` test that is proposed by the **Quick start** page available at www.scalacheck.org:

```
import org.scalacheck.Properties
import org.scalacheck.Prop.forAll

object StringSpecification extends Properties("String") {

  property("startsWith") = forAll { (a: String, b: String) =>
    (a+b).startsWith(a)
  }

  property("concatenate") = forAll { (a: String, b: String) =>
    (a+b).length > a.length && (a+b).length > b.length
  }

  property("substring") = forAll { (a: String, b: String, c: String)
  =>
    (a+b+c).substring(a.length, a.length+b.length) == b
  }

}
```

In this code snippet, ScalaCheck produces (randomly) a number of strings and verifies that the properties are correct; the first one is straightforward; it should verify that adding two strings a and b should produce a string that starts with a. It probably sounds obvious that this test will pass, no matter what the values of the strings are, but the second property that verifies the length of the concatenation of the two strings is not always true; feeding both a and b with the empty value " " is a counter example that shows that the property is not verified. We can illustrate that by running the test via SBT as follows:

```
> test-only se.chap4.StringSpecification
[info] + String.startsWith: OK, passed 100 tests.
[info] ! String.concatenate: Falsified after 0 passed tests.
[info] > ARG_0: ""
[info] > ARG_1: ""
[info] + String.substring: OK, passed 100 tests.
[error] Failed: : Total 3, Failed 1, Errors 0, Passed 2, Skipped 0
[error] Failed tests:
[error]         se.chap4.StringSpecification
```

```
[error] (test:test-only) sbt.TestsFailedException: Tests unsuccessful
[error] Total time: 1 s, completed Nov 19, 2013 4:30:37 PM
>
```

ScalaCheck conveniently outputs a counter example, `ARG_0: ""` and `ARG_1: ""` that makes the test fail.

We can add a few more tests on more complex objects than just strings. Let's add a new test class named `ConverterSpecification` as part of our test suite, to test the `Converter` that we have created in the *Mocking with ScalaMock* section:

```scala
package se.chap4

import org.scalacheck._
import Arbitrary._
import Gen._
import Prop.forAll

object ConverterSpecification extends Properties("Converter") with
Converter {

  val currencies = Gen.oneOf("EUR","GBP","SEK","JPY")

  lazy val conversions: Gen[(BigDecimal,String,String)] = for {
    amt <- arbitrary[Int] suchThat {_ >= 0}
    from <- currencies
    to <- currencies
  } yield (amt,from,to)

  property("Conversion to same value") = forAll(currencies) { c:String
=>
    val amount = BigDecimal(200)
    val convertedAmount = convert(amount,c,c)
    convertedAmount == amount
  }

  property("Various currencies") = forAll(conversions) { c =>
    val convertedAmount = convert(c._1,c._2,c._3)
    convertedAmount >= 0
  }
}
```

If we run the test in SBT, the following output is displayed:

```
> ~test-only se.chap4.ConverterSpecification
[info] + Converter.Conversion to same value: OK, passed 100 tests.
[info] + Converter.Various currencies: OK, passed 100 tests.
[info] Passed: : Total 2, Failed 0, Errors 0, Passed 2, Skipped 0
[success] Total time: 1 s, completed Nov 19, 2013 9:40:40 PM
1. Waiting for source changes... (press enter to interrupt)
```

In this specification, we added two specific generators; the first one named `currencies` is able to generate only a few strings taken from a list of valid currencies that we want to test, as otherwise, a randomly generated string would produce strings that are not part of the `Map`. Let's add an invalid item `"DUMMY"` to the generated list to verify that the test is failing:

```
val currencies = Gen.oneOf("EUR","GBP","SEK","JPY","DUMMY")
```

On saving this, the tests are rerun automatically as we specified the ~ sign in front of `test-only`. This is shown as follows:

```
[info] ! Converter.Conversion to same value: Exception raised on property
evaluation.
[info] > ARG_0: "DUMMY"
[info] > Exception: java.util.NoSuchElementException: key not found:
DUMMY
[info] ! Converter.Various currencies: Exception raised on property
evaluation.
[info] > ARG_0: (1,,)
[info] > ARG_0_ORIGINAL: (1,DUMMY,SEK)
[info] > Exception: java.util.NoSuchElementException: key not found:
[error] Error: Total 2, Failed 0, Errors 2, Passed 0, Skipped 0
[error] Error during tests:
[error]     se.chap4.ConverterSpecification
[error] (test:test-only) sbt.TestsFailedException: Tests unsuccessful
[error] Total time: 1 s, completed Nov 19, 2013 9:48:36 PM
2. Waiting for source changes... (press enter to interrupt)
```

The second generator named `conversions` illustrates the construction of a more complex generator that takes advantage of the power of for comprehensions. In particular, notice the `suchThat {_ >= 0}` filter method that makes sure that the arbitrary chosen integer has a positive value. This generator returns a `Tuple3` triplet that contains all the necessary values to test the `Converter.convert` method.

Summary

In this chapter, we covered some of the major testing frameworks available in Scala, which largely inherit from the rich Java ecosystem. Moreover, by applying property-based testing via ScalaCheck, we explored novel approaches to enhance the testing quality. To further improve the quality of the software, interested readers can look at additional SBT plugins that are listed on the `http://www.scala-sbt.org/` website, notably `scalastyle-sbt-plugin` to check the coding style or the various code-coverage plugins. In the next chapter, we are going to dive into the huge area of web development and take advantage of the power of the Scala language to make the development of portals and web apps a productive and fun activity.

5
Getting Started with the Play Framework

This chapter commences our journey into web development in Scala. Web development has become an area where the choice of architectures and frameworks is tremendous. Finding the right tool for the job is not always a straightforward task as it ranges from traditional Java EE or Spring-based architectural styles to more recent Ruby on Rails-like approaches. Most of the existing solutions still rely on the adoption of the servlet-container model, whether they use lightweight containers such as Jetty/Tomcat or support **EJBs (Enterprise JavaBeans)** such as JBoss, Glassfish, WebSphere, or WebLogic. Many online articles and conference talks have tried to compare some of the alternatives, and as these frameworks evolve rapidly and sometimes focus on different aspects (such as frontend versus backend), compiling a fair and accurate list remains difficult. In the Scala world, alternatives to create web applications range from lightweight frameworks such as Unfiltered, Spray, or Scalatra to full-featured solutions such as the Lift or the Play Frameworks.

We have chosen to concentrate on the Play Framework, because it embraces important features that we think are the key to maintainable, modern software development. Some of the advantages of the Play Framework are:

- The Play Framework is scalable and robust. It can handle large loads because it is built on a fully asynchronous model on the top of technologies that are ready to handle multicore architectures such as Akka, a framework to build concurrent and distributed applications that we will cover in *Chapter 8, Essential Properties of Modern Applications – Asynchrony and Concurrency*.

- It provides us with enhanced developer productivity by promoting ease of use, promoting the **DRY** (short for **Don't Repeat Yourself**) principle, and taking advantage of the expressiveness and conciseness of Scala. In addition to that, the hit refresh workflow of Play by which you can simply refresh your browser and get instant feedback on the changes you make is a real boost in the productivity, in contrast with the longer deployment cycles of the Java servlet and EJB containers.

- It provides good integration with the existing legacy of infrastructure based on the JVM.

- It provides good integration with modern, client-side development trends that heavily rely on JavaScript/CSS and their surrounding ecosystem, including frameworks such as AngularJS or WebJars. Moreover, the **LESS** (short for **Leaner CSS**) dynamic stylesheet language as well as CoffeeScript, a small and elegant language that compiles to JavaScript, are supported by Play Framework without any additional integration.

The Play Framework Version 2.*x* exists both for Java and Scala, which is an additional strength as Java developers will probably get acquainted with the differences more quickly and may have previous experience with the Java version before moving on to Scala.

Several alternatives are offered to rapidly get you started with the Play Framework and create a minimalistic `helloworld` project. Note that all these alternatives create projects based on SBT, as we mentioned briefly in *Chapter 3, Understanding the Scala Ecosystem.*

Getting started with the classic Play distribution

Download the classic Play distribution from `http://www.playframework.com/download`, and unpack the `.zip` archive in a directory of your choice. Add this directory to your path (so that running the `play` command anywhere on your filesystem will create a new application). With this alternative, you can open a terminal window and enter the following command:

```
> play new <PROJECT_NAME>    (for example  play new playsample)
```

The following output will be displayed:

```
 _ _     _
| _ \| | __ _ _  _ 
|  _/| |/ _` | || |
|_|  |_|\__,_|\_, |
             |__/

play 2.2.1 built with Scala 2.10.2 (running Java 1.7.0_11), http://
www.playframework.com

The new application will be created in /Users/thomas/playsample

What is the application name? [playsample]
>
```

We just need to press *Enter* as we have already given a project name on the previous command. The following will be displayed on pressing *Enter*:

```
Which template do you want to use for this new application?
  1            - Create a simple Scala application
  2            - Create a simple Java application
> 1
OK, application playsample is created.


Have fun!
```

That's all; in less than a minute, we already have a fully working web app that we can now execute. As it is an SBT project (where the sbt command has been renamed play instead), we can just navigate to the root of the created project and start our Play session as if we were working on an SBT project. This is done as follows:

```
> cd playsample
> play run
[info] Loading project definition…
--- (Running the application from SBT, auto-reloading is enabled) ---

[info] play - Listening for HTTP on /0:0:0:0:0:0:0:0:9000

(Server started, use Ctrl+D to stop and go back to the console...)
```

Notice that the application is started on port 9000 by default. If you want a different port, you can type the following command instead:

```
> play
```

This will bring you to the Play (SBT) session, and from there, you can choose the port to listen to. This can be done as follows:

```
[playsample] $ run 9095
[info] play - Listening for HTTP on /0:0:0:0:0:0:0:0:9095
```

Another alternative is to enter `> play "run 9095"` in the terminal.

Launch a browser at `http://localhost:9095/` (9000 if you are running using the default port), and you should see the **Welcome to Play** page on your running portal:

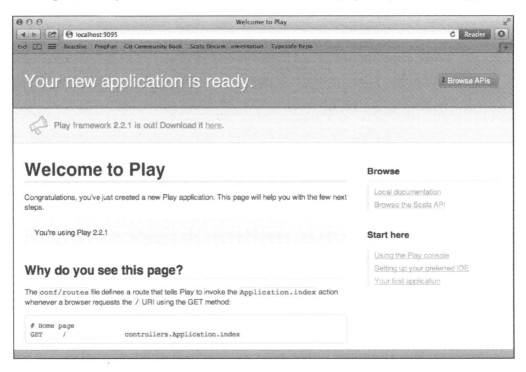

Getting started with the Typesafe Activator

Using the same method that we used earlier in the book to create projects based on the Activator templates, getting started with a Play project through the Activator is very straightforward. Just go to the Typesafe Activator installation directory and enter the following command:

```
> ./activator ui
```

This will launch the activator in a browser window. The most basic Scala Play project is found in the `hello-play-scala` template. Once you have selected the template, notice the default location that indicates where the project will be created and then click on **Create**.

Let's run our sample project either directly from the activator browser view or from a terminal window by navigating to the root directory of the created project and entering the following command in the command prompt:

```
> ./activator run
```

Once the server is listening on port 9000, you can open the `http://localhost:9000/` URL in a browser. Compilation is triggered only once you access the URL, so it may take a few seconds for the application to show up. What should come up in your browser is similar to the following screenshot:

Architecture of a Play application

To perceive in a better way how a Play application is built, we first need to understand a few of its architectural aspects.

Visualizing the framework stack

Before we start exploring the code behind a typical sample Play application, let's visualize the architecture of the framework using a couple of diagrams. First, the overall diagram of the technology stack composed of Play is shown as follows:

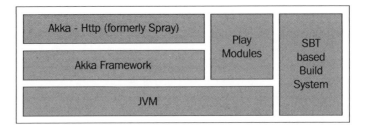

On top of the JVM resides the Akka Framework, a framework to manage concurrent operations based on the actor model, which we will cover later in *Chapter 8, Essential Properties of Modern Applications – Asynchrony and Concurrency*. While most web frameworks today still rely on servlet containers such as Tomcat or JBoss, the novelty of Play is to avoid following this model by focusing on making applications stateless when code can be **hot swapped**, that is, replaced at runtime. Although widely used and deployed in commercial environments, servlet containers suffer from additional overheads, such as the one thread per request problem, which can limit the scalability when handling large loads. For a developer, the time gained by avoiding the redeployment of a partial or full .ear or .war archive every time a change in the code is made can be significant.

On top of Akka resides a REST/HTTP integration layer, based on Spray (an open source toolkit to build REST/HTTP-based integration layers, now called Akka-Http), which produces and consumes embeddable REST services. This makes Play pertinent to the modern ways of writing web applications, where the backend and frontend communicate through HTTP REST services, exchanging mostly JSON/XML messages that can be rendered as HTML5 and, therefore, embrace the full power of frontend JavaScript frameworks.

Finally, to be able to integrate with many other technologies of all kinds, such as relational or NoSQL-based databases, security frameworks, social networks, cloud-based or Big Data solutions, a large list of Play plugins and modules are listed at http://www.playmodules.net.

Exploring the request-response lifecycle

Play follows the well-known MVC pattern, and the lifecycle of the web request can be seen as follows:

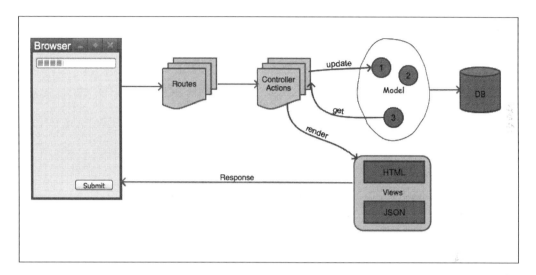

To go through the various steps of this workflow, we are going to explore a sample `helloworld` application that is part of the Play distribution. This `helloworld` application is a little more sophisticated and, therefore, more interesting than the pure getting started examples that we launched previously either via the Typesafe Activator or the plain `> play new <project>` command to create a project from scratch.

The `helloworld` application that we consider here can be found under the `<play installation root>/samples/scala/helloworld` directory (we have used the Play 2.2.1 distribution at the time of this writing).

As for any Play project within the distribution that already contains the `sbteclipse` plugin, we can directly generate Eclipse-related files by entering the following command in a command prompt (at the level of the project root directory):

```
> play eclipse
```

Note that as Play commands are just a thin layer on the top of SBT, we can reuse the same syntax, that is, > `play eclipse` rather than > `sbt eclipse`. Once these are imported into the IDE, you can see the general source layout of a Play application in the **Package Explorer** panel on the left-hand side, as shown in the following screenshot:

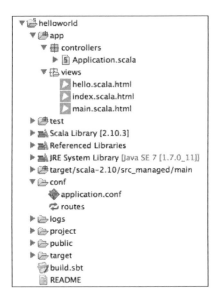

Let's first run the application to see what it looks like using the following command:

```
> play run
```

Open a browser at `http://localhost:9000/` and you should see a small web form similar to the following screenshot:

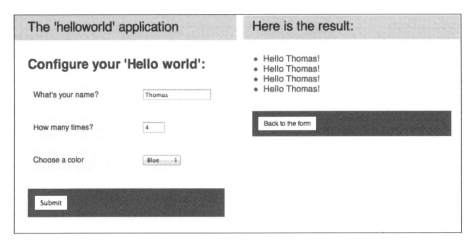

Enter the required information and click on **Submit** to verify that you get your name displayed a specified number of times.

The first step in the request flow appears in the `conf/routes` file, which is shown as follows:

```
# Routes
# This file defines all application routes (Higher priority routes
first)
# ~~~~

# Home page
GET     /                   controllers.Application.index

# Hello action
GET     /hello              controllers.Application.sayHello

# Map static resources from the /public folder to the /assets URL path
GET     /assets/*file  controllers.Assets.at(path="/public", file)
```

This is the place where we can define a mapping between HTTP request URLs and the controller code that needs to handle the request on the Play server, shown in the following format:

```
<REQUEST_TYPE(GET, POST...)> <URL_RELATIVE_PATH> <CONTROLLER_METHOD>
```

For instance, accessing the `http://localhost:9000/hello` URL in the browser matches the following route:

```
GET  /  controllers.Application.index
```

The `index` method, taking no arguments, will be called on the `controller.Application.scala` class.

This way of presenting the routing of the URLs to the controllers is different from the standard Java way found, for instance, in JAX-RS or Spring MVC, where each controller is annotated instead. In our opinion, the routing file approach gives us a clear overview of what the API supports, that is, the documentation, and it makes a Play application RESTful by default.

Even if it seems that the `routes` file is a configuration file, it is indeed compiled and any typo or reference to a nonexistent controller method will be quickly identified. Replace `controllers.Application.index` with `controllers.Application.wrongmethod`, save the file, and just click on the reload button in the browser (*Ctrl* + *R*). You should get the error nicely displayed in the browser, as seen in the following screenshot:

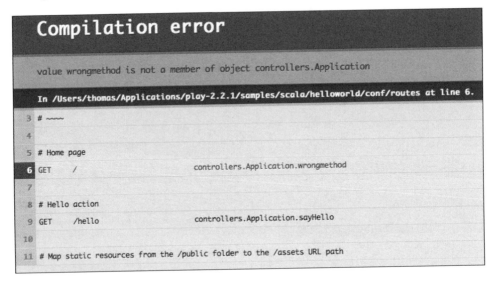

Notice how precise the error message is and how the exact failing line in the file is pointed out. This great way to display error messages on reloading the browser is one of the many features that makes programmers more productive. Similarly, even if there is no mapping error in the routes file, accessing a nonmapped URL that is under development (such as `http://localhost:9000/hi`) will display an error as well as the content of the `routes` file to show us which URLs are possible to invoke. This can be seen in the following screenshot:

Handling a request in the controller

Moving on, let's take a look at the `Application` class that receives and processes the GET request:

```
object Application extends Controller {
  /**
   * Describes the hello form.
   */
  val helloForm = Form(
    tuple(
      "name" -> nonEmptyText,
      "repeat" -> number(min = 1, max = 100),
      "color" -> optional(text)
    )
  )


  // -- Actions
  /**
   * Home page
   */
  def index = Action {
    Ok(html.index(helloForm))
  }

  /**
   * Handles the form submission.
   */
  def sayHello = Action { implicit request =>
    helloForm.bindFromRequest.fold(
      formWithErrors => BadRequest(html.index(formWithErrors)),
      {case (name, repeat, color) => Ok(html.hello(name, repeat.toInt,
color))}
    )
  }
}
```

The `index` method performs the `Action` block, which is a function
(`Request[AnyContent] => Result`), that takes the request and returns a `Result`
object. The input parameter of the `Request` type is not shown here in the `index`
method as it is implicitly passed and we are not using it in the body of the function;
we could have written `def index = Action { implicit request =>` instead, if
we wanted to. The one liner `Ok(html.index(helloForm))` means that the returned
result should have an HTTP status equal to 200, that is, `Ok`, and consist of binding the
`html.index` view to the `helloForm` model.

The model in this tiny example consists of a `Form` object defined in `val` earlier in the file. This can be seen as follows:

```
val helloForm = Form(
  tuple(
    "name" -> nonEmptyText,
    "repeat" -> number(min = 1, max = 100),
    "color" -> optional(text)
  )
)
```

Each parameter is described as a `key -> value` pair, where `key` is the name of the parameter and `value` is the result of a function applied to the parameter that will produce a `play.api.data.Mapping` object. Such mapping functions are very useful to be able to perform a validation on the form parameters. Here, the `Form` parameters are expressed as a tuple object, but we could create more complex objects such as case classes. The sample project named *forms* in the Play distribution contains examples of this more advanced way of handling validation. The `fold` method encountered in the `sayHello` method of the controller is a way to accumulate validation errors to be able to report all of these errors at once. Let's enter a few mistakes (such as leaving the `name` field blank or entering characters when numbers are required) when filling out the form to verify how errors are displayed. This can be seen in the following screenshot:

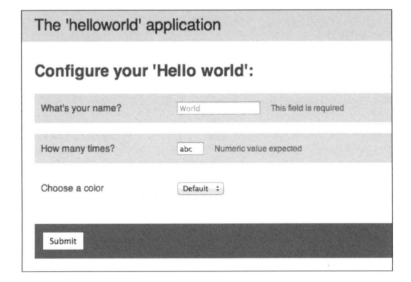

Rendering the view

The template used to render the view is found under the views/index.scala.html file. This template is shown as follows:

```
@(helloForm: Form[(String,Int,Option[String])])
@import helper._

@main(title = "The 'helloworld' application") {

    <h1>Configure your 'Hello world':</h1>

    @form(action = routes.Application.sayHello, args = 'id ->
"helloform") {
        @inputText(
            field = helloForm("name"),
            args = '_label -> "What's your name?", 'placeholder ->
"World"
        )

        @inputText(
            field = helloForm("repeat"),
            args = '_label -> "How many times?", 'size -> 3,
'placeholder -> 10
        )

        @select(
            field = helloForm("color"),
            options = options(
                "" -> "Default",
                "red" -> "Red",
                "green" -> "Green",
                "blue" -> "Blue"
            ),
            args = '_label -> "Choose a color"
        )

        <p class="buttons">
            <input type="submit" id="submit">
        <p>
    }
}
```

One of the strengths of the Play template engine is that it is based on the Scala language itself. This is good news because we do not need to learn any new templating syntax; we can reuse the Scala constructs, without any additional integration. Moreover, the templates are compiled so that we get compile-time errors whenever we make a mistake; the errors will show up in the browser in the same way that they showed up for routes or the plain controller Scala code. This fast feedback can save us a lot of time compared to the more traditional techniques of using **JSPs (JavaServer Pages)** in Java web development.

The declarations at the top of the template contain the bound variables that will be populated throughout the template. The template markup can produce an output of any kind, such as HTML5, XML, or plain text. Templates can also include other templates.

In the previous example, the @main(title = "The 'helloworld' application") { <block> ...} statement refers to the main.scala.html view file itself, displayed as follows:

```
@(title: String)(content: Html)

<!DOCTYPE html>
<html>
    <head>
        <title>@title</title>
        <link rel="stylesheet" media="screen" href="@routes.Assets.
at("stylesheets/main.css")">
        <link rel="shortcut icon" type="image/png" href="@routes.
Assets.at("images/favicon.png")">
        <script src="@routes.Assets.at("javascripts/jquery-1.6.4.min.
js")" type="text/javascript"></script>
    </head>
    <body>
        <header>
            <a href="@routes.Application.index">@title</a>
        </header>

        <section>
            @content
        </section>
    </body>
</html>
```

As you can see, @(title: String)(content: Html) at the top of this file matches (title = "The 'helloworld' application"){ <block of template with code> ...} from the previous template. This is how templates call each other.

The @ sign indicates that the Scala code follows either directly with the name of a variable or a method to be invoked, or with a full block of code given between brackets, that is, @{ ...code ... }.

The response (views/hello.scala.html) template, once the web form has been submitted, contains a for loop to display the name field a number of times. This is shown as follows:

```
@(name: String, repeat: Int, color: Option[String])
@main("Here is the result:") {
    <ul style="color: @color.getOrElse("inherited")">
        @for(_ <- 1 to repeat) {
            <li>Hello @name!</li>
    }
    </ul>
    <p class="buttons">
        <a href="@routes.Application.index">Back to the form</a>
    </p>
}
```

Playing with authentication

A frequent piece of functionality needed when designing a new web application involves authentication and authorization. Authentication usually requires that the user provide the credentials to log in to the application in the form of a username/password. Authorization is the mechanism by which the system can ensure that a user can perform only the operations that he/she is entitled to. In this section, we are going to extend our helloworld sample with security features that are part of the Play distribution, as a way to demonstrate how the usage of traits in Scala can provide an elegant solution to conventional problems.

Let's define a new controller that we will call Authentication, which contains common methods such as login to retrieve a sign-in page, authenticate and check to perform the verification of the authentication, and logout to go back to the login page. This is done as follows:

```
object Authentication extends Controller {

  val loginForm = Form(
    tuple(
      "email" -> text,
      "password" -> text
    ) verifying ("Invalid email or password", result => result match {
      case (email, password) => check(email, password)
```

```
    })
  )

  def check(username: String, password: String) = {
    (username == "thomas@home" && password == "1234")
  }

  def login = Action { implicit request =>
    Ok(html.login(loginForm))
  }

  def authenticate = Action { implicit request =>
    loginForm.bindFromRequest.fold(
      formWithErrors => BadRequest(html.login(formWithErrors)),
      user => Redirect(routes.Application.index).withSession(Security.
username -> user._1)
    )
  }

  def logout = Action {
    Redirect(routes.Authentication.login).withNewSession.flashing(
      "success" -> "You are now logged out."
    )
  }
}
```

Similar to the index method that belongs to the Application controller from the previous section, the login method here consists of binding a form (named loginForm) to a view (named html.login, corresponding to the file views/login. scala.html). A simple template for a view that consists of two text fields to capture an e-mail/username and password is shown as follows:

```
@(form: Form[(String,String)])(implicit flash: Flash)

@main("Sign in") {

    @helper.form(routes.Authentication.authenticate) {

        @form.globalError.map { error =>
            <p class="error">
                @error.message
            </p>
        }

        @flash.get("success").map { message =>
```

```
                    <p class="success">
                        @message
                    </p>
                }

                <p>
                    <input type="email" name="email" placeholder="Email"
id="email" value="@form("email").value">
                    </p>
                    <p>
                        <input type="password" name="password" id="password"
placeholder="Password">
                    </p>
                    <p>
                        <button type="submit" id="loginbutton">Login</button>
                    </p>

                }

            <p class="note">
                Try login as <em>thomas@@home</em> with <em>1234</em> as
password.
            </p>

        }
```

Notice how the `thomas@@home` username shows us that you can escape the special `@` character by entering it twice.

Now we have the logic to handle an HTML login page with the submission of the credentials to be authenticated, but we are still lacking the missing piece that will wrap a conventional invocation of a method from any controller that we want to protect. Moreover, this logic will redirect us to the login page in case the username (a property stored in our `request.session` object and retrieved from a cookie) is not present. It can be described in a trait as follows:

```
trait Secured {

    def username(request: RequestHeader) = request.session.get(Security.
username)

    def onUnauthorized(request: RequestHeader) = Results.
Redirect(routes.Authentication.login)

    def withAuth(f: => String => Request[AnyContent] => SimpleResult) =
{
```

```
      Security.Authenticated(username, onUnauthorized) { user =>
        Action(request => f(user)(request))
      }
    }
  }
```

We can add this trait to the same `Authentication.scala` controller class. The `withAuth` method wraps our `Action` invocations by applying the `Security.Authenticated` method around them. To be able to use this trait, we just need to mix it in in our controller class as follows:

```
object Application extends Controller with Secured {
    ...
}
```

Once the trait is part of our controller, we can replace an `Action` method with a `withAuth` method instead. For example, when invoking the `index` method, we replace the `Action` method, as follows:

```
/**
 * Home page
 */
def index = withAuth { username => implicit request =>
  Ok(html.index(helloForm))
}
```

To be able to execute our new functionality, we should not forget to add the extra methods from the `Authentication.scala` controller to the routes' definitions (the compiler will flag this if we omit them):

```
# Authentication
GET    /login     controllers.Authentication.login
POST   /login     controllers.Authentication.authenticate
GET    /logout    controllers.Authentication.logout
```

Let's rerun the application and invoke the `http://localhost:9000/` page. We should be routed to the `login.html` page rather than the `index.html` page. This is shown in the following screenshot:

Try to log in with both the erroneous and correct e-mail/password combinations to verify that the authentication has been implemented correctly.

This basic authentication mechanism is just an example of how you can easily extend the applications in Play. It demonstrates the use of the Action composition, a technique that can also be applied to many other aspects—for example, logging or modifying requests—and is a good alternative to interceptors.

There are, of course, external modules that you can use with Play if you need to achieve authentication through other services; for instance, modules based on standards such as OAuth, OAuth2, or OpenID. The SecureSocial module is a good example to do this and is available at `http://securesocial.ws`.

Practical tips when using Play

We will conclude this chapter with a couple of recommendations that will help with the daily usage of the Play Framework.

Debugging with Play

Due to the declarative nature of functional programming and the powerful type checking mechanism of the compiler, debugging should happen less often when dealing with Scala code. However, if you need to debug a Play application in a situation, you might as well run a remote debugging session as you would in Java. To achieve this, just start your Play application with an extra debug command:

```
> play debug run
```

You should see an extra information line in the output that displays the following command line:

```
Listening for transport dt_socket at address: 9999
```

From here, you can add break points in your code and start a remote debugging configuration in Eclipse by navigating to the menu named **Run | Debug Configurations...**

Right-click on **Remote Java Application** and select **New**. Just make sure that you enter `Port:9999` in the **Connection Properties** form and then start debugging by clicking on the **Debug** button.

Dealing with version control

Typical files that can be ignored when maintaining the code under version control tools such as GIT are located as follows:

- `logs`
- `project/project`
- `project/target`
- `target`
- `tmp`
- `dist`
- `.cache`

Summary

In this chapter, we introduced the Play Framework and covered typical examples where requests are routed to controllers and rendered through views following the well-known MVC pattern. We saw that the usage of the Scala syntax inside the definition of routes and templates gives us the extra benefit of compile-time safety. Such help provided to the programmer largely increases productivity and avoids spelling mistakes while refactoring, making the whole experience more enjoyable.

We also added some basic HTTP authentication to a `helloworld` application sample. In the next chapter, we are going to tackle the issue of Persistence/ORM, a part that is essential in any web application, involving the usage of a database in the backend to store and retrieve data. We will see how to integrate the existing persistence standards used in Java, such as JPA, and will introduce a novel but powerful approach to Persistence through the Slick framework.

6
Database Access and the Future of ORM

An essential component found in almost any web application involves the storage and retrieval of data in a persistent store. Whether relational or NoSQL based, a database often occupies the most important place since it holds the application data. When a technology stack becomes a legacy and needs to be refactored or ported to a new one, the database is usually the starting point since it holds the domain knowledge.

In this chapter, we are first going to study how to integrate and reuse persistence frameworks inherited from Java that deal with **Object Relational Mapping (ORM)** such as those supporting **Java Persistence API (JPA)**, for example, Hibernate and EclipseLink. We will then experiment with the default persistence framework available in the Play Framework, Anorm. Finally, we will introduce and discover a Scala alternative to ORM and a rather novel approach that adds type safety and composition to the more traditional SQL-based queries, the Slick framework. We will experiment with Slick in the context of Play web development. We will also cover the generation of CRUD-like applications out of existing relational databases that can be a boost in productivity when starting out from a legacy database.

Integrating an existing ORM – Hibernate and JPA

As defined by Wikipedia:

> *"Object-relational mapping (ORM, O/RM, and O/R mapping) in computer software is a programming technique for converting data between incompatible type systems in object-oriented programming languages".*

The popular adoption of ORM frameworks in Java such as Hibernate is largely due to the simplicity and diminution of code you need to write to persist and query data.

Making JPA available in Scala

Although Scala has its own modern standard for data persistence (that is, Slick, which we will introduce later on), in this section, we will cover a possible integration of JPA (Java Persistence API, documented at http://docs.oracle.com/javaee/6/tutorial/doc/bnbpz.html) within the Scala world by building an SBT project that uses JPA-annotated Scala classes to persist data in a relational database. It is derived from an online sample available at http://www.brainoverload.nl/scala/105/jpa-with-scala, which should be particularly interesting to Java developers since it illustrates how to use the Spring framework both for dependency injection and configuration of beans in the context of a Scala project at the same time. As a reminder, the Spring framework, created by Rod Johnson, came out in 2002 as a way to provide inversion of control, that is, dependency injection increased in popularity to become a full-featured framework now containing many aspects of Java EE 7. More information about Spring is available at http://projects.spring.io/spring-framework/.

We are going to connect to the already existing CustomerDB sample database that we have introduced in *Chapter 2, Code Integration*, to show both how to read existing data and create new entities/tables to persist data.

As we have seen in *Chapter 3, Understanding the Scala Ecosystem*, creating a blank Scala SBT project is a matter of opening a command terminal, creating a directory to put the project in, and running SBT as follows:

```
> mkdir sbtjpasample
> cd sbtjpasample
> sbt
> set name:="sbtjpasample"
> session save
```

We can navigate to the `project/` folder that SBT created, and add a `plugins.sbt` file containing the following one-liner to import the `sbteclipse` plugin so that we can work with the project under the Eclipse IDE:

```
addSbtPlugin("com.typesafe.sbteclipse" % "sbteclipse-plugin" % "2.4.0")
```

Since we are going to use Hibernate- and Spring-related classes, we need to include such dependencies into our `build.sbt` build file (as well as the derby-client driver to connect to the `CustomerDB sample` database) so that it looks like the following code snippet:

```
name:="sbtjpasample"

scalaVersion:="2.10.3"

libraryDependencies ++= Seq(
    "junit" % "junit" % "4.11",
    "org.hibernate" % "hibernate-core" % "3.5.6-Final",
    "org.hibernate" % "hibernate-entitymanager" % "3.5.6-Final",
    "org.springframework" % "spring-core" % "4.0.0.RELEASE",
    "org.springframework" % "spring-context" % "4.0.0.RELEASE",
    "org.springframework" % "spring-beans" % "4.0.0.RELEASE",
    "org.springframework" % "spring-tx" % "4.0.0.RELEASE",
    "org.springframework" % "spring-jdbc" % "4.0.0.RELEASE",
    "org.springframework" % "spring-orm" % "4.0.0.RELEASE",
    "org.slf4j" % "slf4j-simple" % "1.6.4",
    "org.apache.derby" % "derbyclient" % "10.8.1.2",
    "org.scalatest" % "scalatest_2.10" % "2.0.M7"
)
```

As a reminder to make these dependencies available in Eclipse, we have to run the > `sbt eclipse` command again and refresh our project in the IDE.

Now, from the root directory of the project, enter > `sbt eclipse` and import the project into the IDE.

Now let's add a couple of domain entities (under a new package `se.sfjd`) that we want to annotate with Java-based JPA annotations. The `Customer` entity defined in a `Customer.scala` file in the `se.sfjd` package will map (at least partially) to the existing CUSTOMER database table:

```
import javax.persistence._
import scala.reflect.BeanProperty

@Entity
@Table(name = "customer")
class Customer(n: String) {

    @Id
    @GeneratedValue(strategy = GenerationType.AUTO)
    @Column(name = "CUSTOMER_ID")
```

```
    @BeanProperty
    var id: Int = _

    @BeanProperty
    @Column(name = "NAME")
    var name: String = n

    def this() = this(null)

    override def toString = id + " = " + name
}
```

Notice the underscore (_) representing a default value when declaring `var id: Int = _`. The default value will be set according to the type `T` of a variable, as defined by the Scala specification:

- `0` if `T` is `Int` or one of its subrange types
- `0L` if `T` is `Long`
- `0.0f` if `T` is `Float`
- `0.0d` if `T` is `Double`
- `false` if `T` is `Boolean`
- `()` if `T` is `Unit`
- `null` for all other types of `T`

The `Language` entity corresponds to the addition of a new concept we want to persist and therefore requires a new database table, as follows:

```
@Entity
@Table(name = "language")
class Language(l: String) {

    @Id
    @GeneratedValue(strategy = GenerationType.AUTO)
    @Column(name = "ID")
    @BeanProperty
    var id: Int = _

    @BeanProperty
    @Column(name = "NAME")
    var name: String = l

    def this() = this(null)

    override def toString = id + " = " + name
}
```

As we saw in *Chapter 2, Code Integration,* the `@BeanProperty` annotation is a way to generate getters and setters conforming to Java, and the `this()` method is a no argument constructor needed by Hibernate.

Moving on, the controller class or **DAO (Data Access Object)** class captures the behavior we want to provide for the `Customer` entity such as CRUD functionality in the form of `save` and `find` methods following an interface, or in this case, a Scala trait:

```
trait CustomerDao {
    def save(customer: Customer): Unit
    def find(id: Int): Option[Customer]
    def getAll: List[Customer]
}
```

The implementation of the `CustomerDao` class relies on the methods of the JPA entity manager that we as Java developers are probably familiar with:

```
import org.springframework.beans.factory.annotation._
import org.springframework.stereotype._
import org.springframework.transaction.annotation.{Propagation,
Transactional}
import javax.persistence._
import scala.collection.JavaConversions._


@Repository("customerDao")
@Transactional(readOnly = false, propagation = Propagation.REQUIRED)
class CustomerDaoImpl extends CustomerDao {

    @Autowired
    var entityManager: EntityManager = _

    def save(customer: Customer):Unit = customer.id match{
        case 0 => entityManager.persist(customer)
        case _ => entityManager.merge(customer)
    }

    def find(id: Int): Option[Customer] = {
        Option(entityManager.find(classOf[Customer], id))
    }

    def getAll: List[Customer] = {
        entityManager.createQuery("FROM Customer", classOf[Customer]).
getResultList.toList
    }
}
```

In a similar manner, we can define a `Language` trait and its implementation as follows, with the addition of a `getByName` method:

```
trait LanguageDao {
    def save(language: Language): Unit
    def find(id: Int): Option[Language]
    def getAll: List[Language]
    def getByName(name : String): List[Language]
}

@Repository("languageDao")
@Transactional(readOnly = false, propagation = Propagation.REQUIRED)
class LanguageDaoImpl extends LanguageDao {

  @Autowired
  var entityManager: EntityManager = _

  def save(language: Language): Unit = language.id match {
    case 0 => entityManager.persist(language)
    case _ => entityManager.merge(language)
  }

  def find(id: Int): Option[Language] = {
    Option(entityManager.find(classOf[Language], id))
  }

  def getAll: List[Language] = {
     entityManager.createQuery("FROM Language", classOf[Language]).
getResultList.toList
  }

  def getByName(name : String): List[Language] = {
     entityManager.createQuery("FROM Language WHERE name = :name",
classOf[Language]).setParameter("name", name).getResultList.toList
  }
}
```

Before we can execute the project, we still have a couple of steps to follow: first we need a test class, we can therefore create a `CustomerTest` class following the `ScalaTest` syntax, as we have seen earlier in *Chapter 4, Testing Tools*:

```
import org.junit.runner.RunWith
import org.scalatest.junit.JUnitRunner
import org.scalatest.FunSuite
import org.springframework.context.support.
```

```
lassPathXmlApplicationContext

@RunWith(classOf[JUnitRunner])
class CustomerTest extends FunSuite {

   val ctx = new ClassPathXmlApplicationContext("application-context.
xml")

   test("There are 13 Customers in the derby DB") {

     val customerDao = ctx.getBean(classOf[CustomerDao])
     val customers = customerDao.getAll
     assert(customers.size === 13)
     println(customerDao
       .find(3)
       .getOrElse("No customer found with id 3"))
   }

   test("Persisting 3 new languages") {
     val languageDao = ctx.getBean(classOf[LanguageDao])
     languageDao.save(new Language("English"))
     languageDao.save(new Language("French"))
     languageDao.save(new Language("Swedish"))
     val languages = languageDao.getAll
     assert(languages.size === 3)
     assert(languageDao.getByName("French").size ===1)
   }
}
```

Last but not least, we have to define some configuration, both a META-INF/
persistence.xml file required by JPA that we can put under src/main/resources/
and a Spring application-context.xml where all beans are wired and the database
connection is defined. The persistence.xml file will look as simple as follows:

```
<?xml version="1.0" encoding="UTF-8"?>
<persistence version="2.0" xmlns="http://java.sun.com/xml/ns/
persistence" xmlns:xsi="http://www.w3.org/2001/XMLSchema-instance"
    xsi:schemaLocation="http://java.sun.com/xml/ns/persistence http://
java.sun.com/xml/ns/persistence/persistence_2_0.xsd">

    <persistence-unit name="JpaScala" transaction-type="RESOURCE_
LOCAL">
        <provider>org.hibernate.ejb.HibernatePersistence</provider>
    </persistence-unit>
</persistence>
```

The `application-context.xml` file, directly available under `src/main/resources/`, is a bit more elaborate and is given as follows:

```xml
<?xml version="1.0" encoding="UTF-8"?>
<beans xmlns="http://www.springframework.org/schema/beans"
       xmlns:xsi="http://www.w3.org/2001/XMLSchema-instance"
       xmlns:context="http://www.springframework.org/schema/context"
       xmlns:p="http://www.springframework.org/schema/p"
xmlns:tx="http://www.springframework.org/schema/tx"
       xsi:schemaLocation="
           http://www.springframework.org/schema/beans http://www.
springframework.org/schema/beans/spring-beans.xsd
           http://www.springframework.org/schema/context http://www.
springframework.org/schema/context/spring-context.xsd
           http://www.springframework.org/schema/tx http://www.
springframework.org/schema/tx/spring-tx.xsd
       ">

    <tx:annotation-driven transaction-manager="transactionManager"/>

    <context:component-scan base-package="se.sfjd"/>

    <bean id="dataSource"
          class="org.springframework.jdbc.datasource.
DriverManagerDataSource"
          p:driverClassName="org.apache.derby.jdbc.ClientDriver"
p:url="jdbc:derby://localhost:1527/sample"
          p:username="app" p:password="app"/>

    <bean id="entityManagerFactory"
          class="org.springframework.orm.jpa.
LocalContainerEntityManagerFactoryBean">
        <property name="persistenceUnitName" value="JpaScala"/>
        <property name="persistenceProviderClass" value="org.
hibernate.ejb.HibernatePersistence"/>
        <property name="jpaDialect">
            <bean class="org.springframework.orm.jpa.vendor.
HibernateJpaDialect"/>
        </property>

        <property name="dataSource" ref="dataSource"/>
        <property name="jpaPropertyMap">
            <map>
                <entry key="hibernate.dialect" value="org.hibernate.
dialect.DerbyDialect"/>
```

```
                    <entry key="hibernate.connection.charSet"
    value="UTF-8"/>
                    <entry key="hibernate.hbm2ddl.auto" value="update"/>
                    <entry key="hibernate.show.sql" value="true"/>
                </map>
            </property>
        </bean>


        <bean id="entityManager"
                class="org.springframework.orm.jpa.support.
    SharedEntityManagerBean">
            <property name="entityManagerFactory"
    ref="entityManagerFactory"/>
        </bean>


        <bean id="transactionManager" class="org.springframework.orm.jpa.
    JpaTransactionManager">
            <property name="entityManagerFactory"
    ref="entityManagerFactory"/>
            <property name="dataSource" ref="dataSource"/>
        </bean>
    </beans>
```

Before running the test, we need to make sure the database server is up and running; this was explained in *Chapter 2, Code Integration,* while using the NetBeans IDE.

Now we can execute the example either by right-clicking on the `CustomerTest` class and navigating to **Debug As | Scala JUnit Test** or from the command prompt by entering the following command:

```
> sbt test
3 = Nano Apple
[info] CustomerTest:
[info] - There are 13 Customers in the derby DB
[info] - Persisting 3 new languages
[info] Passed: : Total 2, Failed 0, Errors 0, Passed 2, Skipped 0
[success] Total time: 3 s
```

Dealing with persistence in the Play Framework

The Play Framework can be run with any sort of ORM, whether it is Java based such as JPA or Scala specific. There are related-but-separate Java and Scala flavors of the framework. As described in the Play documentation, the Java version uses Ebean as its ORM, whereas the Scala alternative does not use ORM but runs with Anorm, a Scala-ish abstraction layer on top of JDBC that interacts with a database using plain SQL.

A simple example using Anorm

To illustrate the usage of Anorm, we are going to make a small Play example that connects to the existing `CustomerDB` database from the NetBeans distribution that we have used in the previous section and introduced in *Chapter 2, Code Integration*.

The most straightforward way to start is to create a default Play Scala project from a terminal window by entering the following command:

```
> play new anormsample
```

Once created and imported into Eclipse (after creating Eclipse-related files once again using the `> play eclipse` command; refer to *Chapter 5, Getting Started with the Play Framework*, if you need more details) we can see that the dependency to Anorm is already part of the `built.sbt` file. However, we need to add the dependency to the `derby-client` database driver to this file to be able to communicate with the database through jdbc. The dependency can be added as follows:

```
libraryDependencies ++= Seq(
  jdbc,
  anorm,
  cache,
  "org.apache.derby" % "derbyclient" % "10.8.1.2"
)
```

We can now define a `Customer` case class that will represent the CUSTOMER table from the database and implement some behaviors in the form of methods defined in its companion object, as follows:

```
package models

import play.api.db._
import play.api.Play.current
```

```
import anorm._
import anorm.SqlParser._
import scala.language.postfixOps

case class Customer(id: Pk[Int] = NotAssigned, name: String)

object Customer {
  /**
    * Retrieve a Customer from an id.
    */
  def findById(id: Int): Option[Customer] = {
    DB.withConnection { implicit connection =>
      println("Connection: "+connection)
      val query = SQL("SELECT * from app.customer WHERE customer_id =
{custId}").on('custId -> id)
      query.as(Customer.simple.singleOpt)
    }
  }


  /**
    * Parse a Customer from a ResultSet
    */
  val simple = {
    get[Pk[Int]]("customer.customer_id") ~
    get[String]("customer.name") map {
      case id~name => Customer(id, name)
    }
  }
}
```

The Anorm SQL query conforms to a string-based SQL statement where variables are bound to values. Here we bind the `customer_id` column to the `id` input parameter. Since we want to return an `Option[Customer]` to handle the case where the SQL query did not return any result, we first need to parse the `ResultSet` object to create a `Customer` instance and invoke the `singleOpt` method that will make sure we wrap the result into an `Option` (which can return `None` instead of a potential error).

The `Application` controller is given as follows:

```
package controllers

import play.api._
import play.api.mvc._
import play.api.db._
import play.api.Play.current
```

```
import models._

object Application extends Controller {
  def index = Action {
    val inputId = 2   //  Hardcoded input id for the example
    val result =
      DB.withConnection { implicit c =>
        Customer.findById(inputId) match {
          case Some(customer) => s"Found the customer: ${customer.
name}"
          case None => "No customer was found."
        }
      }
    Ok(views.html.index(result))
  }
}
```

It simply surrounds the database query with a database connection and does some pattern matching on the Option[Customer] entity to display different messages whether the queried customer id is found or not.

You may have noticed the keyword, implicit, sometimes while reading the Scala code in general (such as the implicit c parameter given in the previous code example). As clearly explained in the Scala documentation:

> "*a method with implicit parameters can be applied to arguments just like a normal method. In this case, the implicit label has no effect. However, if such a method misses arguments for its implicit parameters, such arguments will be automatically provided*".

In our previous case, we could have omitted this implicit parameter since we are not using the database connection c variable further in the body of our method.

Running the application with inputId=2 can be replaced by inputId=3000; for example, to demonstrate the case where no customer is found. To avoid changing anything in the view, we have reused the welcome message location of the default index.html page; therefore, you will see the result in the browser in the green header at the top of the HTML page.

This sample only shows a basic usage of Anorm; it is derived from the much more complete computer-database example that is part of the samples of the Play Framework distribution. You can refer to it if you need a deeper knowledge of the Anorm framework.

Replacing ORM

As Java developers, we are used to handling relational database persistence through the use of mature and well-established JPA frameworks such as Hibernate or EclipseLink. Despite the fact that these frameworks are convenient to use and hide a lot of the complexity for retrieving or updating data that is spread over several tables, Object-Relational Mapping suffers from the **Object-Relational Impedance Mismatch** problem; in an object-oriented model, you traverse objects via their relationships, whereas in a relational database, you join the data rows of tables, resulting sometimes in an inefficient and cumbersome retrieval of data. (This is further explained on the Wikipedia page, `http://en.wikipedia.org/wiki/ Object-relational_impedance_mismatch`.)

In contrast, the `Slick` framework that is part of the Typesafe stack proposes to solve the persistence of data to relational databases through a Functional Relational Mapping, which strives for a more natural fit. Some of the additional benefits of Slick include the following two aspects:

- **Conciseness and Type Safety**: Instead of running SQL queries by expressing them through strings in Java code, Slick uses plain Scala code to express queries. In JPA, the Criteria API or languages such as **JPQL (Java Persistence Query Language)** or **HQL (Hibernate Query Language)** have long tried to make string-based queries more type checked, but are still difficult to comprehend and produce verbose code. With Slick, queries are written concisely using the power of Scala `for comprehensions`. Type safety of SQL queries was introduced a long time ago in the .Net world through the popular LINQ Framework.

- **Composable and reusable queries**: The functional approach adopted by Slick makes composition a natural behavior, a feature that lacks when considering plain SQL as an alternative to ORM.

Learning about Slick

Let's explore the behavior of the Slick framework through code examples to see how we can enhance and replace more traditional ORM solutions.

The first example we can study is part of the `test-patterns-scala` activator template project that we have analyzed in *Chapter 4, Testing Tools*. The `scalatest/Test012.scala` file found inside the project exhibits a typical usage of Slick as follows:

```scala
package scalatest

import org.scalatest._
import scala.slick.driver.H2Driver.simple._
import Database.threadLocalSession

object Contacts extends Table[(Long, String)]("CONTACTS") {
  def id = column[Long]("CONTACT_ID", O.PrimaryKey)
  def name = column[String]("CONTACT_NAME")
  def gender = column[String]("GENDER")
  def * = id ~ name
}

class Test12 extends FunSuite {
  val dbUrl = "jdbc:h2:mem:contacts"
  val dbDriver = "org.h2.Driver"

  test("Slick, H2, embedded") {
    Database.forURL(dbUrl, driver = dbDriver) withSession {
    Contacts.ddl.create
    Contacts.insertAll(
      (1, "Bob"),
      (2, "Tom"),
      (3, "Salley")
    )

    val nameQuery =
      for(
        c <- Contacts if c.name like "%o%"
      ) yield c.name
    val names = nameQuery.list
    names.foreach(println)
    assert(names === List("Bob","Tom"))
    }
  }
}
```

The most interesting part in the code has to do with the SQL query. The immutable variable `names` contains the result of a query to the database; instead of expressing the SQL query as a `String` or through the Java Criteria API, pure Scala code is used through a `for comprehension`, as shown in the following screenshot:

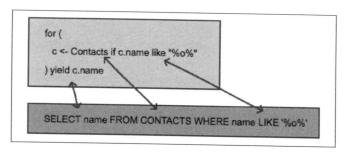

Unlike string-based SQL queries, any typo or reference to tables or fields that do not exist will be immediately pointed out by the compiler. More complex queries will be very naturally translated into for expressions in a readable manner compared to the verbose and hard-to-read output code resulting from the JPA Criteria API.

This sample only contains one table, `Contacts`, that we define by extending the `scala.slick.driver.H2Driver.simple.Table` class. The CONTACTS database table includes three columns, one primary key `id` defined as a `Long` datatype, and two other properties of type `String`, name, and gender respectively. The method `*` defined in the `Contacts` object specifies a default projection, that is, all the columns (or computed values) we are usually interested in. The expression `id ~ name` (using the `~` sequence operator) returns a `Projection2[Long,String]` which can be thought of as a Tuple2, but for the representation of relations. The default projection of `(Int, String)` leads to a `List[(Int, String)]` for simple queries.

Since the datatypes of columns in relational databases are not the same as Scala types, they need to be mapped (similar to the mappings needed when dealing with ORM frameworks or pure JDBC access). As stated in Slick's documentation, the primitive types supported out of the box are as follows (with a few limitations depending on the database driver used for each database type):

- **Numeric types**: `Byte`, `Short`, `Int`, `Long`, `BigDecimal`, `Float`, `Double`
- **LOB types**: `java.sql.Blob`, `java.sql.Clob`, `Array[Byte]`
- **Date types**: `java.sql.Date`, `java.sql.Time`, `java.sql.Timestamp`
- `Boolean`
- `String`
- `Unit`
- `java.util.UUID`

Once the domain entity is defined, the next steps are to create the database, insert some test data in it, and then run a query as we would do with any other persistence framework.

All of the code we run in the `Test12` test is surrounded by the following block:

```
Database.forURL(dbUrl, driver = dbDriver) withSession {
   < code accessing the DB...>
}
```

The `forURL` method specifies a JDBC database connection, which normally consists of a driver class corresponding to the specific database to use and a connection URL defined by its `host`, `port`, `database` name as well as an optional `username`/ `password`. In the example, a local in-memory database (H2) named `contacts` is used so that the connection URL is `jdbc:h2:mem:contacts`, exactly as we would write it in Java. Note that a Slick `Database` instance only encapsulates a "how-to" on how connections are created, the physical connection being created only at the `withSession` call.

The `Contacts.ddl.create` statement will create the database schema and the `insertAll` method will populate the `Contacts` table with three rows each consisting of its primary key `id` and `name`.

We can execute this test alone to verify that it runs as expected, by entering the following command in a terminal window in the root directory of the `test-patterns-scala` project:

```
> ./activator
> test-only scalatest.Test12
Bob
Tom
[info] Test12:
[info] - Slick, H2, embedded (606 milliseconds)
[info] ScalaTest
[info] Run completed in 768 milliseconds.
[info] Total number of tests run: 1
[info] Suites: completed 1, aborted 0
[info] Tests: succeeded 1, failed 0, canceled 0, ignored 0, pending 0
[info] All tests passed.
[info] Passed: Total 1, Failed 0, Errors 0, Passed 1
[success] Total time: 1 s, completed Dec 7, 2013 1:43:28 PM
```

Currently, the `test-patterns-scala` project includes a dependency to the `slf4j-nop` implementation of the SLF4J logging framework that disables any logging. Since it can be useful to visualize the exact SQL statement produced by Scala `for comprehension` statements, let's replace `sl4j-nop` with a logback implementation. In your `build.sbt` build file, replace the line `"org.slf4j" % "slf4j-nop" % "1.6.4"` with a reference to logback, for example, `"ch.qos.logback" % "logback-classic" % "0.9.28" % "test"`.

Now, if you rerun the test, you will probably see much more logging info than you actually want. We can therefore add a `logback.xml` file to the project (in the `src/test/resources/` folder) as follows:

```xml
<?xml version="1.0" encoding="UTF-8"?>
<configuration>

    <appender name="STDOUT" class="ch.qos.logback.core.
ConsoleAppender">
        <encoder>
            <pattern>%d{HH:mm:ss.SSS} [%thread] %-5level %logger{36} -
%msg%n</pattern>
        </encoder>
    </appender>

    <root level="debug">
        <appender-ref ref="STDOUT" />
    </root>

    <logger name="scala.slick.compiler"       level="${log.qcomp:-warn}"
/>
    <logger name="scala.slick.compiler.QueryCompiler" level="${log.
qcomp.phases:-inherited}" />

    ...

    <logger name="scala.slick.compiler.CodeGen"
level="${log.qcomp.codeGen:-inherited}" />
    <logger name="scala.slick.compiler.InsertCompiler"
level="${log.qcomp.insertCompiler:-inherited}" />
    <logger name="scala.slick.jdbc.JdbcBackend.statement"
level="${log.session:-info}" />

    <logger name="scala.slick.ast.Node$"
level="${log.qcomp.assignTypes:-inherited}" />
    <logger name="scala.slick.memory.HeapBackend$"
level="${log.heap:-inherited}" />
    <logger name="scala.slick.memory.QueryInterpreter"
level="${log.interpreter:-inherited}" />
</configuration>
```

This time if we enable only the `"scala.slick.jdbc.JdbcBackend.statement"` logger, the output from the test will show all the SQL queries, similar to the following output:

```
> test-only scalatest.Test12
19:00:37.470 [ScalaTest-running-Test12] DEBUG scala.slick.session.
BaseSession - Preparing statement: create table "CONTACTS" ("CONTACT_
ID" BIGINT NOT NULL PRIMARY KEY,"CONTACT_NAME" VARCHAR NOT NULL)
19:00:37.484 [ScalaTest-running-Test12] DEBUG scala.slick.session.
BaseSession - Preparing statement: INSERT INTO "CONTACTS" ("CONTACT_
ID","CONTACT_NAME") VALUES (?,?)
19:00:37.589 [ScalaTest-running-Test12] DEBUG scala.slick.session.
BaseSession - Preparing statement: select x2."CONTACT_NAME" from
"CONTACTS" x2 where x2."CONTACT_NAME" like '%o%'
Bob
Tom
[info] Test12:
[info] - Slick, H2, embedded (833 milliseconds)
[info] ScalaTest
[info] Run completed in 952 milliseconds.
[info] Total number of tests run: 1
[info] Suites: completed 1, aborted 0
[info] Tests: succeeded 1, failed 0, canceled 0, ignored 0, pending 0
[info] All tests passed.
[info] Passed: Total 1, Failed 0, Errors 0, Passed 1
[success] Total time: 1 s, completed Dec 10, 2013 7:00:37 PM
>
```

Finally, to verify whether database schema validation has been enforced, let's try to modify one of the keys of the inserted data so that we have duplicate keys, as shown in the following lines of code:

```
Contacts.insertAll(
      (1, "Bob"),
      (2, "Tom"),
      (2, "Salley")
   )
```

If we run the test again, it fails with a message similar to the following:

```
[info] Test12:
[info] - Slick, H2, embedded *** FAILED *** (566 milliseconds)
[info]    org.h2.jdbc.JdbcBatchUpdateException: Unique index or primary
key violation: "PRIMARY_KEY_C ON PUBLIC.CONTACTS(CONTACT_ID)"; SQL
statement:
[info] INSERT INTO "CONTACTS" ("CONTACT_ID","CONTACT_NAME") VALUES (?,?)
[23505-166]...
```

Scaffolding a Play application

In this section, we are going to further experiment with Slick and Play by automatically creating a full Play application with basic CRUD functionality out of a relational database, including Models, Views, Controllers, as well as test data and configuration files such as Play routes.

Any web application that needs to connect to a database generally requires most of the CRUD functionality at least in the backend. Furthermore, being able to generate a default frontend can avoid you having to make one from scratch. In particular, a Play frontend consisting of HTML5 views is highly reusable since most of the display of columns, fields, buttons, and forms can be re-arranged with limited copy/paste in an HTML editor.

Let's apply this reverse engineering on the sample customer database from the NetBeans distribution that we have already covered in *Chapter 2, Code Integration*.

The generation of the Play app is done in two steps:

1. Creation of a regular Play project.
2. Usage of an external tool named `playcrud` that is itself a Play app and will generate all the required MVC and configuration files on top of the new Play project structure.

Having this approach in two steps has a better guarantee that the generated application will follow the latest changes in the Play distribution, in particular with regards to the evolution of the look and feel in Play that comes with every new release.

To get started with the `playcrud` utility, clone the project from GitHub by entering in a command terminal in a directory of your choice (assuming GIT is installed, visit `http://git-scm.com/` if you don't have it already):

```
> git clone https://github.com/ThomasAlexandre/playcrud
```

This should create a directory, `playcrud`, with the content of the project being a regular Play application, including the plugin to generate an Eclipse project. We can therefore run the following commands:

```
> cd playcrud
```

```
> play eclipse
```

Then, import the project into Eclipse to better visualize what it consists of. The application is made of just one controller found in the `Application.scala` file located at `samplecrud\app\controllers`, and its corresponding view found in `index.scala.html` under `samplecrud\app\views`. Only two routes are defined in the `routes` file under `samplecrud\conf`:

```
# Home page
GET     /       controllers.Application.index


# CRUD action
GET     /crud       controllers.Application.generateAll
```

The first route will display a form in the browser where we can enter information about the database from which we want to create a Play app. The form is fairly straightforward to understand by looking at its template:

```
@(dbForm: Form[(String,String,String,String)])
@import helper._
@main(title = "The 'CRUD generator' application") {
    <h1>Enter Info about your existing database:</h1>
    @form(action = routes.Application.generateAll, args = 'id ->
"dbform") {

        @select(
            field = dbForm("driver"),
            options = options(
                "com.mysql.jdbc.Driver" -> "MySQL",
                "org.postgresql.Driver" -> "PostgreSQL",
                "org.h2.Driver" -> "H2",
                "org.apache.derby.jdbc.ClientDriver" -> "Derby"
            ),
            args = '_label -> "Choose a DB"
        )


        @inputText(
            field = dbForm("dburl"),
            args = '_label -> "Database url", 'placeholder ->
"jdbc:mysql://localhost:3306/slick"
        )


        @inputText(
            field = dbForm("username"),
            args = '_label -> "DB username", 'size -> 10, 'placeholder
-> "root"
        )


        @inputText(
            field = dbForm("password"),
            args = '_label -> "DB password", 'size -> 10, 'placeholder
-> "root"
        )
```

```
<p class="buttons">
    <input type="submit" id="submit">
<p>
}
}
```

The second is the `generateAll` action performed once we submit the form that will create all files needed to execute the newly created Play app.

To be able to generate all files in the right place, we just need to edit one configuration property called `baseDirectory`, currently found in the `Config.scala` file in the `utilities/` folder. This property specifies the root directory of the Play application we want to generate. Before we edit it, we can generate a blank Play project that the `baseDirectory` variable will refer to:

```
> cd ~/projects/internal (or any location of your choice)
> play new samplecrud
...
What is the application name? [samplecrud]
> [ENTER]
Which template do you want to use for this new application?
  1            - Create a simple Scala application
  2            - Create a simple Java application
> [Press 1]
```

Just to verify we have our blank Play application correctly created we can launch it with:

```
> cd samplecrud
> play run
```

Now, open the `http://localhost:9000` URL in a web browser.

Now that we have our `baseDirectory` (`~/projects/internal/samplecrud`), we can add it to the `Config.scala` file. The other properties concerning the database are just default values; we do not need to edit them here since we will instead specify them when we fill out the HTML form while running the `playcrud` app.

In a new terminal window, let's execute the `playcrud` app by entering the following commands:

```
> cd <LOCATION_OF_PLAYCRUD_PROJECT_ROOT>
> play "run 9020" (or any other port than 9000)
```

Here, we need to choose a different port than `9000` as it is already taken by the blank application.

Now, point your web browser to the `playcrud` URL, `http://localhost:9020/`. You should get an HTML form where you can edit the properties of the source database to access for CRUD generation, as shown in the following screenshot (this database will only be read from):

Submitting the form will most likely generate some logging output in the terminal console, and once it is done with the generation, the browser will be redirected to port `9000` to display the newly generated CRUD app. Since this is the first time we generate the app, it will fail because the `build.sbt` file of the generated app was updated and needs to be reloaded with some new dependencies.

To fix that, interrupt the currently running Play app by pressing *Ctrl + D*. Once it has stopped, simply re-launch it:

```
> play run
```

If everything goes well, you should be able to access `http://localhost:9000` and see a list of clickable controllers corresponding to the entities that were generated from the database, including `Product`, `Manufacturer`, and `Purchase Order`.

Let's open one of them, for instance, the Manufacturer view, as shown in the following screenshot:

The resulting screen shows the READ part of the CRUD functionality by displaying a list of all the manufacturer rows from the database. The paging functionality is set to 3 by default, that is why only three out of the 30 available manufacturers are seen at once, but one can navigate to the other pages by clicking on the **Previous** and **Next** buttons. This default page size is editable in each individual controller (look for a pageSize val declaration), or can be modified in the controller template before code generation to update all controllers at once. Moreover, the headers of the HTML table are clickable to sort elements according to each specific column.

Clicking on the **Add New Manufacturer** button will invoke a new screen containing a form used to create a new entry in the database.

Importing test data

The generated app is running with an H2 in-memory database, by default, which is populated at startup with some test data. During generation, we have exported content from the source database into an XML file using the functionality of DBUnit, a JUnit-based framework in Java. DBUnit is useful when there is enough database data involved in your tests that you want to avoid mocking everything by producing XML sample files containing some data extracted from a real database instead. The exported test data is stored in testdata.xml under samplecrud\test\. When running the generated application, this file will be loaded by DBUnit in the onStart method of the Global.scala after the DB schema has been created.

To be able to persist the data to a real database and therefore avoid importing the XML file on every restart, we can replace the in-memory data by a real database on disk. For example, we can replace the database driver properties in the `application.conf` file under `samplecrud\conf` with the following lines:

```
db.default.driver=org.h2.Driver
db.default.url="jdbc:h2:tcp://localhost/~/customerdb"
db.default.user=sa
db.default.password=""
```

The new database is built once we have restarted the play app:

```
> play run
```

Accessing the `http://localhost:9000` URL in the browser will this time create the database schema on disk and populate test data as well. Since the database is persisted between restarts, from now on we have to comment out the `ddl.create` statement in `Global.scala` as well as the lines referring to the DBUnit import of `testdata.xml`.

Visualizing the database in the H2browser

A convenient feature of Play is that you can access the `h2-browser` to visualize the database content in your browser directly from SBT. This is true even if you are using most databases other than H2. Open a terminal window and navigate to the root of the generated project:

```
> play
```
```
> h2-browser
```

Connect to the database by filling out the connection properties as shown in the following screenshot:

Assuming that clicking on the **Test Connection** button displayed **Test successful** as shown in the previous screenshot, we can visualize and send SQL queries to the `customerdb` database as shown in the following screenshot:

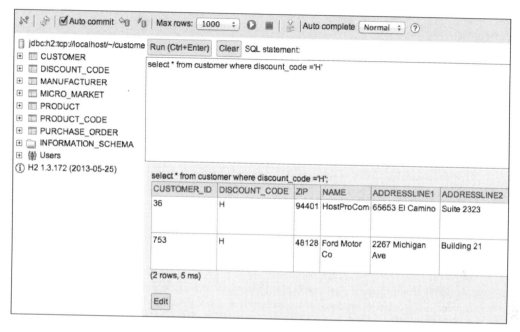

Exploring the code behind the app generation

Every table from the source database leads to the generation of a number of artifacts:

- One `model`, one `controller`, and several `view` classes
- A set of `route` entries inserted in the `conf.routes` file, as shown in the following code for the PURCHASE_ORDER table:

```
# PurchaseOrder
#
# PurchaseOrder list (look at the default values for pagination
parameters)

GET      /purchaseorder              controllers.
PurchaseOrderController.list(p:Int ?= 0, s:Int ?= 2, f ?= "")
# Add purchaseorder
GET      /purchaseorder/new          controllers.
PurchaseOrderController.create
POST     /purchaseorder              controllers.
PurchaseOrderController.save
```

```
# Edit existing purchaseorder
GET      /purchaseorder/:pk              controllers.
PurchaseOrderController.edit(pk:Int)
POST     /purchaseorder/:pk              controllers.
PurchaseOrderController.update(pk:Int)


# Delete purchaseorder
POST     /purchaseorder/:pk/delete       controllers.
PurchaseOrderController.delete(pk:Int)
```

Models consist of the domain entities, each being defined in Slick by a combination of a case class representing a row together with a driver specific `slick.driver.H2Driver.simple.Table` of rows. We could have avoided the usage of the case class and directly written tuples of the involved columns as we have seen in the earlier `Test12` example from the `test-patterns-scala` activator template, but encapsulating the columns in a case class is convenient for later use of pattern matching and usage in the views. The model class representing a `PurchaseOrder` entity is generated as follows:

```
package models

case class PurchaseOrderRow(orderNum : Option[Int], customerId : Int,
productId : Int, quantity : Option[Int], shippingCost : Option[Int],
salesDate : Option[Date], shippingDate : Option[Date], freightCompany
: Option[String])

// Definition of the PurchaseOrder table
object PurchaseOrder extends Table[PurchaseOrderRow]("PURCHASE_ORDER")
{

  def orderNum = column[Int]("ORDER_NUM", O.PrimaryKey)
  def customerId = column[Int]("CUSTOMER_ID")
  def productId = column[Int]("PRODUCT_ID")
  def quantity = column[Option[Int]]("QUANTITY")
  def shippingCost = column[Option[Int]]("SHIPPING_COST")
  def salesDate = column[Option[Date]]("SALES_DATE")
  def shippingDate = column[Option[Date]]("SHIPPING_DATE")
  def freightCompany = column[Option[String]]("FREIGHT_COMPANY")

  def * = orderNum.? ~ customerId ~ productId ~ quantity ~
shippingCost ~ salesDate ~ shippingDate ~ freightCompany <>
(PurchaseOrderRow.apply _, PurchaseOrderRow.unapply _)

  def findAll(filter: String = "%") = {
    for {
      entity <- PurchaseOrder
      // if (entity.name like ("%" + filter))
    } yield entity
```

```
    }

    def findByPK(pk: Int) =
       for (
          entity <- PurchaseOrder if entity.orderNum === pk
       ) yield entity
       ...
```

The complete code for the PurchaseOrder entity as well as the definition of the CRUD methods of the corresponding PurchaseOrderController class is available for download on the Packt Publishing website and can also be reproduced by executing the scaffolding playcrud GitHub project on the CustomerDB sample database as we have explained in this section.

Finally, templates to generate views for a specific entity are gathered under the same directory named views.<entity_name>/ and consist of three files, list.scala.html, createForm.scala.html, and editForm.scala.html for the READ, CREATE, and UPDATE operations, respectively. They embed a mix of plain HTML5 markup together with minimal Scala code to loop over and display elements from the controller queries. Notice in the view the addition of a specific play.api.mvc.Flash implicit object: this useful feature of Play makes it possible to display some information in the resulting views to inform the user on the outcome of the performed actions. You can see in the controller that we referred to it via the statement Home.flashing {... }, where we display various information depending on pattern matching on the success or failure of an action.

Limitations of the playcrud utility

In the current release of the experimental playcrud utility, a few limitations have been found, which are explained as follows:

- The playcrud project does not always work out of the box with all JDBC databases, especially since the mappings of some databases are customized. However, with only few changes, it is flexible enough to adapt to new mappings. Furthermore, it allows the generation of only a partial database by specifying the tables that need to be generated in an external file. To enable this functionality, we only need to add a file in our playcrud project under conf/, name it tables, and write the table names of tables we want to include (one table name per row in the file, case insensitive). For instance, consider a tables file that includes the following code:

  ```
  product
  purchaseorder
  manufacturer
  ```

  This code will create MVC classes and HTML views for these three tables only.

- In case the mapping of a specific database datatype is not handled by `playcrud`, you will get a compiler error in the browser window that will most likely refer to the missing datatype. The place in the `playcrud` code where mappings are handled is the `utilities/DBUtil.scala` class. A later release of `playcrud` should make these configurations more flexible per database type and put them in external files, but for now they are embedded in the code.

- The available code generation is inspired and built upon two already existing samples, one being the sample named `computer-database` part of the Play Framework distribution (which exhibits a CRUD app but with Anorm as persistence, a SQL-based persistence framework, which is the default in Play), the other being a sample of usage of Slick done by Typesafe's Slick Team (the `Coffee` database with its `Suppliers` showing one-to-many relationships). If you wish to generate the code differently, all the templates are found under `views/`. Some of them mostly contain static data, such as the generation of `build.sbt` based on the `build.scala.txt` template.

- In commercial applications, it is not unusual to encounter database tables that have more than 22 columns. Since we encapsulate these columns into case classes and Scala 2.10 has a restriction that limits the creation of a case class of more than 22 elements, it is not possible at the moment to generate Slick mappings exceeding that size. Hopefully, starting with Scala 2.11, this limitation should be lifted.

Summary

In this chapter, we have covered several approaches to deal with relational database persistence. We first went through an example of integration between Scala and traditional JPA-based ORM persistence. The example also illustrated the integration between the Spring framework and a Scala codebase. We then introduced Anorm, the default persistence framework available in the Play Framework that relies on direct SQL queries. Because of some limitations of ORM, mainly related to scalability and performance, and limitations as well of plain SQL queries in terms of lack of type safety and lack of composability, we moved towards the adoption of the Slick framework, a unique approach to persistence that targets a more functional way to persist data in relational databases. Finally, we considered the case where we can generate a full Play web app with basic CRUD functionality out of an existing database as a way of rapidly getting started integrating Slick into Play. The future releases of Slick starting with 2.0 enhance support for code generation and strive for even more readable syntax for writing database queries through the usage of Scala macros.

In the next chapter, we are going to consider how to use Scala when integrating external systems together, in particular through Web Services and REST APIs, supporting data formats such as JSON and XML.

7
Working with Integration and Web Services

Because technology stacks evolve continuously, a large area to consider when developing commercial software is the integration between systems. The flexibility and scalability of the Web have seen the proliferation of services built on top of HTTP to integrate systems in a loosely-coupled fashion. Moreover, to be able to navigate through secure networks accessible via firewalls and additional security mechanisms, the HTTP model has been increasingly popular. In this chapter, we are going to cover how to involve Scala when integrating with systems either via Web Services or REST Services exchanging messages in formats such as XML and JSON. In particular, we will consider running such services through the Play Framework.

In this chapter, we will cover the following topics:

- Generating data bindings from XML schemas as well as SOAP web service classes out of their WSDL description

- Manipulating XML and JSON in Scala and in particular in the context of the Play Framework

- Invoking other REST web services from Play, and validating and displaying their response

Binding XML data in Scala

Even if XML has recently stepped down a bit from its ubiquitous position due to the increasing popularity of JSON, both formats will continue to be heavily used to structure data.

In Java, it is a common practice to use the JAXB libraries to create classes that are able to serialize and deserialize XML data and construct XML documents through an API.

In a similar manner, the scalaxb library available for Scala can generate help classes for working with XML and web services. As an example, let's consider a small XML schema, Bookstore.xsd, that defines a set of books as part of a book store as follows:

```
<?xml version="1.0" encoding="UTF-8"?>
<xsd:schema xmlns:xsd="http://www.w3.org/2001/XMLSchema"
            targetNamespace="http://www.books.org"
            xmlns="http://www.books.org"
            elementFormDefault="qualified">
    <xsd:element name="book_store">
        <xsd:complexType>
            <xsd:sequence>
                <xsd:element name="book" type="book_type"
                             minOccurs="1" maxOccurs="unbounded"/>
            </xsd:sequence>
        </xsd:complexType>
    </xsd:element>
    <xsd:complexType name="book_type">
        <xsd:sequence>
            <xsd:element name="title" type="xsd:string"/>
            <xsd:element name="author" type="xsd:string"/>
            <xsd:element name="date" minOccurs="0"
type="xsd:string"/>
            <xsd:element name="publisher" type="xsd:string"/>
        </xsd:sequence>
        <xsd:attribute name="ISBN" type="xsd:string"/>
    </xsd:complexType>
</xsd:schema>
```

A typical book is defined by its title, author, date of publication, and ISBN number, as shown in the following example:

```
<book ISBN="9781933499185">
  <title>Madame Bovary</title>
  <author>Gustave Flaubert</author>
  <date>1857</date>
  <publisher>Fonolibro</publisher>
</book>
```

There are several ways one can run scalaxb documented on the www.scalaxb.org website: either directly as a command line tool, through plugins from SBT or Maven, or as a web API hosted on heroku. Since we have essentially used SBT so far and should be comfortable with it, let's use the SBT plugin to create the bindings.

First create a new SBT project entitled wssample by running the following commands in a new terminal window:

```
> mkdir wssample
> cd wssample
> sbt
> set name:="wssample"
> session save
>
```

Now we need to add the scalaxb plugin dependency to a plugins.sbt file under project/ (and at the same time we will add the sbteclipse plugin that enables us to generate an Eclipse project out of the SBT project). The resulting plugins.sbt file will look similar to the following code:

```
addSbtPlugin("com.typesafe.sbteclipse" % "sbteclipse-plugin" %
"2.4.0")

addSbtPlugin("org.scalaxb" % "sbt-scalaxb" % "1.1.2")

resolvers += Resolver.sonatypeRepo("public")
```

Additionally, we have to slightly modify the build.sbt file to notably include a command that will generate scalaxb XML bindings when compiling with SBT. The resulting build.sbt file will look similar to the following code:

```
import ScalaxbKeys._

name:="wssample"

scalaVersion:="2.10.2"

scalaxbSettings
```

```
libraryDependencies += "net.databinder.dispatch" %% "dispatch-core" %
"0.11.0"

libraryDependencies += "org.scalatest" %% "scalatest" % "2.0.M7" %
"test"

sourceGenerators in Compile <+= scalaxb in Compile

packageName in scalaxb in Compile := "se.wssample"
```

Add the `Bookstore.xsd` schema shown previously to a new `src/main/xsd` directory created within the project. From now on, each time you invoke the SBT command > `compile`, `scalaxb` will generate some Scala classes under the `target/scala-2.10/src_managed` directory (in the package given in the `build.sbt` file that is, `se.wssample`), unless no changes have been made. For instance, in the case of our small example, `scalaxb` generates the following case classes:

```
package se.wssample

case class Book_store(book: se.wssample.Book_type*)

case class Book_type(title: String,
    author: String,
    date: Option[String] = None,
    publisher: String,
    ISBN: Option[String] = None)
```

Note the * at the end of the first case class declaration, which is used to specify varargs (that is, an unspecified number of arguments, so here the `Book_store` constructor can take several `Book_type` instances). A possible test class illustrating the usage of the generated code to parse an XML document is given in the `BookstoreSpec.scala` class as follows:

```
package se.wssample

import org.scalatest._
import org.scalatest.matchers.Matchers

class BookstoreSpec extends FlatSpec with Matchers {
    "This bookstore" should "contain 3 books" in {

        val bookstore =
        <book_store xmlns="http://www.books.org">
```

```
<book ISBN="9781933499185">
    <title>Madame Bovary</title>
    <author>Gustave Flaubert</author>
    <date>1857</date>
    <publisher>Fonolibro</publisher>
</book>
<book ISBN="9782070411207">
    <title>Le malade imaginaire</title>
    <author>Moliere</author>
    <date>1673</date>
    <publisher>Gallimard</publisher>
</book>
<book ISBN="1475066511">
    <title>Fables</title>
    <author>Jean de La Fontaine</author>
    <date>1678</date>
    <publisher>CreateSpace</publisher>
</book>
</book_store>

val bookstoreInstance = scalaxb.fromXML[Book_store](bookstore)

println("bookstoreInstance: "+ bookstoreInstance.book)

bookstoreInstance.book.length should be === 3
    }
}
```

The expected output from this test when invoking the `> sbt test` command is as follows:

```
bookstoreInstance: List(Book_type(Madame Bovary,Gustave Flaubert,Some(185
7),Fonolibro,Some(9781933499185)), Book_type(Le malade imaginaire,Molièr
e,Some(1673),Gallimard,Some(9782070411207)), Book_type(Fables,Jean de La
Fontaine,Some(1678),CreateSpace,Some(1475066511)))
```

```
[info] BookstoreSpec:
[info] This bookstore
[info] - should contain 3 books
[info] Passed: : Total 1, Failed 0, Errors 0, Passed 1, Skipped 0
[success] Total time: 4 s
```

Running scalaxb from a SOAP web service

Since `scalaxb` supports the **Web Services Description Language (WSDL)**, we can also generate a full web service API in addition to the XML data-only related classes. To achieve this functionality, we just need to copy our WSDL service description file to `src/main/wsdl`. All the files with the `.wsdl` extension will be processed at compile time by the `scalaxb` plugin that will create the following three types of output:

- The service API specific to your application.

- Classes specific to the SOAP protocol.

- Classes responsible for sending the SOAP messages to the endpoint URL via HTTP. `scalaxb` uses the dispatch library that we introduced in *Chapter 3, Understanding the Scala Ecosystem*. This is why we added it as a dependency into the `build.sbt` file.

Let's take an online SOAP web service as a way to illustrate the usage of `scalaxb` from a WSDL description. `www.webservicex.net` is a site that contains many different samples of such web services in various market segments. Here, we will focus on their Stock Quote service that returns quotes given by a stock symbol. The API is very straightforward since it consists of only one request method, `getQuote`, and the data it returns is limited in size. You might want to try any other available service (later on as you can have multiple WSDL files in your same project). Its WSDL description looks similar to the following code:

```
<?xml version="1.0" encoding="utf-8"?>
<wsdl:definitions … // headers >
  <wsdl:types>
    <s:schema elementFormDefault="qualified" targetNamespace="http://
www.webserviceX.NET/">
      <s:element name="GetQuote">
        <s:complexType>
          <s:sequence>
            <s:element minOccurs="0" maxOccurs="1" name="symbol"
type="s:string" />
          </s:sequence>
        </s:complexType>
      </s:element>
      <s:element name="GetQuoteResponse">
        <s:complexType>
          <s:sequence>
            <s:element minOccurs="0" maxOccurs="1"
name="GetQuoteResult" type="s:string" />
          </s:sequence>
        </s:complexType>
      </s:element>
```

```
            <s:element name="string" nillable="true" type="s:string" />
        </s:schema>
    </wsdl:types>
    <wsdl:message name="GetQuoteSoapIn">
        <wsdl:part name="parameters" element="tns:GetQuote" />
    </wsdl:message>
    <wsdl:message name="GetQuoteSoapOut">
        <wsdl:part name="parameters" element="tns:GetQuoteResponse" />
    </wsdl:message>
    ...
```

The first part of the WSDL file contains the description of the XML schema. The second part defines the various web service operations as follows:

```
    <wsdl:portType name="StockQuoteSoap">
        <wsdl:operation name="GetQuote">
            <wsdl:documentation xmlns:wsdl="http://schemas.xmlsoap.org/
wsdl/">Get Stock quote for a company Symbol</wsdl:documentation>
            <wsdl:input message="tns:GetQuoteSoapIn" />
            <wsdl:output message="tns:GetQuoteSoapOut" />
        </wsdl:operation>
    </wsdl:portType>
    <wsdl:portType name="StockQuoteHttpGet">
        <wsdl:operation name="GetQuote">
            <wsdl:documentation xmlns:wsdl="http://schemas.xmlsoap.org/
wsdl/">Get Stock quote for a company Symbol</wsdl:documentation>
            <wsdl:input message="tns:GetQuoteHttpGetIn" />
            <wsdl:output message="tns:GetQuoteHttpGetOut" />
        </wsdl:operation>
    </wsdl:portType>

    <wsdl:binding name="StockQuoteSoap12" type="tns:StockQuoteSoap">
        <soap12:binding transport="http://schemas.xmlsoap.org/soap/http"
/>
        <wsdl:operation name="GetQuote">
            <soap12:operation soapAction="http://www.webserviceX.NET/
GetQuote" style="document" />
            <wsdl:input>
                <soap12:body use="literal" />
            </wsdl:input>
            <wsdl:output>
                <soap12:body use="literal" />
            </wsdl:output>
        </wsdl:operation>
    </wsdl:binding>
    ...
```

Finally, the last part of the WSDL file defines the coupling between web service operations and physical URLs:

```
<wsdl:service name="StockQuote">
  ...
  <wsdl:port name="StockQuoteSoap12" binding="tns:StockQuoteSoap12">
    <soap12:address location="http://www.webservicex.net/stockquote.asmx" />
  </wsdl:port>
  ...
</wsdl:service>
</wsdl:definitions>
```

As you can see, the WSDL files are often pretty verbose, but the Scala contract resulting from the `scalaxb` generation boils down to this one method trait:

```
// Generated by <a href="http://scalaxb.org/">scalaxb</a>.
package se.wssample

trait StockQuoteSoap {
  def getQuote(symbol: Option[String]): Either[scalaxb.Fault[Any],
se.wssample.GetQuoteResponse]
}
```

Notice how the resulting type is nicely wrapped into an `Either` class that represents a value of one of the two possible types, `Left` and `Right`, where the `Right` object corresponds to a successful invocation of the service whereas the `Left` object contains a `scalaxb.Fault` value in case of failure, as we have briefly described in *Chapter 2, Code Integration*.

Since the generated classes concerning the SOAP protocol and the HTTP dispatch-related classes are not specific to the service we are defining, they can be reused and therefore have been generated as stackable traits including data types and interface, SOAP bindings, and full SOAP clients. A typical usage scenario of these traits to invoke a SOAP web service is given in the following `StockQuoteSpec.scala` test sample:

```
package se.wssample

import org.scalatest._
import org.scalatest.matchers.Matchers
import scala.xml.{ XML, PrettyPrinter }

class StockQuoteSpec extends FlatSpec with Matchers {
  "Getting a quote for Apple" should "give appropriate data" in {
```

```
      val pp = new PrettyPrinter(80, 2)

      val service =
        (new se.wssample.StockQuoteSoap12Bindings
          with scalaxb.SoapClients
          with scalaxb.DispatchHttpClients {}).service

      val stockquote = service.getQuote(Some("AAPL"))

      stockquote match {
        case Left(err) => fail("Problem with stockquote invocation")
        case Right(success) => success.GetQuoteResult match {
          case None => println("No info returned for that quote")
          case Some(x) => {
            println("Stockquote: "+pp.format(XML.loadString(x)))
            x should startWith ("<StockQuotes><Stock><Symbol>AAPL</
Symbol>")
          }
        }
      }
    }
  }
```

In this example, once we have instantiated the service, we will just call the API method `service.getQuote(Some("AAPL"))` for retrieving the stock quote of the AAPL symbol (Apple, Inc). We then pattern match on the result to extract the XML data out of the `Either` object that was returned by the service. Finally, since the retrieved data is given as a string of XML, we parse it and format it for better reading. We can execute the test using the following code to see what comes out of it:

```
> sbt
> test-only se.wssample.StockQuoteSpec
Stockquote: <StockQuotes>
  <Stock>
    <Symbol>AAPL</Symbol>
    <Last>553.13</Last>
    <Date>1/2/2014</Date>
    <Time>4:00pm</Time>
    <Change>-7.89</Change>
    <Open>555.68</Open>
    <High>557.03</High>
    <Low>552.021</Low>
```

```
    <Volume>8388321</Volume>

    <MktCap>497.7B</MktCap>

    <PreviousClose>561.02</PreviousClose>

    <PercentageChange>-1.41%</PercentageChange>

    <AnnRange>385.10 - 575.14</AnnRange>

    <Earns>39.75</Earns>

    <P-E>14.11</P-E>

    <Name>Apple Inc.</Name>

  </Stock>
</StockQuotes>
[info] StockQuoteSpec:
[info] Getting a quote for Apple
[info] - should give appropriate data
[info] Passed: : Total 1, Failed 0, Errors 0, Passed 1, Skipped 0
[success] Total time: 3 s
```

Working with XML and JSON

XML and JSON are the dominant formats to structure data that can be exchanged between parts of a system such as backend-frontend or between external systems. In Scala, there is some out-of-the-box support in the Scala library to manipulate both.

Manipulating XML

We have briefly seen earlier in this chapter as well as in *Chapter 3, Understanding the Scala Ecosystem*, when working with HTTP that XML documents can be created as literals and transformed in many ways. For instance, if we launch an REPL by typing > `play console` from a Play project root directory, we can start experimenting with XML:

```
scala> val books =
       <Library>
         <book title="Programming in Scala" quantity="15" price="30.00"
/>
         <book title="Scala for Java Developers" quantity="10"
price="25.50" />
       </Library>
```

```
books: scala.xml.Elem =
<Library>
   <book title="Programming in Scala" quantity="15" price="30.00"/>
   <book title="Scala for Java Developers" quantity="10" price="25.50"/>
</Library>
```

The `books` variable is of type `Elem`, which represents an XML structure. Rather than directly writing an XML literal, we could also construct the XML `Elem` using utility methods to parse a file or just parse a string, as follows:

```
scala> import scala.xml._
scala> val sameBooks = XML.loadString("""
        <Library>
            <book title="Programming in Scala" quantity="15"
price="30.00"/>
            <book title="Scala for Java Developers" quantity="10"
price="25.50"/>
        </Library>
      """)
sameBooks: scala.xml.Elem =
<Library>
<book price="30.00" quantity="15" title="Programming in Scala"/>
<book price="25.50" quantity="10" title="Scala for Java Developers"/>
</Library>
```

The triple quote used in the preceding command lets us express a preformatted string where the characters are escaped (for example, the " within a regular string would have been noted \").

Processing such an XML structure can, for example, consist of computing the total price for the books. This operation can be achieved with a Scala `for comprehension` leading to the following code:

```
scala> val total = (for {
        book <- books \ "book"
        price = ( book \ "@price").text.toDouble
        quantity = ( book \ "@quantity").text.toInt
      } yield price * quantity).sum
total: Double = 705.0
```

Retrieving and transforming XML structures happens all the time when dealing with the integration of diverse external systems. Accessing the various XML tags through XPath expressions as we have done earlier is very handy and produces concise and readable code. Programmatically, creating XML out of information exported from Excel in the form of CSV data is also a common operation and can be achieved as follows:

```
scala> val books =
       <Library>
          { List("Programming in Scala,15,30.00","Scala for Java
Developers,10,25.50") map { row => row split "," } map { b => <book
title={b(0)} quantity={b(1)} price={b(2)} /> }}
       </Library>
books: scala.xml.Elem =
<Library>
   <book title="Programming in Scala" quantity="15" price="30.00"/><book
title="Scala for Java Developers" quantity="10" price="25.50"/>
</Library>
```

Manipulating JSON

JSON is supported in the Scala library and you just need to import the appropriate library. An example of some REPL usage is illustrated as follows:

```
scala> import scala.util.parsing.json._
import scala.util.parsing.json._
scala> val result = JSON.parseFull("""
        {
          "Library": {
            "book": [
              {
                "title": "Scala for Java Developers",
                "quantity": 10
              },
              {
                "title": "Programming Scala",
                "quantity": 20
              }
            ]
```

```
        }
    }
    """)
```

```
result: Option[Any] = Some(Map(Library -> Map(book -> List(Map(title ->
Scala for Java Developers, quantity -> 10.0), Map(title -> Programming
Scala, quantity -> 20.0)))))
```

Any valid JSON message can be transformed into a structure made of `Maps` and `Lists`. However, it is often desirable to create meaningful classes, that is, expressing the business domain out of the JSON messages. The online service available at `http://json2caseclass.cleverapps.io` does exactly that; it is a convenient JSON to Scala case class converter. We can, for example, copy our preceding JSON message into the **Json paste** text area and click on the **Let's go!** button to try it out as shown in the following screenshot:

The converter produces the following output:

```
case class Book(title:String, quantity:Double)
case class Library(book:List[Book])
case class R00tJsonObject(Library:Library)
```

Among the very interesting features of case classes that we have already introduced in *Chapter 1, Programming Interactively within Your Project*, is a decomposition mechanism for pattern matching. Once JSON messages have been deserialized into case classes, we can, for instance, manipulate them using this mechanism, as the sequence of the following command illustrates:

```
scala> case class Book(title:String, quantity:Double)
defined class Book
scala> val book1 = Book("Scala for Java Developers",10)
book1: Book = Book(Scala for Java Developers,10.0)
```

```
scala> val book2 = Book("Effective Java",12)
book2: Book = Book(Effective Java,12.0)
scala> val books = List(book1,book2)
books: List[Book] = List(Book(Scala for Java Developers,10.0),
Book(Effective Java,12.0))
```

First, we defined two instances of books and put them into a list.

```
scala> def bookAboutScala(book:Book) = book match {
        case Book(a,_) if a contains "Scala" => Some(book)
        case _ => None
      }
bookAboutScala: (book: Book)Option[Book]
```

The method defined previously does pattern matching on the Book constructor, which also contains a guard (that is, the if condition). Since we do not use the second constructor parameter, we have put an underscore instead of creating an anonymous variable. Calling this method on both the book instances that we defined earlier will show the following result:

```
scala> bookAboutScala(book1)
res0: Option[Book] = Some(Book(Scala for Java Developers,10.0))
scala> bookAboutScala(book2)
res1: Option[Book] = None
```

We can mix case class pattern matching together with other patterns. Let's, for instance, define the following regular expression (note the usage of the triple quotes as well as the use of .r to specify that it is a regular expression):

```
scala> val regex = """(.*)(Scala|Java)(.*)""".r
regex: scala.util.matching.Regex = (.*)(Scala|Java)(.*)
```

This regular expression will match any string that contains either Scala or Java.

```
scala> def whatIs(that:Any) = that match {
        case Book(t,_) if (t contains "Scala") =>
          s"${t} is a book about Scala"
        case Book(_,_) => s"$that is a book "
        case regex(_,word,_) => s"$that is something about ${word}"
        case head::tail => s"$that is a list of books"
        case _ => "You tell me !"
      }
```

```
whatIs: (that: Any)String
```

We can now try out this method on a number of different inputs and observe the result:

```
scala> whatIs(book1)
res2: String = Scala for Java Developers is a book about Scala
scala> whatIs(book2)
res3: String = "Book(Effective Java,12.0) is a book "
scala> whatIs(books)
res4: String = List(Book(Scala for Java Developers,10.0), Book(Effective
Java,12.0)) is a list of books
scala> whatIs("Scala pattern matching")
res5: String = Scala pattern matching is something about Scala
scala> whatIs("Love")
res6: String = You tell me !
```

Using Play JSON

There are many alternative libraries one can use to manipulate JSON in addition to the default implementation of the Scala library. In addition to the ones built on top of the known Java libraries such as Jerkson (built on top of Jackson) and other known implementations such as sjson, json4s, or Argonaut (functional programming oriented), many web frameworks have created their own including lift-json, spray-json, or play-json. Since in this book we are mostly covering the Play Framework to build web applications, we are going to focus on the play-json implementation. Note that play-json can also be run as standalone since it consists of a single jar without other dependencies to Play. Running an REPL console from within a Play project already includes the play-json dependency so that we can directly experiment with it in a console terminal window.

 If you want to run the following samples into an REPL different from the Play console (for instance, a regular SBT project or a Typesafe activator project) then you will have to add the following dependency to your `build.sbt` file:

```
libraryDependencies += "com.typesafe.play" %% "play-
json" % "2.2.1"
```

```
scala> import play.api.libs.json._
import play.api.libs.json._
scala> val books = Json.parse("""
```

```
    {
      "Library": {
        "book": [
          {
            "title": "Scala for Java Developers",
            "quantity": 10
          },
          {
            "title": "Programming Scala",
            "quantity": 20
          }
        ]
      }
    }
    """)
```

```
books: play.api.libs.json.JsValue = {"Library":{"book":[{"title":
"Scala for Java Developers","quantity":10},{"title":"Programming
Scala","quantity":20}]}}
```

The `JsValue` type is the super type of the other JSON data types included in play-json and is listed as follows:

- `JsNull` to represent a null value

- `JsString`, `JsBoolean`, and `JsNumber` to describe strings, booleans, and numbers respectively: numbers include short, int, long, float, double, and BigDecimal as seen in the following commands:

  ```
  scala> val sfjd = JsString("Scala for Java Developers")

  sfjd: play.api.libs.json.JsString = "Scala for Java Developers"

  scala> val qty = JsNumber(10)

  qty: play.api.libs.json.JsNumber = 10
  ```

- `JsObject` represents a set of name/value pairs as follows:

  ```
  scala> val book1 = JsObject(Seq("title"->sfjd,"quantity"->qty))

  book1: play.api.libs.json.JsObject = {"title":"Scala for Java
  Developers","quantity":10}

  scala> val book2 = JsObject(Seq("title"->JsString("Programming in
  Scala"),"quantity"->JsNumber(15)))

  book2: play.api.libs.json.JsObject = {"title":"Programming in
  Scala","quantity":15}
  ```

- `JsArray` represents a sequence of any JSON value types (which can be heterogenous, that is, of different types):

```
scala> val array =
          JsArray(Seq(JsString("a"),JsNumber(2),JsBoolean(true)))
array: play.api.libs.json.JsArray = ["a",2,true]
```

Programmatically, creating a JSON **Abstract Syntax Tree (AST)** equivalent to our list of books can therefore be expressed as follows:

```
scala> val books = JsObject(Seq(
          "books" -> JsArray(Seq(book1,book2))
       ))
books: play.api.libs.json.JsObject = {"books":[{"title":"Scala
for Java Developers","quantity":10},{"title":"Programming in
Scala","quantity":15}]}
```

Play has recently been enhanced to provide a slightly simpler syntax when creating the JSON structure we have just described. The alternative syntax to construct the same JSON object is given as follows:

```
scala> val booksAsJson = Json.obj(
          "books" -> Json.arr(
            Json.obj(
              "title" -> "Scala for Java Developers",
              "quantity" -> 10
            ),
            Json.obj(
              "title" -> "Programming in Scala",
              "quantity" -> 15
            )
          )
       )
booksAsJson: play.api.libs.json.JsObject = {"books":[{"title":"Scala
for Java Developers","quantity":10},{"title":"Programming in
Scala","quantity":15}]}
```

Serializing the JsObject to its string representation can be achieved with the following statement:

```
scala> val booksAsString = Json.stringify(booksAsJson)
booksAsString: String = {"books":[{"title":"Scala for Java Developers","q
uantity":10},{"title":"Programming in Scala","quantity":15}]}
```

Finally, since a `JsObject` object represents a tree structure, you can navigate within the tree by using XPath expressions to retrieve various elements, such as the following example to access the titles of both our books:

```
scala> val titles = booksAsJson \ "books" \\ "title"
titles: Seq[play.api.libs.json.JsValue] = ArrayBuffer("Scala for Java
Developers", "Programming in Scala")
```

As the return type is a sequence of `JsValue` objects, it can be useful to convert them into Scala types and the `.as[...]` method would be convenient to achieve that:

```
scala> titles.toList.map(x=>x.as[String])
res8: List[String] = List(Scala for Java Developers, Programming in Scala)
```

Handling Play requests with XML and JSON

Now that we are familiar with the JSON and XML formats, we can start using them to handle HTTP requests and responses in the context of a Play project.

To exhibit these behaviors, we are going to call an online web service, the iTunes media library, which is available and documented at `http://www.apple.com/itunes/affiliates/resources/documentation/itunes-store-web-service-search-api.html`.

It returns JSON messages on search invocations. We can, for instance, call the API with the following URL and parameters:

`https://itunes.apple.com/search?term=angry+birds&country=se&entity=software`

The term parameter filters every item in the library that has to do with *Angry Birds* and the entity parameter retains only software items. We also apply an additional filter to query only the Swedish App Store.

If you don't have it already in your `build.sbt` file, you may need to add the dispatch dependency at this point, the same way we did while working with HTTP in *Chapter 3, Understanding the Scala Ecosystem*:

```
libraryDependencies += "net.databinder.dispatch" %%
"dispatch-core" % "0.11.0"
```

```
scala> import dispatch._
import dispatch._
```

```
scala> import Defaults._

import Defaults._

scala> val request = url("https://itunes.apple.com/search")

request: dispatch.Req = Req(<function1>)
```

Parameters that will be part of our GET method call can be expressed as `(key,value)` tuples in a Scala `Map`:

```
scala> val params = Map("term" -> "angry birds", "country" -> "se",
"entity" -> "software")

params: scala.collection.immutable.Map[String,String] = Map(term -> angry
birds, country -> se, entity -> software)

scala> val result = Http( request <<? params OK as.String).either

result: dispatch.Future[Either[Throwable,String]] = scala.concurrent.
impl.Promise$DefaultPromise@7a707f7c
```

The type of result in this case is `Future[Either[Throwable,String]]`, which means we can extract a successful invocation as well as a failed execution by pattern matching as follows:

```
scala> val response = result() match {
        case Right(content)=> "Answer: "+ content
        case Left(StatusCode(404))=> "404 Not Found"
        case Left(x)  => x.printStackTrace()
    }

response: Any =
"Answer:


{
 "resultCount":50,
 "results": [
{"kind":"software", "features":["gameCenter"],
"supportedDevices":["iPhone5s", "iPad23G", "iPadThirdGen",
"iPodTouchThirdGen", "iPadFourthGen4G", "iPhone4S", "iPad3G", "iPhone5",
"iPadWifi", "iPhone5c", "iPad2Wifi", "iPadMini", "iPadThirdGen4G",
"iPodTouchourthGen", "iPhone4", "iPadFourthGen", "iPhone-3GS",
"iPodTouchFifthGen", "iPadMini4G"], "isGameCenterEnabled":true,
"artistViewUrl":"https://itunes.apple.com/se/artist/rovio-entertainment-
ltd/id298910979?uo=4", "artworkUrl60":"http://a336.phobos.apple.com/us/
r30/Purple2/v4/6c/20/98/6c2098f0-f572-46bb-f7bd-e4528fe31db8/Icon.png",
"screenshotUrls":["http://a2.mzstatic.com/eu/r30/Purple/v4/c0/eb/59/
c0eb597b-a3d6-c9af-32a7-f107994a595c/screen1136x1136.jpeg", "http://
a4.mzst...
```

Mocking Play responses with JSON

Whenever you need to integrate your services with external systems that you do not own or that are not available until you deploy them in production, it can be cumbersome to test the interaction of messages that are sent and received. An efficient way to avoid calling a real service is to replace it with mock messages, that is, hardcoded responses that will cut short the real interaction, especially if you need to run your tests as part of an automated process (for instance, daily as a Jenkins job). Returning a plain JSON message from within a Play controller is very straightforward, as the following example illustrates:

```scala
package controllers

import play.api.mvc._
import play.api.libs.json._
import views._

object MockMarketplaceController extends Controller {

  case class AppStoreSearch(artistName: String, artistLinkUrl: String)
  implicit val appStoreSearchFormat = Json.format[AppStoreSearch]

  def mockSearch() = Action {
    val result = List(AppStoreSearch("Van Gogh", " http://www.
vangoghmuseum.nl/"), AppStoreSearch("Monet", " http://www.
claudemonetgallery.org "))
    Ok(Json.toJson(result))
  }
}
```

The `Json.format[. . .]` declaration that involves Reads, Writes, and Format will be explained later on in this section when we invoke web services, so we can skip discussing that part for the moment.

To try out this controller, you can either create a new Play project, or, as we did before, just add this controller to the application we generated out of an existing database in the last section of *Chapter 6, Database Access and the Future of ORM.* You also need to add a route to the `route` file under `conf/` as follows:

```
GET /mocksearch  controllers.MockMarketplaceController.mockSearch
```

Once the app is running, accessing the `http://localhost:9000/mocksearch` URL in a browser will return the following mock JSON message:

```
⊟ [
    ⊟ {
        "artistName":"Van Gogh",
        "artistLinkUrl":"
        http://www.vangoghmuseum.nl/"
    },
    ⊟ {
        "artistName":"Monet",
        "artistLinkUrl":"
        http://www.claudemonetgallery.org "
    }
]
```

Another convenient way to obtain a JSON test message that you can use to mock a response is to use the online service found at http://json-generator.appspot.com. It consists of a JSON generator that we can use as it is by simply clicking on the **Generate** button. By default, it will generate a JSON sample including random data in the panel to the right of the browser window, but adhering to the structure defined in the panel to the left, as illustrated in the following screenshot:

You can click on the **Copy to clipboard** button and paste the resulting mock message directly into the response of the Play controller.

Calling web services from Play

In the previous section, to quickly experiment with the App Store search API, we have used the `dispatch` library; we have already introduced this library in *Chapter 3, Understanding the Scala Ecosystem.* Play provides its own HTTP library to be able to interact with other online web services. It is also built on top of the Java `AsyncHttpClient` library (https://github.com/AsyncHttpClient/async-http-client), as `dispatch` is.

Before we dive into invoking REST web services from Play controllers, let's experiment a little bit with Play web services from the REPL. In a terminal window, either create a new Play project or go to the root directory of the one we have used in the previous sections. Once you get a Scala prompt after having typed the > `play console` command, enter the following commands:

```scala
scala> import play.api.libs.ws._
import play.api.libs.ws._
scala> import scala.concurrent.Future
import scala.concurrent.Future
```

Since we are going to invoke a web service asynchronously, we need an execution context to handle the `Future` placeholder:

```scala
scala> implicit val context = scala.concurrent.ExecutionContext.
Implicits.global
context: scala.concurrent.ExecutionContextExecutor = scala.concurrent.
impl.ExecutionContextImpl@44d8bd53
```

We can now define a service URL that needs to be called. Here, we will take a simple web service that returns the geographic location of a site given as a parameter, according to the following signature:

```
http://freegeoip.net/{format}/{site}
```

The format parameter can either be `json` or `xml`, and the `site` will be a reference to a website:

```scala
scala> val url = "http://freegeoip.net/json/www.google.com"
url: String = http://freegeoip.net/json/www.google.com
scala> val futureResult: Future[String] = WS.url(url).get().map {
        response =>
```

```
        (response.json \ "region_name").as[String]
    }
```

```
futureResult: scala.concurrent.Future[String] = scala.concurrent.impl.
Promise$DefaultPromise@e4bc0ba
scala> futureResult.onComplete(println)
Success(California)
```

As we saw earlier in *Chapter 3, Understanding the Scala Ecosystem,* when working with the `dispatch` library, a `Future` is a placeholder that contains the result of an asynchronous computation and can be in two states, either `completed` or `not`. Here, we want to print the result once it is available.

We have only extracted the `region_name` item from the response; the whole JSON document is as follows:

```
{
    "ip":"173.194.64.106",
    "country_code":"US",
    "country_name":"United States",
    "region_code":"CA",
    "region_name":"California",
    "city":"Mountain View",
    "zipcode":"94043",
    "latitude":37.4192,
    "longitude":-122.0574,
    "metro_code":"807",
    "areacode":"650"
}
```

We can encapsulate part of the response if we want to by creating a `case` class as follows:

```
scala> case class Location(latitude:Double, longitude:Double,
region:String, country:String)
defined class Location
```

The `play-json` library includes support to read/write JSON structures via `Reads`/`Writes`/`Format` combinators based on `JsPath` so that validation can be made on the fly. If you are interested in all the details behind the use of these combinators, you may want to read through the blog at http://mandubian.com/2012/09/08/unveiling-play-2-dot-1-json-api-part1-jspath-reads-combinators/.

```
scala> import play.api.libs.json._
import play.api.libs.json._
```

```
scala> import play.api.libs.functional.syntax._

import play.api.libs.functional.syntax._

scala> implicit val locationReads: Reads[Location] = (
        (__ \ "latitude").read[Double] and
        (__ \ "longitude").read[Double] and
        (__ \ "region_name").read[String] and
        (__ \ "country").read[String]
      ) (Location.apply _)

locationReads: play.api.libs.json.Reads[Location] = play.api.libs.json.
Reads$$anon$8@4a13875b

locationReads: play.api.libs.json.Reads[Location] = play.api.libs.json.
Reads$$anon$8@5430c881
```

Now, invoking the validate method on the JSON response will verify that the data we receive is well-formed and with acceptable values.

```
scala> val futureResult: Future[JsResult[Location]] = WS.url(url).get().
map {
        response => response.json.validate[Location]
      }

futureResult: scala.concurrent.Future[play.api.libs.
json.JsResult[Location]] = scala.concurrent.impl.
Promise$DefaultPromise@3168c842


scala> futureResult.onComplete(println)

Success(JsError(List((/country,List(ValidationError(error.path.
missing,WrappedArray())))))))
```

The previous JsError object illustrates a validation that failed; it detected that the country element is not found in the response. In fact, the correct spelling is country_name instead of country, which we can correct in our locationReads declaration. This time validation goes through and what we get as a response is a JsSuccess object containing the latitude and longitude information as we expect it:

```
scala> implicit val locationReads: Reads[Location] = (
        (__ \ "latitude").read[Double] and
        (__ \ "longitude").read[Double] and
        (__ \ "region_name").read[String] and
        (__ \ "country_name").read[String]
      ) (Location.apply _)
```

```
locationReads: play.api.libs.json.Reads[Location] = play.api.libs.json.
Reads$$anon$8@70aab9ed

scala> val futureResult: Future[JsResult[Location]] = WS.url(url).get().
map {
        response => response.json.validate[Location]
    }
futureResult: scala.concurrent.Future[play.api.libs.
json.JsResult[Location]] = scala.concurrent.impl.
Promise$DefaultPromise@361c5860

scala> futureResult.onComplete(println)

scala> Success(JsSuccess(Location(37.4192,-122.0574,California,United
States),))
```

Now, let's create a sample controller that invokes a web service to retrieve some data from the App Store:

```
package controllers

import play.api._
import play.api.mvc._
import play.api.libs.ws.WS
import scala.concurrent.ExecutionContext.Implicits.global
import play.api.libs.json._
import play.api.libs.functional.syntax._
import scala.concurrent.Future
import views._
import models._

object MarketplaceController extends Controller {

  val pageSize = 10
  val appStoreUrl = "https://itunes.apple.com/search"

  def list(page: Int, orderBy: Int, filter: String = "*") = Action.
async { implicit request =>
    val futureWSResponse =
      WS.url(appStoreUrl)
        .withQueryString("term" -> filter, "country" -> "se", "entity"
-> "software")
        .get()

      futureWSResponse map { resp =>
        val json = resp.json
```

```
val jsResult = json.validate[AppResult]
jsResult.map {
  case AppResult(count, res) =>
    Ok(html.marketplace.list(
      Page(res,
        page,
        offset = pageSize * page,
        count),
      orderBy,
      filter))
}.recoverTotal {
  e => BadRequest("Detected error:" + JsError.toFlatJson(e))
}
      }
    }
  }
}
```

Here, the call to the web service is illustrated by invoking methods on the WS class, first the url method giving the URL, then the withQueryString method with input parameters given as a sequence of key->value pairs. Notice that the returned type is a Future, meaning our web service is asynchronous. recoverTotal takes a function that will return a default value after managing the error. The line json.validate[AppResult] makes the JSON response validated against an AppResult object that is specified here (as part of a Marketplace.scala file in app/models/ folder):

```
package models

import play.api.libs.json._
import play.api.libs.functional.syntax._

case class AppInfo(id: Long, name: String, author: String,
authorUrl:String,
    category: String, picture: String, formattedPrice: String, price:
Double)
object AppInfo {
  implicit val appInfoFormat = (
    (__ \ "trackId").format[Long] and
    (__ \ "trackName").format[String] and
    (__ \ "artistName").format[String] and
    (__ \ "artistViewUrl").format[String] and
    (__ \ "primaryGenreName").format[String] and
    (__ \ "artworkUrl60").format[String] and
    (__ \ "formattedPrice").format[String] and
```

```
      (__ \ "price").format[Double])(AppInfo.apply, unlift(AppInfo.
   unapply))
   }


   case class AppResult(resultCount: Int, results: Array[AppInfo])
   object AppResult {
     implicit val appResultFormat = (
       (__ \ "resultCount").format[Int] and
       (__ \\ "results").format[Array[AppInfo]])(AppResult.apply,
   unlift(AppResult.unapply))
   }
```

The `AppResult` and `AppInfo` case classes are created to encapsulate the elements that
we care about for our service. As you may have seen when first experimenting with
the API, most of the search queries to the App Store return a large amount of elements,
most of which we may not need. This is why, using some Scala syntactic sugar with
combinators, we can validate the JSON response on the fly and directly extract the
elements of interest. Before trying out this web service call, we just need to add the
needed route to the `routes` file under `conf/`, as shown in the following code:

```
GET /marketplace  controllers.MarketplaceController.list(p:Int ?= 0,
s:Int ?= 2, f ?= "*")
```

Finally, before launching the application in a web browser, we also need the
sample view that is referred to in the `MarketplaceController.scala` file by
`html.marketplace.list` and created in a `list.scala.html` file under `views/`
`marketplace/` in several parts as shown in the following code:

```
@(currentPage: Page[AppInfo], currentOrderBy: Int, currentFilter:
String)(implicit flash: play.api.mvc.Flash)
...
@main("Welcome to Play 2.0") {

<h1>@Messages("marketplace.list.title", currentPage.total)</h1>

@flash.get("success").map { message =>
<div class="alert-message warning">
  <strong>Done!</strong> @message
</div>
}
<div id="actions">

  @helper.form(action=routes.MarketplaceController.list()) { <input
    type="search" id="searchbox" name="f" value="@currentFilter"
    placeholder="Filter by name..."> <input type="submit"
```

```
            id="searchsubmit" value="Filter by name" class="btn primary">
    }
</div>
...
```

The first part of the view only consists of helper methods to navigate and is generated the same way as we did for the CRUD sample generation in *Chapter 6, Database Access and the Future of ORM*. The second part of the view includes the JSON elements we have retrieved from the web service:

```
...
@Option(currentPage.items).filterNot(_.isEmpty).map { entities =>
<table class="computers zebra-striped">
  <thead>
    <tr>
      @header(2, "Picture")
      @header(4, "Name")
      @header(5, "Author")
      @header(6, "IPO")
      @header(7, "Category")
      @header(8, "Price")
    </tr>
  </thead>
  <tbody>
    @entities.map{ entity =>
    <tr>
      <td>
        <img
          src="@entity.picture"
          width="60" height="60" alt="image description" />
      </td>
      <td>@entity.name</td>
      <td><a href="@entity.authorUrl" class="new-btn btn-back">@
entity.author</a></td>
```

```
        <td>@entity.category</td>
        <td>@entity.formattedPrice</td>
      </tr>
      }
    </tbody>
</table>
...
```

The third and final part of the view is handling pagination:

```
...
<div id="pagination" class="pagination">
  <ul>
     @currentPage.prev.map { page =>
     <li class="prev"><a href="@link(page)">&larr; Previous</a></li>
     }.getOrElse {
     <li class="prev disabled"><a>&larr; Previous</a></li> }
     <li class="current"><a>Displaying @(currentPage.offset + 1)
         to @(currentPage.offset + entities.size) of @currentPage.
total</a></li>
     @currentPage.next.map { page =>
     <li class="next"><a href="@link(page)">Next &rarr;</a></li>
     }.getOrElse {
     <li class="next disabled"><a>Next &rarr;</a></li> }
  </ul>
</div>
}.getOrElse {
<div class="well">
  <em>Nothing to display</em>
</div>
} }
```

Once we re-launch the Play app with `> play run` and access (through a web browser) our local `http://localhost:9000/marketplace?f=candy+crush` URL that includes a default search from the App Store (the `f` parameter stands for `filter`), we will obtain a page similar to the following screenshot:

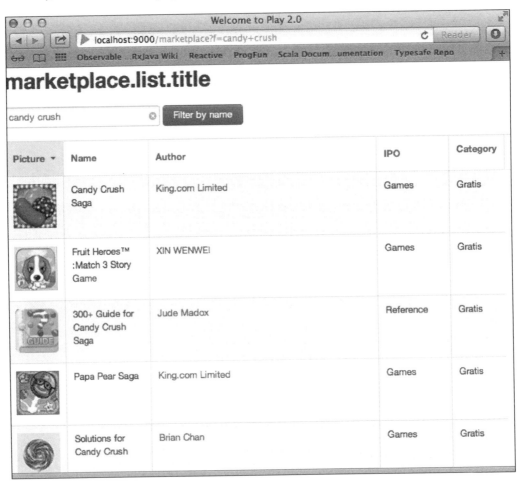

Summary

In this chapter, we saw some examples on how to manipulate the XML and JSON formats in Scala and how to connect to other systems via web services. In the case of XML, we also covered how to generate SOAP bindings out of a WSDL description as well as Scala classes to encapsulate the XML domain included in an XML schema. Web services in the Play Framework run asynchronously, which means that the caller is not waiting for the answer to come back before he continues to do other useful processing (such as serving other requests). In the next chapter, we are going to study this notion of asynchronous invocations more precisely. It is based on the concepts of `Future` and `Promise` that are also emerging in the Java world to deal with the execution of concurrent code. In particular, we will go through the Akka framework, an open source toolkit and runtime simplifying the construction of concurrent applications. Designed and written in Scala, Akka contains both Scala and Java APIs and is the basis of the Play Framework infrastructure that makes the Play Framework an ideal candidate for running scalable web applications on multicore architectures.

8
Essential Properties of Modern Applications – Asynchrony and Concurrency

Availability and performance are two words that often characterize the requirements found behind most commercial software. As the volume of processed information continues to grow together with the rise of social networks and added complexity of online services, web servers are now increasingly confronted with heavy loads and higher numbers of concurrent requests. In this chapter, we will explore different ways to deal with better performance and scalability by covering the following topics:

- The Async library, a new way to simplify asynchronous code, including examples of web services composition

- Akka, a toolkit and runtime that simplifies the building of concurrent, distributed, and fault-tolerant applications based on the actor paradigm

The pillars of Concurrency

Concurrency and asynchrony are the techniques that most programming languages use to enhance response time and scalability, and Java is no exception. Asynchronous method calls is a technique by which the caller of a potentially time-consuming computation does not wait for a response, but rather continues to proceed with other code while the computation is ongoing. The caller will be notified once running has completed, receiving notification of either a successful result or a failure message.

The traditional way to deal with asynchronous code in Java has mostly been through the registration of callbacks, that is, placeholders that are called upon completion. Complexity tends to increase when working with asynchronous code as the sequence of execution is not deterministic, that is, the order of execution is not guaranteed. Executing code concurrently is, therefore, more difficult to test since it may not produce the same result on successive invocations. Furthermore, as callbacks are not composable (which means that they can't be chained and combined in a flexible way), it can be cumbersome to mix several asynchronous computations together to achieve more advanced scenarios, resulting in the well-known problem of callback hell when such projects increase in size (cases where the complexity is at such a high level that it is difficult to maintain and guarantee the proper execution of a piece of code).

Concurrency is also encountered when code is executed on multiple cores. Recent hardware architectures are now embedding several cores into the same machine as a way to continue achieving better performance when the minimal physical size of transistors has been reached.

Another consequence of dealing with concurrent code is that multiple threads of execution can get into conflicts when trying to access the same resources. Mutable state in a program, which is not protected against shared access, has a higher risk of being incorrect. Making sure that the concurrent code executes correctly often comes at the cost of increased complexity. Java thread synchronization mechanisms, for example, using locks, have led to solutions that are difficult to understand and maintain.

The functional approach of Scala striving for immutability is a first step towards easier concurrency. **Scala Improvement Process (SIP)**, which can be seen as the equivalent to the Java JSR process in Scala, has proposed an SIP concerning *SIP-14-Futures and Promises*. These notions are not new as they have already been used in many other languages when writing concurrent code, but the new proposal tries to merge the various Scala implementations of Futures.

 Futures and Promises are objects through which you can later retrieve the result of some asynchronous execution after it finishes. To learn more, visit `http://en.wikipedia.org/wiki/Futures_and_promises`.

As stated in *SIP-14-Futures and Promises*:

> *Futures provide a nice way to reason about performing many operations in parallel – in an efficient and non-blocking way.*

From this proposal, an implementation has been created, which is now the basis of many Scala libraries that deal with concurrent and asynchronous code.

The Async library – SIP-22-Async

In *Chapter 7, Working with Integration and Web Services*, we have briefly seen how to call asynchronous web services that return a `Future` object. The aim of Async is to simplify asynchronous code by providing a couple of powerful constructs to deal with asynchronous code blocks and, in particular, combining several such blocks. It consists of only two constructs:

- `async { <expression> }`: In this construct, `<expression>` is the code to be executed asynchronously.

- `await { <expression returning a Future> }`: This construct is included in an `async` block. It suspends the execution of the enclosing `async` block until the argument `Future` is completed.

An interesting characteristic of the whole `async`/`await` mechanism is that it is totally nonblocking. Although it is not really required to understand how `async`/`await` works, the exact signature of the two methods `async[]` and `await[]` are given for reference, as follows:

```
def async[T](body: => T) : Future[T]
def await[T](future:Future[T]):T
```

`T` refers to arbitrary types (such as `Int` or `String`) or container types (such as `List` or `Map`), which is how we describe generic types in Scala. Although we will not cover too much programming with generic types, which has already been extensively described in other books such as *Programming in Scala, Artima* by *Martin Odersky*, *Lex Spoon* and *Bill Venners*, it is important to understand that they exist and they form part of the core of the Scala language.

To better understand what Async is all about, we will use the examples that we can run in the REPL. Create a new `Play` project by running the command `> play new ch8samples` and choose, of course, Scala as the language used for the project. Once the project is created, add the Async library as a dependency by adding one line inside the `build.sbt` file, which now looks like the following lines:

```
name := "ch8samples"


version := "1.0-SNAPSHOT"


libraryDependencies ++= Seq(
  jdbc,
  anorm,
  cache,
```

```
  "org.scala-lang.modules" %% "scala-async" % "0.9.0"
)
```

```
play.Project.playScalaSettings
```

We can run the REPL console, as usual, in a terminal window by entering the following command from the root directory of the project:

```
> play console
```

First, we need to perform some imports, which are as shown in the following command lines:

```
scala> import scala.async.Async.{async, await}
import scala.async.Async.{async, await}
scala> import scala.concurrent.ExecutionContext.Implicits.global
import scala.concurrent.ExecutionContext.Implicits.global
```

Similarly, for a thread pool, an execution context is needed to handle how and when the asynchronous computation should be executed.

Second, we can specify an asynchronous computation by enclosing the computation into an `async` block:

```
scala> val computation = async { 3 * 2 }
computation: scala.concurrent.Future[Int] = scala.concurrent.impl.
Promise$DefaultPromise@545c484c
scala> computation.value
res0: Option[scala.util.Try[Int]] = Some(Success(6))
```

As you can see that the type of the result is `Option[scala.util.Try[Int]]`, recollect the brief discussion on the `Try` class in *Chapter 2, Code Integration*. We learned that it builds upon an `Either` class that can take the value `Success` or `Failure` that corresponds respectively to the `Left` and `Right` values of the `Either` class.

In our case, the computation was quite immediate and resulted in the success value of `6`.

Let us make the computation that takes a longer time (for example, 10 seconds), as shown in the following command lines:

```
scala> val longComputation = async { Thread.sleep(10000); 3*2 }
longComputation: scala.concurrent.Future[Int] = scala.concurrent.impl.
Promise$DefaultPromise@7b5ab834
```

Also, during those 10 seconds, we access its result value:

```
scala> longComputation.value
res1: Option[scala.util.Try[Int]] = None
```

We will get the answer None, which is what we expect, as the computation is not completed yet.

If we wait for 10 seconds and perform the same query again, we'll get our result:

```
scala> longComputation.value
res2: Option[scala.util.Try[Int]] = Some(Success(6))
```

Note that once a Future is completed and given a value, it cannot be modified.

An alternative to polling for the result is to be informed or execute some code when the Future is completed. We can do that by invoking the onComplete method, immediately after rerunning our computation, as follows:

```
scala> val longComputation = async { Thread.sleep(10000); 3*2 }
longComputation: scala.concurrent.Future[Int] = scala.concurrent.impl.
Promise$DefaultPromise@1c6b985a
scala> longComputation.onComplete(println)
scala>    (no immediate result)
```

In other words, while the computation is not finished, we can proceed executing other statements:

```
scala> val hello = "Hello"
```

Eventually, we will see the value 6 on the screen, once the time of 10 seconds elapses:

```
scala> Success(6)
```

So far, we've seen that the async method performs the same way as the future method, which is part of the scala.concurrent package; for this reason, we could just replace async with future.

The preferred way is to use async in conjunction with await. The await method is taking a Future object as an input argument. It wraps the rest of the async, blocks in a closure and passes it as a callback on completion of the Future object we're waiting on (the one we passed as argument). Although await will wait for the invoked Future object until it is completed, the whole async/await execution is nonblocking, which means we can compose the Future objects in a totally nonblocking way.

Let's illustrate composing two computations where the input of one depends on the output of the other. A typical example is the invocation of two web services to query a weather forecast service: one that returns our current geo location and the other that needs our position (coordinates or the city name). The following lines of command explain the invocation:

```
scala> import play.api.libs.json._
import play.api.libs.json._
scala> import play.api.libs.ws._
import play.api.libs.ws._
scala> import play.api.libs.functional.syntax._
import play.api.libs.functional.syntax._
scala> import scala.util.{Success, Failure}
import scala.util.{Success, Failure}
scala> val locationURL = "http://freegeoip.net/xml/www.aftonbladet.se"
locationURL: String = http://freegeoip.net/xml/www.aftonbladet.se
scala> val futureLocation = WS.url(locationURL).get().map { response =>
        (response.xml \ "City").text
      }
futureLocation: scala.concurrent.Future[String] = scala.concurrent.impl.
Promise$DefaultPromise@6039c183
```

Wait for a couple of seconds to make sure that the web service `Future` gets completed, then press *Enter*; you'll see the following result:

```
scala> val location = futureLocation.value
location: Option[scala.util.Try[String]] = Some(Success(Stockholm))
```

The first service returns the XML text where we extracted only the `City` element.

Now, let's try a second service from the `http://openweathermap.org` website, a useful resource for testing web service code in general. The following web service call returns the weather as a JSON message, given a particular location (we will use a hardcoded `Paris` city here to first experiment with this service alone without composing the two services):

```
scala> val weatherURL = "http://api.openweathermap.org/data/2.5/
weather?q="
weatherURL: String = http://api.openweathermap.org/data/2.5/weather?q=
scala> val futureWeather = WS.url(weatherURL+"Paris").get().map{ response
=>
        response.json
```

```
        }
futureWeather: scala.concurrent.Future[play.api.libs.json.JsValue] =
scala.concurrent.impl.Promise$DefaultPromise@4dd5dc9f
```

Wait for a couple of seconds to make sure that the web service `Future` gets completed, then enter the following statement:

```
scala> val weather = futureWeather.value
weather: Option[scala.util.Try[play.api.libs.json.JsValue]] = Some(Succes
s({"coord":{"lon":2.35,"lat":48.85},
"sys":{"message":0.0052,"country":"FR","sunrise":1389166933,
"sunset":1389197566},"weather":[{"id":803,"main":"Clouds",
"description":"broken clouds","icon":"04n"}],
"base":"cmc stations","main":{"temp":284.36,"pressure":1013,
"temp_min":284.15,"temp_max":284.82,"humidity":86},
"wind":{"speed":5.37,"deg":193},"clouds":{"all":80},
"dt":1389221871,"id":2988507,"name":"Paris","cod":200}))
```

Combining web services

We are now ready to combine two services using `async`/`await`.

Let's copy and paste the following lines at once in the REPL. To do this, we can use the convenient `:paste` command of the REPL, as shown in the following command lines:

```
scala> :paste
// Entering paste mode (ctrl-D to finish)

val futureLocation =
  WS.url(locationURL).get().map(resp => (resp.xml \ "City").text)
val futureWeather2 = async {
  await(WS.url(weatherURL+await(futureLocation)).get()).body
}
futureWeather2.onComplete(println)


// once the block is copied from somewhere using ctrl-C/ctrl-D, press
ctrl-D


// Exiting paste mode, now interpreting.
futureLocation: scala.concurrent.Future[String] = scala.concurrent.impl.
Promise$DefaultPromise@1e111066
futureWeather2: scala.concurrent.Future[String] = scala.concurrent.impl.
Promise$DefaultPromise@724ba7f5
```

```
scala> Success({"coord":{"lon":18.06,"lat":59.33},
"sys":{"message":0.0251,"country":"SE",
"sunrise":1395808197,"sunset":1395854197},
"weather":[{"id":800,"main":"Clear",
"description":"Sky is Clear","icon":"01d"}],
"base":"cmc stations","main":{"temp":277.29,
"pressure":1028,"humidity":69,"temp_min":276.15,"temp_max":278.15},
"wind":{"speed":5.1,"deg":60},"rain":{"3h":0},
"clouds":{"all":0},"dt":1395852600,"id":2673730,
"name":"Stockholm","cod":200}
)
```

What happens in this code is that the `await` construct ensures that the location city will be available to the weather service.

Combining services without await

If we do not put an `await` method around the `futureLocation` web service call while defining the `futureWeather2` variable, we get a different answer. This is because, in such a case, the `Future` object that contains the location service answer is not yet populated when querying for the weather service. You can verify this behavior by copying and pasting the three following statements at once into the REPL (assuming the `locationURL` variable is still valid, it was created earlier while introducing the location service):

```
scala> :paste
// Entering paste mode (ctrl-D to finish)

val futureLocation =
    WS.url(locationURL).get().map(resp => (resp.xml \ "City").text)
val futureWeather2 = async {
    await(WS.url(weatherURL + futureLocation).get()).body
}
futureWeather2.onComplete(println)

// once the block is copied from somewhere using ctrl-C/ctrl-D, press
ctrl-D
// Exiting paste mode, now interpreting.
```

```
futureLocation: scala.concurrent.Future[String] = scala.concurrent.impl.
Promise$DefaultPromise@705a7c28

futureWeather2: scala.concurrent.Future[String] = scala.concurrent.impl.
Promise$DefaultPromise@448d5fb8

scala> Success({"message":"Error: Not found city","cod":"404"}
)
```

This time, the output shows that the city was not entered correctly into the
weather service.

Getting started with Akka

Akka is a toolkit to simplify writing concurrent and distributed applications, tasks
that can be complex to achieve, as we described at the beginning of this chapter.
As Akka is largely documented both by a number of books as well as extensive
online documentation, our goal here is mostly to experiment with the technology.
We will see how to elegantly write Scala code to solve problems that might otherwise
be error-prone and hard to understand if written in more conventional ways such
as thread synchronization and other languages such as Java. Akka is written in
Scala, but provides to both Java and Scala APIs.

Understanding the Actor model

Akka relies on the Actor paradigm to create concurrent applications. The Actor
model has already been introduced decades ago in the original paper of Carl Hewitt,
Peter Bishop, and Richard Steiger entitled *A Universal Modular Actor Formalism for
Artificial Intelligence, 1973, IJCAI.* Erlang is an example of language that has been
made famous using this model of computation and achieved very good scalability
and reliability figures (the well-known nine nines of availability).

Without going too much into details, we can say that the Actor model is a model
based on message passing rather than method calls. Each unit of computation, called
actor, encapsulates its own behavior and communicates with other actors through
asynchronous immutable messages. It is quite straightforward to reason about actor
systems since they mimic the way humans communicate, exchanging immutable
messages between each other. Since the footprint of actors is very minimal compared
to threads, and state is not shared, they are very suited to writing concurrent and
distributed applications.

In the gold mine of Typesafe activator templates, a number of projects concerning
Akka are available. Let's dig into a couple of them to better understand how to make
programs using Akka actors. First, we can take a look at the `hello-akka` project to
get an idea on how to run a simple actor.

If you haven't got the Typesafe activator in place, follow the instructions from *Chapter 3, Understanding the Scala Ecosystem*, to create the sample project associated with the `hello-akka` template. Once imported into Eclipse, we may start looking at the main class `HelloAkkaScala.scala` in the default package of the `Scala src` directory.

It starts with the following lines (skipping the imports):

```
case object Greet
case class WhoToGreet(who: String)
case class Greeting(message: String)

class Greeter extends Actor {
  var greeting = ""

  def receive = {
    case WhoToGreet(who) => greeting = s"hello, $who"
    case Greet           => sender ! Greeting(greeting)
    // Send the current greeting back to the sender
  }
}
```

As you see, defining an actor consists of extending an `Actor` trait and requires only implementing the abstract `receive` method. This method represents the actor's behavior when it receives a message. It does not need to handle all types of messages, which is why it is a partial function.

The declared mutable variable, `greeting`, shows that you can safely add some mutable state to your actor since the processing of the `receive` method is single threaded.

It is convenient to model the immutable messages sent between actors as case classes, and the `Greeter` actor uses the two messages, `Greet` and `WhoToGreet(who:String)`. Whenever the `Greeter` actor receives a `WhoToGreet(who)` message, it simply updates its state but does not reply anything. In contrast, when this same actor receives a `Greet` message, it uses the saved state to answer the actor that sent the message. The `!` method is also called `tell` (which, by the way, is the name used in the Akka Java API) and represents the sending of a message to an actor, with the signature `actor ! message`.

Also, note the presence of the `sender` variable that is made implicitly available as part of the `Actor` trait, since it is a common pattern that an actor replies to the sender. However, we could have added an `ActorRef` argument to the `Greet` message containing the address of the receiver instead, that is, declared a `case Greet(someone:ActorRef)` class and implemented the processing of `Greet`, as follows:

```
def receive = {
  ...
  case Greet(someone) => someone ! Greeting(greeting)
}
```

The `HelloAkkaScala` object defines the main routine, as shown in the following code snippet:

```
object HelloAkkaScala extends App {

  // Create the 'helloakka' actor system
  val system = ActorSystem("helloakka")

  // Create the 'greeter' actor
  val greeter = system.actorOf(Props[Greeter], "greeter")

  // Create an "actor-in-a-box"
  val inbox = Inbox.create(system)

  // Tell the 'greeter' to change its 'greeting' message
  greeter.tell(WhoToGreet("akka"), ActorRef.noSender)

  // Ask the 'greeter for the latest 'greeting'
  // Reply should go to the "actor-in-a-box"
  inbox.send(greeter, Greet)

  // Wait 5 seconds for the reply with the 'greeting' message
  val Greeting(message1) = inbox.receive(5.seconds)
  println(s"Greeting: $message1")

  // Change the greeting and ask for it again
  greeter.tell(WhoToGreet("typesafe"), ActorRef.noSender)
  inbox.send(greeter, Greet)
```

```
    val Greeting(message2) = inbox.receive(5.seconds)
    println(s"Greeting: $message2")
    val greetPrinter = system.actorOf(Props[GreetPrinter])
    // after zero seconds, send a Greet message every second to the
greeter with a sender of the greetPrinter
    system.scheduler.schedule(0.seconds, 1.second, greeter, Greet)
(system.dispatcher, greetPrinter)
    }
```

A system running actors needs a runtime environment; this is what the `system` variable declares. Creating an actor consists of invoking the `system.actorOf` method with a configuration argument as well as an optional name. This method gives you back an `ActorRef` (actor reference) object, which is the actor address, that is, where messages can be sent. An `ActorRef` object is an immutable and serializable handle to an actor, which may or may not reside on the local host or within the same `ActorSystem` object. As actors only communicate through messages in an asynchronous fashion, each actor has a mailbox where messages can be enqueued if the actor cannot handle them as quickly as they arrive.

The remaining part of the main routine essentially sends orders in the form of `Greet` or `WhoToGreet` messages to the `Greeter` actor. These messages are sent from an `Inbox` object that also expects answers. This `Inbox` object, also referred to as "actor-in-a-box", is a convenient way to write code outside actors that will communicate with actors. Finally, the last actor, `greetPrinter`, sends `Greet` messages (that are scheduled by the environment) to the `Greeter` actor repetitively every second.

You can execute the example code within the project by running the command `> ./activator run` and choosing the `[2] HelloAkkaScala` program. You should see something as is shown in the following code:

```
Multiple main classes detected, select one to run:

[1] HelloAkkaJava
[2] HelloAkkaScala

Enter number: 2

[info] Running HelloAkkaScala
Greeting: hello, akka
Greeting: hello, typesafe
hello, typesafe
hello, typesafe
hello, typesafe
… [press CTRL-C to interrupt]
```

Switching behavior

Actors have the ability to switch their behavior before handling the next message. To illustrate this, let's consider an example of a travel agent actor that needs to reserve both a seat in a flight and a hotel room for its customer. The travel agent is responsible for making sure the booking is transactional, that is, it is only successful if both transport and accommodation are booked, which is illustrated in the following figure:

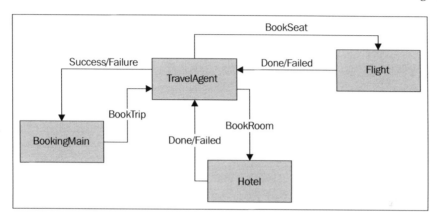

As it is a recognized best practice to declare the messages concerning an actor into its companion object, we will express a `Flight` actor in the following way:

```
package se.sfjd.ch8

import akka.actor.Actor
import akka.event.LoggingReceive

object Flight {
  case class BookSeat(number:Int) {
    require(number > 0)
  }
  case object Done
  case object Failed
}
class Flight extends Actor {
  import Flight._
  var seatsLeft = 50
  def receive = LoggingReceive {
    case BookSeat(nb) if nb <= seatsLeft =>
      seatsLeft -= nb
      sender ! Done
    case _ => sender ! Failed
  }
}
```

Notice the `require` assertion found in the `BookSeat` message declaration. This method is part of `Predef`, a global object that includes many useful functionalities imported by default. It enables to do some *design-by-contract* style specification by checking pre- and post-conditions on methods. The `receive` method of the `Flight` actor is handling one type of message only, `BookSeat(n:Int)`, which means reserving *n* seats as long as there are enough seats left for the flight. The `Flight` actor updates its state and replies with a `Done` message to the sender if there are enough seats left; it replies `Failed` otherwise.

Notice the `LoggingReceive` class that surrounds the block handling the actor messages. It is part of the `akka.event` package and is a convenient way of logging information that reaches this block. We will see later on, while executing the sample code, what these messages look like.

In a similar manner, a `Hotel` actor that takes care of reserving a room for *n* persons can be written as follows:

```
object Hotel {
  case class BookRoom(number:Int) {
    require(number > 0)
  }
  case object Done
  case object Failed
}

class Hotel extends Actor {
  import Hotel._
  var roomsLeft = 15
  def receive = LoggingReceive {
    case BookRoom(nb) if nb <= roomsLeft =>
      roomsLeft -= nb
      sender ! Done
    case _ => sender ! Failed
  }
}
```

The travel agent actor is the one that is going to switch its behavior. Once it has sent orders to book plane seats and hotel rooms for a number of people, it will successively change state while expecting answers. Since the messages sent to both `Flight` and `Hotel` are asynchronous, that is, nonblocking, we do not know which answer will come back first. Furthermore, answers might not come back at all as there is no guarantee at this point that the messages have been delivered or correctly handled. The code for the `TravelAgent` actor is given as follows:

```
object TravelAgent {
  case class BookTrip(transport: ActorRef, accomodation: ActorRef,
  nbOfPersons: Int)
  case object Done
  case object Failed
}
class TravelAgent extends Actor {
  import TravelAgent._

  def receive = LoggingReceive {
    case BookTrip(flightAgent, hotelAgent, persons) =>
      flightAgent ! Flight.BookSeat(persons)
      hotelAgent ! Hotel.BookRoom(persons)
      context.become(awaitTransportOrAccomodation(flightAgent,
  hotelAgent,sender))
  }

  def awaitTransportOrAccomodation(transport: ActorRef, accomodation:
  ActorRef, customer:ActorRef): Receive = LoggingReceive {
    case Flight.Done =>
      context.become(awaitAccomodation(customer))
    case Hotel.Done =>
      context.become(awaitTransport(customer))
    case Flight.Failed | Hotel.Failed =>
      customer ! Failed
      context.stop(self)
  }
```

```scala
  def awaitTransport(customer: ActorRef): Receive = LoggingReceive {
    case Flight.Done =>
      customer ! Done
      context.stop(self)
    case Flight.Failed =>
      customer ! Failed
      context.stop(self)
  }

  def awaitAccomodation(customer: ActorRef): Receive = LoggingReceive
{
    case Hotel.Done =>
      customer ! Done
      context.stop(self)
    case Hotel.Failed =>
      customer ! Failed
      context.stop(self)
  }
}
```

The invocation `context.become(<new behavior method>)` switches the behavior of the actor. In the case of this simple travel agent, the behavior will be switched to the expected messages that can be received in any order from the `Flight` and `Hotel` actors, respectively. If a successful answer is received from either the `Flight` or `Hotel` actors, the `TravelAgent` actor will switch its behavior to expect only the remaining answer.

Now, we only need a main routine to create our initial actors and initiate communication with the `TravelAgent` actor, as exhibited in the following code:

```scala
package se.sfjd.ch8

import akka.actor.Actor
import akka.actor.Props
import akka.event.LoggingReceive

class BookingMain extends Actor {
  val flight = context.actorOf(Props[Flight], "Stockholm-Nassau")
  val hotel = context.actorOf(Props[Hotel], "Atlantis")
```

```
val travelAgent = context.actorOf(Props[TravelAgent], "ClubMed")
travelAgent ! TravelAgent.BookTrip(flight,hotel,10)

def receive = LoggingReceive {
    case TravelAgent.Done =>
      println("Booking Successful")
      context.stop(self)
    case TravelAgent.Failed =>
      println("Booking Failed")
      context.stop(self)
  }
}
```

Once the four actor classes involved in the use case have been written in Eclipse, running the program can be done by running an Eclipse configuration. Navigate to **Run | Run Configuration...** and edit a new **Java Application configuration** window knowing that the main class to run is the akka.Main class of the Akka runtime, as specified in the following screenshot:

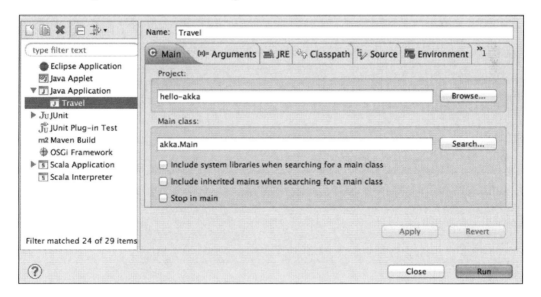

The actual main routine we want to run is passed as an argument. To do that, edit the **Arguments** tab of the same window, as shown in the following screenshot:

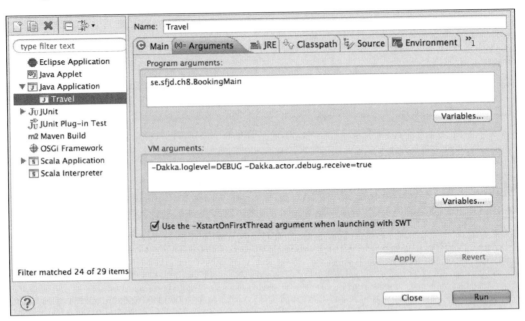

For the debug messages produced by the `LoggingReceive` object to be active, you need to add the VM arguments as specified in the previous screenshot. Clicking on the **Run** button will execute the `BookingMain` class within the Akka runtime environment and display the following flow of messages:

```
[DEBUG] [03/23/2014 15:49:23.668] [main] [EventStream(akka://Main)] logger log1-Logging$DefaultLogger started
[DEBUG] [03/23/2014 15:49:23.669] [main] [EventStream(akka://Main)] Default Loggers started
[DEBUG] [03/23/2014 15:49:23.749] [Main-akka.actor.default-dispatcher-4] [EventStream(akka://booking-system)] logger log1-Logging$DefaultLogger started
[DEBUG] [03/23/2014 15:49:23.749] [Main-akka.actor.default-dispatcher-4] [EventStream(akka://booking-system)] Default Loggers started
[DEBUG] [03/23/2014 15:49:23.824] [Main-akka.actor.default-dispatcher-2] [akka://Main/user/app/ClubMed] received handled message BookTrip(10)
[DEBUG] [03/23/2014 15:49:23.825] [Main-akka.actor.default-dispatcher-4] [akka://Main/user/app/ClubMed/UnreliableFlightAgent] received handled message BookSeat(10)
[DEBUG] [03/23/2014 15:49:23.826] [Main-akka.actor.default-dispatcher-5] [akka://Main/user/app/ClubMed/UnreliableHotelAgent] received handled message BookRoom(10)
[DEBUG] [03/23/2014 15:49:23.827] [Main-akka.actor.default-dispatcher-2] [akka://Main/user/app/ClubMed] received handled message Done
[DEBUG] [03/23/2014 15:49:23.828] [Main-akka.actor.default-dispatcher-2] [akka://Main/user/app/ClubMed] received handled message Done
Booking Successful
```

If you want to test an alternative scenario, for example, to see the booking failed while reserving the hotel, just put a higher number of persons, that is, 20 in `travelAgent ! TravelAgent.BookTrip(flight,hotel,20)`, instead of 10.

Supervising actors to handle failure

In applications that are running actors concurrently, there might sometimes be exceptions that are thrown and those make an actor die eventually. As other actors are still running, it might be difficult to notice partial failures. In traditional architectures, where an object calls methods on other objects, the caller is the one receiving the exception. Since it usually blocks waiting for a response, it is also the one responsible to handle the failure. With actors, as all messages are being handled asynchronously without knowing the time it will take before receiving an answer (if any), the context in regards to the sent messages is usually not around anymore to handle the failure; so, it might be more difficult to react on an exception. In any case, something must be done about the failing actor for the application to function properly as its whole.

This is why Akka embraces the "let it crash" philosophy by providing support to monitor and eventually restart an actor or a group of dependent actors. As actors are normally created by other actors, they can be organized as hierarchies where an actor's parent is also its supervisor. Handling partial failure, therefore, consists of defining some strategies to restart part of the actor hierarchy simultaneously, depending on the situation.

If we go back to our small travel booking application, we can refactor the `TravelAgent` actor to be the supervisor of the `Flight` and `Hotel` booking actors. Therefore, we can declare the following supervisor strategy within the `TravelAgent` class:

```
override val supervisorStrategy = OneForOneStrategy(loggingEnabled =
false) {
    case _: Flight.FlightBookingException =>
      log.warning("Flight Service Failed. Restarting")
      Restart
    case _: Hotel.HotelBookingException =>
      log.warning("Hotel Service Failed. Restarting")
      Restart
    case e =>
      log.error("Unexpected failure", e.getMessage)
      Stop
}
```

The two possible strategies are `OneForOneStrategy` and `AllForOneStrategy`. In the first case, each child of the supervisor will be handled separately, whereas in the second case, all children of the given supervisor will be handled simultaneously.

The `Flight` companion object now contains an additional message that reflects the failure, as shown in the following code:

```
object Flight {
  case class BookSeat(number:Int) {
    require(number > 0)
  }
  case object Done
  case object Failed
  class FlightBookingException extends Exception("Unavailable Flight
Booking Service")
}
```

To simulate the fact that booking the seats on a flight might fail at times, we can introduce the following method call when handling the `receive` method of the `Flight` actor, as shown in the following code snippet:

```
class Flight extends Actor {
  import Flight._
  var seatsLeft = 50
  def receive = LoggingReceive {
    case BookSeat(nb) if nb <= seatsLeft =>
      unreliable()
      seatsLeft -= nb
      sender ! Done
    case _ => sender ! Failed
  }

  private def unreliable(): Unit =
      // the service is only working 75 percent of the time
      if (ThreadLocalRandom.current().nextDouble() < 0.25)
        throw new FlightBookingException
  }
```

Relaunching the booking scenario with the Run configuration will display (since the failure happens only 25 percent of the time) the failing message at times, as shown in the following lines:

...

```
[WARN] [01/24/2014 00:23:50.098] [Main-akka.actor.default-dispatcher-3]
[akka://Main/user/app/ClubMed] Flight Service Failed. Restarting
```

...

For interested readers who want to elaborate more on the topic of supervision, there is a complete and consistent sample called `akka-supervision` that is part of the activator templates. It demonstrates the computation of arithmetic expressions, so that nodes that represent subparts of the total computation may fail and be restarted.

Testing actor systems

Because of their nondeterministic nature, concurrent systems require some special care when testing them in contrast to traditional single-threaded architectures. Actor systems are no exceptions; the messages being sent and received asynchronously, there are multiple paths a program flow can follow. Fortunately, Akka provides a lot of support defined in the akka-testkit module for dealing with tests.

In *Chapter 4, Testing Tools*, we have already covered a number of examples involving the scalatest framework by looking at the test-patterns-scala activator template project. It contains a basic use case regarding the testing of Akka actors through the testkit module. You can reimport this template project into Eclipse or just open it if it is still in the IDE. The Test09.scala file exhibits the usage of a testing actor by providing an ImplicitSender trait that fakes the sending of messages to two actors under test. The first actor under test is a simple echo actor, whereas the second is calling a location service asynchronously that calculates the latitude and longitude of a given address. The syntax of the GeoActor object, given in the following test, should look familiar since it uses the dispatch libraries in the same way as we have seen in *Chapter 3, Understanding the Scala Ecosystem*:

```
package scalatest

import akka.actor.ActorSystem
import akka.actor.Actor
import akka.actor.Props
import akka.testkit.TestKit
import org.scalatest.WordSpecLike
import org.scalatest.matchers.MustMatchers
import org.scalatest.BeforeAndAfterAll
import akka.testkit.ImplicitSender

//http://doc.akka.io/docs/akka/snapshot/scala/testing.html
object Setup {
  class EchoActor extends Actor {
    def receive = {
      case x => sender ! x
    }
  }

  case class Address(street: String,
                     city: String,
                     state: String,
                     zip: String)
```

```
//see https://developers.google.com/maps/documentation/
geocoding/#Limits
class GeoActor extends Actor {
  def receive = {
    case Address(street,city,state,zip) => {
      import dispatch._, Defaults._
      val svc = url(s"http://maps.googleapis.com/maps/api/geocode/xm
l?address=${street},${city},${state},${zip}&sensor=true".replace("
","+"))
      val response = Http(svc OK as.xml.Elem)
      val lat = (for {
        elem <- response() \\ "geometry" \ "location" \ "lat"
      } yield elem.text).head
      val lng = (for {
        elem <- response() \\ "geometry" \ "location" \ "lng"
      } yield elem.text).head
      sender ! s"${lat},${lng}"
    }
    case _ => sender ! "none"
  }
 }
}
```

In the main routine of the test case, we mix in the `ImplicitSender` trait and then invoke the `expectMsg` method :

```
class Test09(asys: ActorSystem) extends TestKit(asys) with
ImplicitSender with WordSpecLike with MustMatchers with
BeforeAndAfterAll {
  import Setup._
  def this() = this(ActorSystem("Setup"))

  override def afterAll {
    TestKit.shutdownActorSystem(system)
  }

  "An Echo actor" must {
    "return messages" in {
```

```
      val echo = system.actorOf(Props[EchoActor])
      echo ! "hello world"
      expectMsg("hello world")
    }
  }

  "Geo actor" must {
    "send back lat,lon" in {
      val geo = system.actorOf(Props[GeoActor])
      geo ! Address("27 South Park Avenue","San
Francisco","CA","94107")
      expectMsg("37.7822991,-122.3930776")
      }
    }
  }
```

The `expectMsg()` method has the role of an assertion that takes duration as a parameter, so that it does not wait forever for the reply to come back. Instead, it will throw an exception if the specified time has passed and it has not yet received the answer it was waiting for.

Exploring further with Akka

In addition to the useful functionalities of actor messaging and supervision, Akka includes support for many other, more advanced features. Among them are the following:

- It monitors the lifecycle of actors through the `DeathWatch` API.

- It persists actor state for recovery after failure.

- It remotes with actors, that is, communicates with actors in a distributed environment and in a transparent way.

- It clusters to handle failure in a distributed environment. A sample of the clustering features is also available as the `akka-clustering` activator template.

These features are out of the scope of this book, but they are extensively documented on the Akka site and available at `http://akka.io/docs/`.

Summary

In this chapter, we have first studied how to deal with asynchronous Scala code using the Async toolkit, which simplifies writing nonblocking code using Futures and Promises. We then moved to the concurrency topic by introducing the Akka framework based on the actor paradigm.

Concurrent and distributed systems is such a large topic that we have only introduced some basic usage scenarios of actor systems. We have learned that since the behavior and state of actors are encapsulated, actor systems are easy to reason about. Moreover, the supervision and clustering support in Akka makes the handling of failure and distribution very robust. The material covered in this chapter is just a glimpse of what the toolkit can achieve; the very extended and well-written documentation of the Akka project will guide you through creating scalable and distributed applications. Programming asynchronous, concurrent, and distributed systems is often a complex task, and the actor model makes it more manageable.

Since Akka is also the foundation of the Play Framework, we will continue to use it through the next chapter. We will build reactive web applications in Play to illustrate how to create modern applications that need to handle streams of data and push information into the browser.

9
Building Reactive Web Applications

Modern web applications increasingly require us to move from static web content to a more dynamic paradigm where a lot of integration happens in the background and the user interaction is more and more sophisticated. At the same time, the provided online services need to adapt to the changing business requirements and scale to elastic loads, that is, handling peak hour traffic. Finally, in addition to the service they provide, web applications now tend to collect extra information concerning user interaction to better understand customer behavior. In this chapter, we are going to tackle the following topics:

- Understanding what makes applications reactive
- Introducing the processing of streams in Play Framework with the *Iteratees* pattern
- Writing reactive applications including web sockets

Describing reactive applications

The traditional pull model adopted by the Web, which is used to browse HTML pages now needs to be seconded by two-way communication. This includes a push model where users, for example, receive confirmation of asynchronous and long-running services or just get notifications of various natures.

The recently created Reactive Manifesto, which is available at `http://www.reactivemanifesto.org`, aims to summarize the criteria that characterize reactive applications in a technology-agnostic way:

- **React to events**: Message-passing architecture, not wasting the time waiting for resources

- **React to load**: Focuses on scalability by avoiding contention on shared resources

- **React to failure**: Build resilient systems with the ability to recover at all levels

- **React to users**: Honor response time guarantees regardless of load

Without going into the details of the manifesto that you are encouraged to read, we can directly see that the notion of message-driven architecture, which was used by Akka in the previous chapter, fits very well with this reactive model. In the following sections, we are going to focus on examples of building such web applications on top of the Play Framework.

Handling streams reactively

Whenever you need to consume and transform streams of data in web applications, such as watching stock updates or monitoring log activities on a service, you need mechanisms to manipulate chunks of data that can be pushed from a server to a browser, for instance, using Comet (http://en.wikipedia.org/wiki/Comet_ (programming)) or WebSocket (http://en.wikipedia.org/wiki/WebSocket) technologies. The Iteratee pattern available within the Play framework is such a mechanism. It was borrowed from the Haskell functional language initially.

Understanding Iteratees in Play

An Iteratee construct aims at providing a composable and nonblocking way of handling streams produced by its counterpart called Enumerator.

Let's launch a Scala REPL to explore the Iteratee/Enumerator constructs in more detail. To create a new play project as we have done several times before, notably in *Chapter 5, Getting Started with the Play Framework*, use the following command:

```
> play new ch9samples (then choose Scala as language)
> cd ch9samples
> play console
```

First, we will remind ourselves how an iteration is done within an imperative language such as Java. The following statements written in Scala describe the use of a mutable variable total that will be updated at each step of the iteration:

```
scala> val numbers = List(1,4,7,8,10,20)
numbers: List[Int] = List(1, 4, 7, 8, 10, 20)
scala> var total = 0
total: Int = 0
scala> var iterator = numbers.iterator
```

```
iterator: Iterator[Int] = non-empty iterator
scala> while (iterator.hasNext) {
          total += iterator.next
      }
scala> total
res2: Int = 50
```

As explained in the blog post available at http://mandubian. com/2012/08/27/understanding-play2-iteratees-for-normal-humans/, we need to take care of the following when iterating:

- The state of the iteration (are there more elements to follow or is it finished)?
- A context (here the total accumulator)
- An action, updating the context, that is, the total += iterator.next

We have seen in *Chapter 1, Programming Interactively within Your Project,* that we can implement the same operation in a concise and more functional way by using the foldLeft Scala construct in the following way:

```
scala> List(1,4,7,8,10,20).foldLeft(0){ (total,elem) =>
      total + elem }
res3: Int = 50
```

The foldLeft construct is a powerful construct that is applied to Scala collections such as Lists. If we want to process other forms of input such as a file, a network, a database connection, or a flow produced by an Akka actor for instance, then the Enumerator/Iteratee comes into play. An Enumerator construct can be seen as the producer of data (similar to the previous List) and an Iteratee as the consumer of that data, processing each step of the iteration. The preceding example involving the foldLeft method on a List could just be rewritten using an Enumerator/Iteratee construct. As the iteratee library is already available within Play, it can be imported directly by using the following command:

```
scala> import play.api.libs.iteratee._
import play.api.libs.iteratee._
scala> import play.api.libs.concurrent.Execution.Implicits._
import play.api.libs.concurrent.Execution.Implicits._
```

After importing the *iteratee* library and a global execution context for the `iteratee` variables to work with, we can define our first `Enumerator` as follows:

```
scala> val enumerator = Enumerator(1,4,7,8,10,20)

enumerator: play.api.libs.iteratee.Enumerator[Int] = play.api.libs.
iteratee.Enumerator$$anon$19@27a21c85...
```

The `iteratee` variable defined as follows indicates the computation step to be performed while accepting an input from the `enumerator`:

```
scala> val iteratee = Iteratee.fold(0){ (total, elem:Int) => total + elem
}

iteratee: play.api.libs.iteratee.Iteratee[Int,Int] = play.api.libs.
iteratee.ContIteratee@e07a406
```

Combining the `enumerator` construct with the `iteratee` construct is a matter of invoking the `run` method of `enumerator` that takes the `iteratee` as an argument:

```
scala> val result = enumerator.run(iteratee)

result: scala.concurrent.Future[Int] = scala.concurrent.impl.
Promise$DefaultPromise@78b5282b
```

As we have an asynchronous computation, we get back a `result` as a `Future` that we can display once it is completed, as follows:

```
scala> result onComplete println

scala> Success(50)
```

The `enumerator` object mentioned previously was an enumerator of integers. We can create producers of data of many different types, such as strings or double values. This is shown in the following code:

```
scala> val stringEnumerator = Enumerator("one","two","four")

stringEnumerator: play.api.libs.iteratee.Enumerator[String] = play.api.
libs.iteratee.Enumerator$$anon$19@1ca7d367

scala> val doubleEnumerator = Enumerator(1.03,2.34,4)

doubleEnumerator: play.api.libs.iteratee.Enumerator[Double] = play.api.
libs.iteratee.Enumerator$$anon$19@a8e29a5
```

To illustrate the creation of an Enumerator from a file, let's add a little text file named `samplefile.txt` in the root of the current project containing, for instance, the following three lines of text:

```
Alice
Bob
Charlie
```

You may use a separate console window to create this file while leaving the REPL running in the original console window. Otherwise, you will have to rerun the import statements. Creating an `Enumerator` from a file is shown in the following commands:

```scala
scala> import java.io.File
import java.io.File

scala> val fileEnumerator: Enumerator[Array[Byte]] = Enumerator.
fromFile(new File("./samplefile.txt"))

fileEnumerator: play.api.libs.iteratee.Enumerator[Array[Byte]] = play.
api.libs.iteratee.Enumerator$$anon$4@33500f2
```

`Enumerator` even comprises some useful methods. For example, a stream of events that are generated at regular intervals each time the `Promise` object, which contains the current time, times out (every 500 milliseconds).

```scala
scala> val dateGenerator: Enumerator[String] = Enumerator.generateM(
        play.api.libs.concurrent.Promise.timeout(
    Some("current time %s".format((new java.util.Date()))),
    500
    ))
```

In a more general way, we can say that `Enumerator[E]` (read enumerator of type E) produces three possible kinds of chunks of data of type E:

- `Input[E]`: It is a chunk of data of type E, for example, `Input[LogData]` is a chunk of `LogData`

- `Input.Empty`: It means that the enumerator is empty, for instance, an `Enumerator` streaming an empty file

- `Input.EOF`: It means that the enumerator has reached its end, for instance, an `Enumerator` construct streaming a file and reaching the end of the file

In addition to the `run` method used to run an `Enumerator` over an `Iteratee`, you can also invoke the constructor, that is, the `apply` method of the enumerator directly. Notice in the following two commands, the different result types you get depending on how you combine `enumerator`/`iteratee`:

```scala
scala> val result = enumerator.run(iteratee)

result: scala.concurrent.Future[Int] = scala.concurrent.impl.
Promise$DefaultPromise@1837220f

scala> val result2=enumerator(iteratee)

result2: scala.concurrent.Future[play.api.libs.
iteratee.Iteratee[Int,Int]] = scala.concurrent.impl.
Promise$DefaultPromise@5261b67f
```

This last `Future` result contains an `Iteratee[Int,Int]`, that is, an `Iteratee[<type contained in chunk>, <result of the iteration>]`.

```
scala> val enumerator = Enumerator(1,4,7,8,10,20)
enumerator: play.api.libs.iteratee.Enumerator[Int] = play.api.libs.
iteratee.Enumerator$$anon$19@7e666ce4
```

The following `Iteratee` consumes all the chunks from the `enumerator` stream and returns them as a `List` collection:

```
scala> val chunksIteratee = Iteratee.getChunks[Int]
chunksIteratee: play.api.libs.iteratee.Iteratee[Int,List[Int]] = play.
api.libs.iteratee.ContIteratee@53af8d86
scala> val list = enumerator.run(chunksIteratee)
list: scala.concurrent.Future[List[Int]] = scala.concurrent.impl.
Promise$DefaultPromise@66e1b41c
scala> list onComplete println
scala> Success(List(1, 4, 7, 8, 10, 20))
```

The examples of `Iteratee` that we have seen so far use the method `fold` pretty much like the `foldLeft` and the `foldRight` methods that are part of the Scala collection. Let's try to build a more sophisticated `Iteratee`: one that, for instance, selects words containing the letter E out of the enumerator streams. This can be done using the following code:

```
scala> def wordsWithE: Iteratee[String,List[String]] = {
  def step(total:List[String])(input:Input[String]):
Iteratee[String,List[String]] = input match {
    case Input.EOF | Input.Empty => Done(total,Input.EOF)
    case Input.El(elem) =>
      if(elem.contains("E")) Cont[String,List[String]](i=>
step(elem::total)(i))
      else Cont[String,List[String]](i=> step(total)(i))
    }
  Cont[String,List[String]](i=> step(List[String]())(i))
}

wordsWithE: play.api.libs.iteratee.Iteratee[String,List[String]]
```

The `step` recursive function is using a `total` accumulator variable, that is, a context to keep some state at each step of the recursion. This is a list of strings containing all the results we are interested in. The second argument to the `step` function is the new chunk from the `enumerator` stream that comes up at each step. This chunk is matched against the possible states; if either the stream is empty or we have reached its end, we return the accumulated result in a `Done` state. Otherwise, we handle the incoming element. If the element verifies the `if` condition, then we add it to the accumulator and invoke the next step in our recursion as part of a `Cont` (continue) state. Otherwise, we just invoke the next step without saving the element.

Finally, the last step initiates the recursion by calling the `step` function on the first element of the stream with an empty accumulator. Applying this newly-defined `Iteratee` on a simple enumerator looks like the following command:

```scala
scala> val output = Enumerator("ONE","TWO","THREE") run wordsWithE

output: scala.concurrent.Future[List[String]] = scala.concurrent.impl.
Promise$DefaultPromise@50e0cc83

scala> output onComplete println

scala> Success(List(THREE, ONE))
```

Every computation step performed on an incoming string either appends that string to the total accumulator or ignores it, depending on whether it matches the `if` condition or not. In this example, it simply checks that the word contains at least one E.

Adapting Enumerator with Enumeratee

It might happen that the data consumed by an `Iteratee` does not match the input produced by an `Enumerator`. The role of an `Enumeratee` is to be an adapter that sits in between the `Enumerator` and `Iteratee` to transform the incoming data before feeding the `Iteratee`.

As an example of simple transformation from an `Enumerator` to another one, we could ,for instance, define an `Enumeratee` that converts an input of the type `String` to `Int`, as illustrated by the following commands:

```scala
scala> val summingIteratee = Iteratee.fold(0){ (total, elem:Int) => total
+ elem }

summingIteratee: play.api.libs.iteratee.Iteratee[Int,Int] = play.api.
libs.iteratee.ContIteratee@196fad1a

scala> Enumerator("2","5","7") through Enumeratee.map(x => x.toInt) run
summingIteratee

res5: scala.concurrent.Future[Int] = scala.concurrent.impl.
Promise$DefaultPromise@5ec418a8
```

```
scala> res5 onComplete println
scala> Success(14)
```

The transformation provided by the `Enumeratee` can be declared in its `map` method.

Adapting the `Enumerator` can also consist of transforming the input data to a different format without changing the type. Considering `wordsWithE` that we defined previously, we could apply an `Enumeratee` that converts all the input data to uppercase so that the consumption of the stream of data by the `Iteratee` would produce a different result than the one obtained without `Enumeratee`. The following code illustrates that behavior:

```
scala> val enumerator = Enumerator("ONE","Two","Three")
scala> enumerator run wordsWithE onComplete println
scala> Success(List(ONE))
scala> enumerator through Enumeratee.map(x=>x.toUpperCase) run wordsWithE
onComplete println
scala> Success(List(THREE, ONE))
```

To summarize, an `Enumerator` is a producer of a data stream, an `Iteratee` a consumer of that data, and an `Enumeratee` an adapter between the two. The *iteratee* pattern has been integrated together with the Play Framework as a way to handle streams of data reactively in a web application. In the next section, we are going to build web applications in such a way, by additionally using WebSockets to communicate between the client and the server in both directions.

Experimenting with WebSockets and Iteratees in Play

In addition to the traditional pull model of getting HTML displayed in a browser when querying a service, most web browsers now support bidirectional communication via WebSockets so that servers can push data without the user having to query for it first. Once a socket is established between client and server, the communication can stay open for further interaction, unlike the HTTP protocol. Modern web apps are using this feature more and more to push data from streams reactively.

As a reminder, a **WebSocket** is a protocol providing bidirectional communication over a single TCP connection, in contrast to the traditional one-way, stateless communication of HTTP (either a request or a response). Let's look at the support that Play provides in this area and demonstrate in a short example how to establish a WebSocket communication between the Play server and a client browser.

As we have already created a `ch9samples` Play project at the beginning of this chapter to experiment with `Iteratees` in the REPL, we can just reuse it. We will start by opening the tiny `controllers/Application.scala` server-side class that is available by default. We can add a new `connect` method to it to create a WebSocket interaction. In a regular Play controller, a method would normally use an `Action` class, as we have seen previously. In this example, we use the `WebSocket` class instead, illustrated in the controller as follows:

```
package controllers

import play.api._
import play.api.mvc._
import play.api.libs.iteratee._
import scala.concurrent.ExecutionContext.Implicits.global

object Application extends Controller {

  def index = Action {
    Ok(views.html.index("Your new application is ready."))
  }

  def connect =  WebSocket.using[String] { request =>

    // Concurrent.broadcast returns (Enumerator, Concurrent.Channel)
    val (out,channel) = Concurrent.broadcast[String]

    // log message to stdout and send response back to client
    val in = Iteratee.foreach[String] { msg =>
      println(msg)
      //the channel will push to the Enumerator
      channel push("RESPONSE: " + msg)
    }
    (in,out)
  }
}
```

In the server-side controller seen in the preceding code, the `in` variable contains the logic to handle messages coming from the client, and it will produce an `Enumerator` to assemble some response data that will be pushed through the channel to each client.

On the client side, the `views/main.scala.html` view is where we are going to add the WebSocket support, as a part of a JavaScript script, whose role is to open a web socket and react to incoming messages. as follows:

```
@(title: String)(content: Html)


<!DOCTYPE html>

<html>
    <head>
        <title>@title</title>
        <link rel="stylesheet" media="screen" href="@routes.Assets.
at("stylesheets/main.css")">
        <link rel="shortcut icon" type="image/png" href="@routes.
Assets.at("images/favicon.png")">
        <script src="@routes.Assets.at("javascripts/jquery-1.9.0.min.
js")" type="text/javascript"></script>


        <script type="text/javascript">
    function WebSocketTest() {
      if ("WebSocket" in window) {
        alert("WebSocket is supported by your Browser!");
        // Let us open a web socket
        var ws = new WebSocket("ws://localhost:9000/connect");
        ws.onopen = function() {
           // Web Socket is connected, send data
               var msg = "Hello Websocket!"
           ws.send(msg);
           alert("Message is sent..."+msg);
        };
        ws.onmessage = function (evt) {
           var received_msg = evt.data;
           alert("Message is received..."+received_msg);
        };
        ws.onclose = function() {
           // websocket is closed.
           alert("Connection is closed...");
        };
      }
      else {
         // The browser doesn't support WebSocket
         alert("WebSocket NOT supported by your Browser!");
      }
    }
```

```
        </script>
    </head>
      <body>
          <div id="sse">
              <a href="javascript:WebSocketTest()">Run WebSocket</a>
          </div>
      </body>
  </html>
```

Now that we have both ends, the only remaining step is to define a route for the controller's `connect` method. Edit the `conf/routes` file to make it look like the following:

```
# Routes
# This file defines all application routes (Higher priority routes
first)
# ~~~~

# Home page
GET   /         controllers.Application.index
GET   /connect      controllers.Application.connect

# Map static resources from the /public folder to the /assets URL path
GET   /assets/*file  controllers.Assets.at(path="/public", file)
```

Now, we are ready to try the demo by starting the play server from the command prompt:

```
> play run
```

Opening a browser at `http://localhost:9000/` (preferably one that supports WebSockets) and clicking on the **Run WebSocket** link should first confirm that the browser is indeed supporting WebSockets. Clicking on **OK** a couple of times will first show you that a message has been sent, and then show that the roundtrip has been achieved by receiving a message from the server. You should also see the `Message to send` log message on the play server prompt.

Learning from activator templates

There is a growing list of reactive applications based on *iteratees* that have been packaged and deployed as activator templates. At the time of writing this book, we have identified more than five templates and you can look at a few of them. They often mix technologies such as WebSockets with Akka for communication and message processing and, on the client side, JavaScript frameworks such as Angular.js, to often provide simple HTML rendering.

As the Typesafe activator templates HTML page lets you select tags to filter out projects depending on some keywords, you may check the appropriate projects by selecting the reactive checkbox.

Reactive stocks

This sample is a project based on the Java version of Play. It graphically demonstrates the real-time update of stock values (that are randomly generated for simplicity). It contains both Java and Scala code. An Akka `StockActor` actor is instantiated for every stock symbol, and its role is to maintain a list of all users watching this stock. Some additional functionality queries a twitter API to retrieve all tweets matching a particular symbol (for example, `http://twitter-search-proxy.herokuapp.com/search/tweets?q=appl`). This knowledge can then be processed to calculate a sentiment index that should help to decide whether to buy this stock or not. The following screenshot illustrates graphically what the app looks like, once it is run:

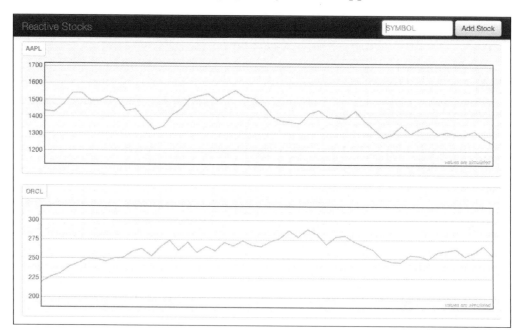

Reactive real-time search

To demonstrate some integration between ElasticSearch and the reactive features of the Typesafe stack through Play iteratees and Akka, this sample exhibits how to push log events to a browser. As a reminder, ElasticSearch (`http://www.elasticsearch.org`) is a distributed real-time search and an analytics engine based on the well-established Apache Lucene (`https://lucene.apache.org`) full-text search engine.

It notably provides a **percolation** feature, that notifies your application when new content matches your search criteria (instead of having to poll the search engine to check regularly for new updates).

To emulate content, an Akka `LogEntryProducerActor` actor is responsible for generating random log entries each time it receives a `Tick` message. These messages are produced at regular intervals by a `MainSearchActor` actor that also acts as a coordinator for the search. Finally, an `ElasticSearchActor` actor implements the percolation feature by interacting with an embedded ElasticSearch server (`EmbeddedESServer`) that is started from the Play `Global` class. Instead of pushing information to the browser via WebSockets, the sample uses **Server Side Events (SSE)** as it only needs one-way communication once the search criteria are known.

Further information on the template and all the code behind it is available at `https://github.com/DrewEaster/realtime-search`. In particular, the query syntax to be entered for a search is defined as Lucene syntax and is specified at `http://lucene.apache.org/core/4_3_1/queryparser/org/apache/lucene/queryparser/classic/package-summary.html#package_description`.

If we execute this sample by installing and running the activator template (with the `> activator run` command from the root of the template project), we can open a browser at `localhost:9000` and enter `GET` as the search criterion. After a few seconds, some browser output should progressively be displayed, as shown in the following screenshot:

Timestamp	Method	Path	Status	Time (ms)	Device	User Agent
2014-02-12T23:43:02.122+01:00	GET	/a	200	780	Desktop	Chrome
2014-02-12T23:42:57.122+01:00	GET	/d	200	988	Desktop	Safari
2014-02-12T23:42:56.122+01:00	GET	/b	200	421	Desktop	Firefox
2014-02-12T23:42:53.123+01:00	GET	/d	200	683	Desktop	Safari
2014-02-12T23:42:52.123+01:00	GET	/b	200	116	Desktop	Firefox
2014-02-12T23:42:50.122+01:00	GET	/a	200	520	Desktop	Chrome
2014-02-12T23:42:32.122+01:00	GET	/d	200	348	Desktop	Safari
2014-02-12T23:42:30.123+01:00	GET	/e	200	144	Desktop	HttpClient

The Play-Akka-Angular-WebSocket template

As another example of reactively pushing information to the browser, this sample updates a clock on the client by scheduling an actor. The role of this actor is to send events in the JSON format via a WebSocket connection by using the Play `WebSocket.async[JsValue]` method call. The Angular.js JavaScript framework is used on the client side and the GUI looks like the following screenshot once it starts running:

The number of activator templates that illustrate reactive applications is growing. Also, you can check out from time to time the new templates that are available, without upgrading the version of the activator each time.

Playing with Actor Room

In the previous section, we have seen a number of projects that are using `Enumerators/Iteratees` to send and receive messages reactively, with various levels of complexity. `Iteratees` are powerful, but using them can sometimes lead to code snippets that are not easy to understand. The Play Actor Room project, which is available at `https://github.com/mandubian/play-actor-room`, proposes to reduce some of the complexity of setting up `Iteratees` by abstracting away this part and letting the programmer focus only on the domain logic, such as processing incoming messages and assembling outgoing messages. This project started from the observation that many applications need the same functionality, which can be seen as a server `Room` (holding state, for instance, and being the middle man between distributed clients). The role of this room is to listen for incoming messages from connected clients, and either broadcast received messages after processing them or just unicast communication to a single client. It is a good illustration of how an application can react to users/events. Typical applications such as a multiuser chat are therefore very straightforward to write, and they are one of the two samples given as examples. Let's experiment with the most basic use of the actor room support, a sample called `simplest`.

To clone the project somewhere on your disk, just enter the following command:

> `git clone https://github.com/mandubian/play-actor-room`

First, we can look at the application once it is running:

> `cd play-actor-room/samples/simplest`

> `play run`

Opening a browser at the default play port (`http://localhost:9000/`) will show you a simple **sign-in** widget, as shown in the following screenshot. Enter your name to log in, type a message in the provided text area, and then press *Enter*.

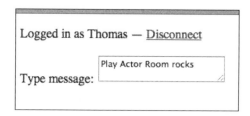

In the console window where you started the actor room application, you should now see the logging information printed by the actor that received messages from the client browser. The information can be seen as follows:

```
[info] play - Application started (Dev)
[info] play - Starting application default Akka system.
[debug] application - Connected Member with ID:Thomas
[info] application - received Play Actor Room rocks
```

On opening several browser windows and logging in with different names, you can see all the messages hitting the server room, that is, at the console. The actor room actually broadcasts the received messages back to all connected browsers, although for now there is nothing in the view to handle the messages.

You can, however, open the console of one browser to see the display of the broadcast messages, as shown in the following screenshot:

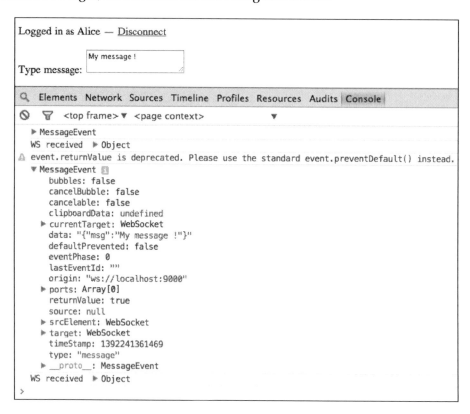

Additionally, invoking the `http://localhost:9000/list/` URL from a third window will return the list of currently connected clients.

Some of the interesting features of this basic application can be observed once we import the project into eclipse (entering the `> play eclipse` command) and open the controller that includes the implementation of the receiving `Actor` class.

The `Receiver` actor that acts as the server has been created by a supervisor `Actor`. It handles messages in JSON format. All the default logic of the receiving `Actor`, which is the only code that we need to care about for processing messages from clients, is as follows:

```
class Receiver extends Actor {
  def receive = {
    case Received(from, js: JsValue) =>
      (js \ "msg").asOpt[String] match {
```

```
      case None => play.Logger.error("couldn't msg in websocket
event")
        case Some(s) =>
          play.Logger.info(s"received $s")
          context.parent ! Broadcast(from, Json.obj("msg" -> s))
      }
    }
  }
```

Note that broadcasting the response from the server to all the clients is done by the supervising actor referenced by `context.parent`. In the previous logic, the `Broadcast` message also includes the originator `from ActorRef` reference.

As a small modification to the default room behavior to fit new business requirements, we can, for instance, reuse the `TravelAgent`, `Flight`, and `Hotel` actors that we created in *Chapter 8, Essential Properties of Modern Applications – Asynchrony and Concurrency*. We want to provide each user with the ability to book a flight, and (at any time) monitor how many seats are still available. To do this, we can involve a slightly bigger JSON message as the exchange format between the server and client.

A useful enhancement to Scala that came with Version 2.10 is the notion of string interpolation. We already used this feature throughout this book and introduced it in *Chapter 1, Programming Interactively within Your Project*. Similarly, JSON interpolation has been created as an extension to the JSON support in Play. We can reuse JSON interpolation, for instance, to do some elegant pattern matching. Just add the following extension dependencies to the `Build.scala` file:

```
val appDependencies = Seq(
    "org.mandubian" %% "play-actor-room" % "0.1",
    "play-json-zipper" %% "play-json-zipper" % "1.0",
    "com.typesafe.play" %% "play-json"          % "2.2.0"
  )
```

Once in place, the JSON pattern matching feature handles the JSON messages coming from the browser client to the `Receiver` actor, as follows

```
case Received(from, js: JsValue) =>
    js match {
      case json"""{
        "booking":"flight",
        "numberOfPersons":$v1
      }""" =>  play.Logger.info(s"received $v1")
        ...
```

Let's add a `Flight` actor to keep the count of seats available. In a new package `actors`, which is directly under the `app/` source directory, we can add a `Flight.scala` class that looks like the following:

```scala
package actors

import akka.actor.Actor
import akka.event.LoggingReceive

object Flight {
  case class BookSeat(number:Int) {
    require(number > 0)
  }
  case object GetSeatsLeft
  case object Done
  case object Failed
}
class Flight extends Actor {
  import Flight._

  def book(seats:Int):Receive = LoggingReceive {
    case BookSeat(nb) if nb <= seats =>
      context.become(book(seats-nb))
      sender ! Done
    case GetSeatsLeft => sender ! seats
    case _ => sender ! Failed
  }

  def receive = book(50) // Initial number of available seats
}
```

Rather than creating a mutable state variable `var seatsLeft`, as we did in *Chapter 8, Essential Properties of Modern Applications – Asynchrony and Concurrency*, we encapsulated this state change as an argument passed while switching context each time we receive a `BookSeat` message. This way of proceeding is a recommended best practice to avoid holding mutable variables. We have added a `GetSeatsLeft` message to be able to query the value of the current state, in which case the state is sent back to the `sender` actor.

On the client side, we can modify the `index.scala.html` view to add a couple of simple widgets to our application. In particular, we can add a placeholder to display the number of available seats left in the flight. This is the information that will be pushed to all connected browsers by the server room actor. An example of such a view is as follows:

```
@(connected: Option[String] = None)

@main(connected) {

  @connected.map { id =>
    <p class="pull-right">
     Logged in as @id
        <a href="@routes.Application.index()">Disconnect</a>
    </p>
    <div>Places left in flight: <input size="10" id="placesLeft"></input></div>

    <div>
      <select id ="booking">
        <option value="flight">Flight</option>
        <option value="hotel">Hotel</option>
      </select>
      Number of persons to book:
      <textarea id ="numberOfPersons" ></textarea>
    </div>

    <script type="text/javascript" charset="utf-8" src="@routes.Application.websocketJs(id)"></script>
  }.getOrElse {
    <form action="@routes.Application.connect(None)" class="pull-right">
      <input id="username" name="id" class="input-small" type="text" placeholder="Username">
        <button class="btn" type="submit">Sign in</button>
    </form>
  }
}
```

We also need to slightly modify the small JavaScript snippet that handles communication between the client browser and the server via the WebSocket so that it handles the new JSON format. The modified websocket.scala.js file is given as follows:

```
@(id: String)(implicit r: RequestHeader)

$(function() {

  var WS = window['MozWebSocket'] ? MozWebSocket : WebSocket;
  var wsSocket = new WS("@routes.Application.websocket(id).webSocketURL()");
```

```
var sendMessage = function() {
  wsSocket.send(JSON.stringify(
    {
      "booking":$("#booking").val(),
      "numberOfPersons":$("#numberOfPersons").val()
    }
  ))
  $("#numberOfPersons").val('');
}

var receiveEvent = function(event) {
  console.log(event);
  var data = JSON.parse(event.data);
  // Handle errors
  if(data.error) {
    console.log("WS Error ", data.error);
    wsSocket.close();
    // TODO manage error
    return;
  } else {
    console.log("WS received ", data);
    // TODO manage display
    $("#placesLeft").val(data.placesLeft);
  }
}

var handleReturnKey = function(e) {
  if(e.charCode == 13 || e.keyCode == 13) {
    e.preventDefault();
    sendMessage();
  }
}

$("#numberOfPersons").keypress(handleReturnKey);

wsSocket.onmessage = receiveEvent;

})
```

Finally, in the `Application.scala` file of the server part, we can extend the `Receiver` actor to handle incoming JSON messages and contact the `Flight` actor to both update and read the current value of its state, as follows:

```
[…imports from the original actor room sample…]
import play.api.libs.json._
```

```
import play.api.libs.functional.syntax._
import play.api.libs.json.extensions._

import actors._

object Receiver {
  val flightBookingActor = Akka.system.actorOf(Props[Flight],"flight")
}
class Receiver extends Actor {
  import Receiver.flightBookingActor

  def receive = LoggingReceive {
    case x:Int =>
      play.Logger.info(s"Received number of seats left: $x")
      val placesLeft:String = if (x<0) "Fully Booked" else x.toString
      context.parent ! Broadcast("flight", Json.obj("placesLeft" ->
placesLeft))
    case Receieved(from, js: JsValue) =>
      js match {
        case json"""{
          "booking":"flight",
          "numberOfPersons":$v1
        }""" =>
          play.Logger.info(s"received $v1")
          val nbOfPersons = v1.as[String]
          flightBookingActor ! Flight.BookSeat(nbOfPersons.toInt)
          val placesCount = flightBookingActor ! Flight.GetSeatsLeft
        case _ => play.Logger.info(s"no match found")
      }
  }
}
```

Now that we have all the pieces in place, let's run the example in a couple of browsers. Notice that we have added the `LoggingReceive` call to both the `Receiver` and `Flight` actors so that we get extensive logging output once we execute the server code. On the command prompt, you may enter the following commands to start the Play application with the additional flags to activate the logging output:

```
> play
> run -Dakka.loglevel=DEBUG -Dakka.actor.debug.receive=true
```

Open two browser windows (possibly using two different browsers) at the URL `http://localhost/9000`. Complete the sign-in step; for instance, use **Alice** and **Bob** as names to connect to the actor room from the two browsers, respectively.

Entering the seats that you want to book from either window will update the global number of seats left in both windows, as illustrated in the following screenshot:

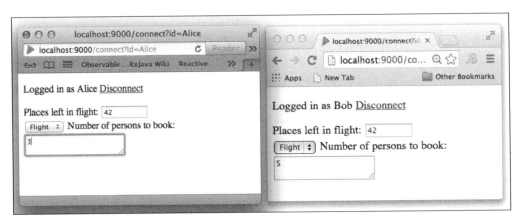

The console output from the server should display the logging information as follows:

```
[info] play - Starting application default Akka system.
[debug] application - Connected Member with ID:Alice
[debug] application - Connected Member with ID:Bob

...

Received(Bob,{"booking":"flight","numberOfPersons":"5"})

...

Received(Alice,{"booking":"flight","numberOfPersons":"3"})

...

[info] application - Received number of seats left: 42
[DEBUG] [02/15/2014 22:51:01.226] [application-akka.actor.default-
dispatcher-7] [akka://application/user/flight] received handled message
GetSeatsLeft
[DEBUG] [02/15/2014 22:51:01.226] [application-akka.actor.default-
dispatcher-6] [akka://application/user/$a/Alice-receiver] received
handled message 42
```

Entering a number of seats that is greater than the number of remaining places will not update the counter, and it will end up in a `Fail` message from the `Flight` actor.

Summary

In this chapter, we have experimented with the *iteratees* pattern supported by the Play Framework to handle streams reactively. We have then used it along with WebSockets and Akka to write a small, reactive web application.

The samples of reactive web applications that we have addressed and discussed in this chapter are just a glimpse of the endless possibilities of making applications that react to events and are resilient to failure and load. As web applications grow in complexity, such architectures should gain in popularity and adoption rate.

Being able to asynchronously process streams in real time is, in our opinion, a big competitive advantage if this functionality is built in a manageable and maintainable way. This is precisely the goal that the Play Framework combined with Akka illustrates.

In the next and the last chapter of this book, we are going to consider a few areas where we think Scala provides additional, convenient help.

10
Scala Goodies

We have covered a number of technologies and toolkits in the previous chapters that, when combined together, offer a great opportunity to build modern and scalable-reactive web applications in Scala. Scala now celebrates 10 years of existence with an active community and large corporations supporting it, leading to a perpetual exploration of innovative ideas touching the language and the ecosystem.

We propose, in this last chapter, to touch upon a few areas where we have found some exciting ongoing projects or technologies and where we feel that Scala can provide elegant solutions to be both productive and fun. We will cover some of the following aspects:

- NoSQL database access through MongoDB
- Introducing DSLs and in particular, a glimpse at Parser Combinators
- Scala.js—compiling Scala to JavaScript on the client side

Exploring MongoDB

As the volume of information to process and store has drastically increased in the past few years, many IT shops have been looking for alternatives to traditional relational databases to store and query data. The **not only SQL (NoSQL)** database movement has gained popularity as a way to trade consistency and structure of the data for more efficient or flexible data storage. MongoDB (`www.mongodb.org`) is a database product designed to store documents in formats, such as JSON, and with no strict database schema. Along with the Java driver built to access and query a MongoDB database, we are going to discover how the Casbah Scala toolkit (`https://github.com/mongodb/casbah`) can be used to conveniently access and query such a database through a DSL.

Entering Casbah

The only requirement to start experimenting with Casbah is to add its `.jar` library dependency to an SBT or Play project. In a new directory on your disk, type `>` `play new ch10samples` from a terminal window and add the Casbah dependency to the `build.sbt` file in the root directory of the project. This dependency is added by adding the following code (note that the given version of Casbah was the latest available at the time of writing this chapter, but should soon be available as the final version 2.7.0):

```
name := "ch10samples"

version := "1.0-SNAPSHOT"

libraryDependencies ++= Seq(
  jdbc,
  anorm,
  cache,
  "org.mongodb" %% "casbah" % "2.7.0-RC1"
)


play.Project.playScalaSettings
```

If you are using an SBT project instead of Play, you may also add a default SLF4J logging implementation, as shown in the following code snippet, as otherwise the default used is a no-operation implementation:

```
libraryDependencies += "org.slf4j" % "slf4j-simple" % "1.7.6"
```

As usual, starting an REPL can be done either by entering the `>` `play` command followed by a `>` `console` command or just `>` `play console`:

```
scala> import com.mongodb.casbah.Imports._
import com.mongodb.casbah.Imports._
```

After some imports, we connect to the MongoDB database on port `27017` using the following code:

```
scala> val mongoClient = MongoClient("localhost", 27017)
mongoClient: com.mongodb.casbah.MongoClient = com.mongodb.casbah.
MongoClient@6fd10428
scala> val db = mongoClient("test")
db: com.mongodb.casbah.MongoDB = test
scala> val coll = db("test")
coll: com.mongodb.casbah.MongoCollection = test
```

These statements have, so far, been executed without a direct contact with the database. From now on, we need to make sure we have a running instance of the MongoDB process before we retrieve any content. Start the `mongod` daemon if it is not running yet (download instructions can be found at `https://www.mongodb.org/downloads`), then enter the following command to fetch the names of the stored collections:

```
scala> db.collectionNames
res0: scala.collection.mutable.Set[String] = Set()
```

We obviously get an empty set as a result, as we haven't stored any document yet. Let's create a couple of entries:

```
scala> val sales   = MongoDBObject("title" -> "sales","amount"->50)
sales: com.mongodb.casbah.commons.Imports.DBObject = { "title" : "sales"
, "amount" : 50}
scala> val sweden   = MongoDBObject("country" -> "Sweden")
sweden: com.mongodb.casbah.commons.Imports.DBObject = { "country" :
"Sweden"}
```

The created items have yet to be added to the database, using the `insert` command as shown in the following commands:

```
scala> coll.insert(sales)
res1: com.mongodb.casbah.TypeImports.WriteResult = { "serverUsed" :
"localhost:27017" , "n" : 0 , "connectionId" : 7 , "err" :  null  , "ok"
: 1.0}
scala> coll.insert(sweden)
res2: com.mongodb.casbah.TypeImports.WriteResult = { "serverUsed" :
"localhost:27017" , "n" : 0 , "connectionId" : 7 , "err" :  null  , "ok"
: 1.0}
scala> coll.count()
res3: Int = 2
```

Retrieving the elements of the `coll` collection can be done using the `find` method:

```
scala> val documents = coll.find() foreach println
{ "_id" : { "$oid" : "530fd91d03645ab9c17d9012"} , "title" : "sales" ,
"amount" : 50}
{ "_id" : { "$oid" : "530fd92703645ab9c17d9013"} , "country" : "Sweden"}
documents: Unit = ()
```

Notice that a primary key for each document has been created as we did not provide any while inserting the document into the collection. You may as well retrieve a single document if you know exactly the object you are looking for and provide it as an argument. For this, the `findOne` method is available, passing a new `SearchedCountry` `MongoDBObject` as expressed in the following command lines:

```
scala> val searchedCountry  = MongoDBObject("country" -> "Sweden")

searchedCountry: com.mongodb.casbah.commons.Imports.DBObject = {
"country" : "Sweden"}

scala> val result = coll.findOne(searchedCountry)

result: Option[coll.T] = Some({ "_id" : { "$oid" :
"530fd92703645ab9c17d9013"} , "country" : "Sweden"})
```

As there might not always be a matching element, the `findOne` method returns `Option`, which in the previous case resulted in `Some(value)`, in contrast to the following empty result:

```
scala> val emptyResult = coll.findOne(MongoDBObject("country" ->
"France"))

emptyResult: Option[coll.T] = None
```

Deleting elements is performed with the `remove` method, which can be used in a manner similar to the `findOne` method:

```
scala> val result = coll.remove(searchedCountry)

result: com.mongodb.casbah.TypeImports.WriteResult = { "serverUsed" :
"localhost:27017" , "n" : 1 , "connectionId" : 9 , "err" :  null  , "ok"
: 1.0}

scala> val countryNoMore = coll.findOne(searchedCountry)

countryNoMore: Option[coll.T] = None
```

Finally, updating a document can be done as follows:

```
scala> sales

res3: com.mongodb.casbah.commons.Imports.DBObject = { "title" : "sales" ,
"amount" : 50}

scala> val newSales = MongoDBObject("title" -> "sales","amount"->100)

newSales: com.mongodb.casbah.commons.Imports.DBObject = { "title" :
"sales" , "amount" : 100

scala> val result = coll.update(sales,newSales)
```

```
result: com.mongodb.casbah.TypeImports.WriteResult = { "serverUsed" :
"localhost:27017" , "updatedExisting" : true , "n" : 1 , "connectionId" :
9 , "err" :  null  , "ok" : 1.0}
scala> coll.find foreach println
{ "_id" : { "$oid" : "530fd91d03645ab9c17d9012"} , "title" : "sales" ,
"amount" : 100}
```

We can see here that the primary key "530fd91d03645ab9c17d9012" is still the one we had when we initially inserted the `sales` document into the database, showing that the `update` operation was not a removal and then inserting a brand new element.

Updating multiple documents at once is also supported and we refer to the documentation available at `http://mongodb.github.io/casbah/guide/index.html` for further operations.

Applying MapReduce transformations

Among the great features of document-oriented databases such as MongoDB, there is the possibility to run the MapReduce functions. **MapReduce** is an approach where you break up a query or task into smaller chunks of work, and then aggregate the results of those chunks. To illustrate how a document-based approach can sometimes be useful in contrast with a traditional relational database, let's take a small example of financial consolidation. In such a domain, aggregating and calculating sales figures globally for a large corporation may involve working with a number of orthogonal dimensions. For instance, sales figures can be gathered from each subsidiary that each has its own geographic location, time intervals, own currency, and specific categories, following some tree-based structures in each dimension as depicted in the following figure:

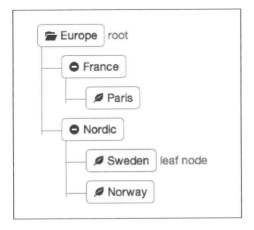

The geographic location might be a decisive factor when it comes to the currency used, and conversion should be done to sum figures consistently. To that extent, the currency used to produce global reports usually follows the root of the company ownership tree. A company tree structure is given in the following figure:

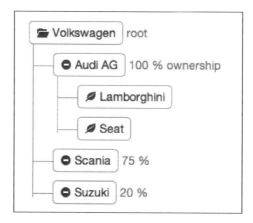

Similarly, various sales categories might define yet another hierarchy, as shown on the following figure:

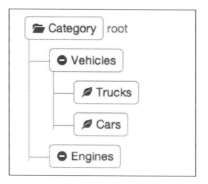

Such reported sales figures may either be very detailed or already accumulated, therefore, reported at various levels of the hierarchies. As large corporations are usually made of smaller groups with various degrees of ownership that are furthermore changing regularly, the consolidation job requires to aggregate and compute data according to all these parameters.

As for a number of data warehousing solutions expressed in relational databases, the heart of the domain model can be a huge table containing facts referring to the various dimensions expressed in the previous figure. For instance, some sample input data for this example can consist in the following list of sales figures (that is, amounts) as XML rows:

```
<dataset>
  <AMT month="2004-12" company="AUDI AG" cur="SEK" acct="A" dim1="CAR" dim2="NOR" amt="12"/>
  <AMT month="2004-12" company="AUDI AG" cur="SEK" acct="A" dim1="CAR" dim2="SWE" amt="24"/>
  <AMT month="2004-12" company="AUDI AG" cur="EUR" acct="A" dim1="CAR" dim2="FRA" amt="36"/>
  <AMT month="2004-12" company="AUDI AG" cur="SEK" acct="A" dim1="ENG" dim2="SWE" amt="48"/>
  <AMT month="2004-12" company="LAMBORGHINI" cur="EUR" acct="B" dim1="CAR" dim2="EUROPE" amt="10"/>
  <AMT month="2004-12" company="LAMBORGHINI" cur="SEK" acct="B" dim1="CAR" dim2="SWE" amt="30"/>
  <AMT month="2004-12" company="LAMBORGHINI" cur="SEK" acct="B" dim1="CAR" dim2="NOR" amt="50"/>
  <AMT month="2004-12" company="LAMBORGHINI" cur="SEK" acct="B" dim1="CAR" dim2="SWE" amt="12"/>
  <AMT month="2004-12" company="SCANIA" cur="EUR" acct="B" dim1="TRUCK" dim2="NORDIC" amt="50"/>
  <AMT month="2004-12" company="SCANIA" cur="SEK" acct="B" dim1="TRUCK" dim2="SWE" amt="36"/>
  <AMT month="2004-12" company="SCANIA" cur="SEK" acct="B" dim1="ENGINE" dim2="NOR" amt="3"/>
  <AMT month="2004-12" company="SCANIA" cur="EUR" acct="B" dim1="ENGINE" dim2="FRA" amt="10"/>
  <AMT month="2004-12" company="SEAT" cur="SEK" acct="B" dim1="CAR" dim2="NOR" amt="2"/>
  <AMT month="2004-12" company="SEAT" cur="EUR" acct="B" dim1="CAR" dim2="FRA" amt="16"/>
  <AMT month="2004-12" company="SUZUKI" cur="SEK" acct="B" dim1="ENGINE" dim2="NOR" amt="4"/>
  <AMT month="2004-12" company="SUZUKI" cur="SEK" acct="B" dim1="CAR" dim2="SWE" amt="20"/>
</dataset>
```

The following construct shows how to represent a tree structure in JSON:

```
{
  "title" : "root",
  "children" : [
    {
      "title" : "node 1",
      "children" : [
        {
          "title" : "node 1.1",
          "children" : [
            ...
          ]
        },
        {
          "title" : "node 1.2",
          "children" : [
            ...
          ]
        }
      ]
    },
    {
      "title" : "node 2",
      "children" : [
        ...
      ]
    }
  ]
}
```

The following is an example of a JSON document that contains sales figures by geographic location:

```
{
  "title" : "sales",
  "regions" : [
    {
      "title" : "nordic",
      "regions" : [
        {
          "title" : "norway",
          "amount" : 150
        },
        {
          "title" : "sweden",
          "amount" : 200
        }
      ]
    },
    {
      "title" : "france",
      "amount" : 400
    }
  ]
}
```

By storing documents coming from various subsidiaries of a large corporation, such as JSON, we can consolidate the figures through MapReduce transformations already supported by the database. Moreover, Casbah takes advantage of the aggregation framework (`http://mongodb.github.io/casbah/guide/aggregation.html`) of MongoDB to be able to aggregate values without having to use MapReduce

To conclude with MongoDB, we will just mention the ReactiveMongo project (`www.reactivemongo.org`) that figures a reactive asynchronous and non-blocking driver for MongoDB. As it uses the Iteratee pattern that we covered in *Chapter 9, Building Reactive Web Applications*, combining it with a stream-friendly framework, such as Play, can result in a number of interesting and scalable demos, as listed on their website.

Scratching the surface of Big Data

Among the recent achievements and trends towards better analysis of data and services lies the Big Data movement. In particular, the Hadoop framework has established some kind of ad hoc standard "for the distributed processing of large datasets across clusters of computers using simple programming models". In addition to a distributed file system called HDFS optimized for high throughput to access data, Hadoop offers MapReduce facilities for processing large datasets in parallel. As setting up and running Hadoop is not always considered a simple task, some other frameworks have been developed on top of Hadoop as a means to simplify the definition of Hadoop jobs. In Java, the Cascading framework is a layer on top of Hadoop that provides a convenient API to facilitate creation of MapReduce jobs. In Scala, the Scalding framework has been developed to further enhance the cascading API by utilizing the concise and expressive Scala syntax, as we can observe by taking a look at the `activator-scalding` Typesafe activator template. The sample code provided with this template illustrates a word counting application, that is, the `hello-world` project of Hadoop MapReduce jobs.

As a reminder on MapReduce jobs, consider reading the original paper from Google, available at `http://static.googleusercontent.com/media/research.google.com/en//archive/mapreduce-osdi04.pdf`

We can express the job of counting words with the following two steps:

- Splitting lines from a file into individual words and creating a key-value pair for each word, where key is the word of the `String` type and value is the constant `1`

- By grouping the elements having the same key (grouping the same words) into a list and reducing the list by summing the values, we obtain our goal

If you run the `> activator ui` command in a terminal window, as we already did a number of times in *Chapter 3, Understanding the Scala Ecosystem*, and create the `activator-scalding` template project, you can verify how concise the word count in scalding is specified. Do not forget to run the `> activator eclipse` command to be able to import the project into the Eclipse IDE:

```
class WordCount(args : Args) extends Job(args) {

    // Tokenize into words by by splitting on non-characters. This
    // is imperfect, as it splits hyphenated words, possessives
```

```
// ("John's"), etc.
val tokenizerRegex = """\W+"""

// Read the file specified by the --input argument and process
// each line by trimming the leading and trailing whitespace,
// converting to lower case,then tokenizing into words.
// The first argument list to flatMap specifies that we pass the
// 'line field to the anonymous function on each call and each
// word in the returned collection of words is given the name
// 'word. Note that TextLine automatically associates the name
// 'line with each line of text. It also tracks the line number
// and names that field 'offset. Here, we're dropping the
// offset.

TextLine(args("input"))
  .read
  .flatMap('line -> 'word) {
    line : String => line.trim.toLowerCase.split(tokenizerRegex)
  }

// At this point we have a stream of words in the pipeline. To
// count occurrences of the same word, we need to group the
// words together. The groupBy operation does this. The first
// argument list to groupBy specifies the fields to group over
// as the key. In this case, we only use the 'word field.
// The anonymous function is passed an object of type
// com.twitter.scalding.GroupBuilder. All we need to do is
// compute the size of the group and we give it an optional
// name, 'count.
  .groupBy('word){ group => group.size('count) }

// In many data flows, we would need to project out just the
// 'word and 'count, since we don't care about them any more,
// but groupBy has already eliminated everything but 'word and
// 'count. Hence, we'll just write them out as tab-delimited
// values.
  .write(Tsv(args("output")))
}
```

Most of the code is indeed comments, which means that the whole algorithm is very close to the description one would do in pseudo code.

If you are interested in Big Data, Scala definitely fits a niche and a number of projects and frameworks handling huge streams of data and Hadoop-like jobs are already pushing the limits. Among them, we can mention Spark (`http://spark.apache.org`) as well as Twitter's open-source projects SummingBird (`https://github.com/twitter/summingbird`) and Algebird (`https://github.com/twitter/algebird`).

Introducing DSLs in Scala

Domain specific language (**DSL**) is usually useful to simplify the interaction with a system by being applied to a small particular domain. They can be targeted to programmers by providing a simplified API to communicate with a system; or they may concern the so-called "business users" who may understand a domain well enough to create some scripts but are not programmers and could have difficulty dealing with a general-purpose programming language. There are, in general, two types of DSLs:

- Internal DSLs
- External DSLs

Observing internal DSLs

Internal DSLs use a host language (for instance, Scala) and the simplified usage is obtained by adding some syntactic sugar, through tricks and special constructs of the language. The book *DSLs in Action* by Debasish Ghosh illustrates the construction of Scala internal DSLs using features of the language such as infix notation and implicit conversions.

He has given the following DSL usage example that represents an executable program expressed in clear English: `200 discount bonds IBM for_client NOMURA on NYSE at 72.ccy(USD)`. Many transformations happen under the hood, but the business user is given a very clean syntax.

Such DSLs have the advantage that you are confident that you can express anything with them as the host language is of generic purpose (such as Scala). This means that sometimes you may be constrained to use a less clean syntax but you know you have the full power of the Scala compiler under your hands. Therefore, you will always succeed in producing a DSL script or program that implements the logic you want.

However, the full power of the compiler may also be something that you would like to avoid in many cases where you want to give your business user the possibility to only perform a few specific actions. For this purpose, you may implement external DSLs instead. There are a number of additional concerns including constrained syntax (for example, you can't avoid parentheses in some cases) and convoluted error messages.

Tackling external DSLs through parser combinators

An external DSL represents a domain language where the syntax is completely up to you. This means you can express things exactly the way you want to and can constrain your business users to only use specific words or meanings. This flexibility comes with a price of much more work to implement it as you need to define a grammar (typically **Backus–Naur Form (BNF)**), that is, define all the rules that apply to parse a meaning or script successfully. In Java, the task to write an external DSL can be cumbersome and it usually involves the ANTLR external framework.

In Scala, parser combinators are a notion very close to the definition of BNF grammars and can provide very concise and elegant code when writing external DSLs.

Once you get acquainted with a few particular operators to deal with the definition of the grammar, you will discover that writing an external DSL is fairly straightforward if your language is not too complex. A good source of information to learn all the symbols and operators involved in parser combinators is available at http://bitwalker.github.io/blog/2013/08/10/learn-by-example-scala -parser-combinators/.

The following experimental code illustrates a small DSL in the domain of finance consolidation where specific money accounts are manipulated as part of predefined formulae. The main method given at the end of the following snippet reflects a formula; for instance, you may parse the formula (3*#ACCOUNT1#) to construct an object-oriented structure that will be able to compute the result of multiplying the content of a given account by three:

```
package parsercombinator

import scala.util.parsing.combinator._
import java.text.SimpleDateFormat
import java.util.Date

object FormulaCalculator {

  abstract class Node

  case class Transaction(amount: Int)
  case class Account(name:String) extends Node {
```

```
    var transactions: Iterable[Transaction] = List.empty
  }

  def addNewTransaction(startingBalance: Int, t: Transaction) =
startingBalance + t.amount
  def balance(account: Account) = account.transactions.foldLeft(0)
(addNewTransaction)

  case class NumberOfPeriods (value: Int) extends Node {
    override def toString = value.toString
  }
  case class RelativePeriod (value:String) extends Node {
    override def toString = value
  }
  case class Variable(name : String) extends Node
  case class Number(value : Double) extends Node
  case class UnaryOp(operator : String, arg : Node) extends Node
  case class BinaryOp(operator : String, left : Node, right : Node)
extends Node
  case class Function(name:String,arguments:List[Node]) extends Node {
    override def toString =
      name+arguments.mkString("(",",",")")
  }...
```

The objects that will result from the parsing of a formula are defined as **case classes**. Hence, continuing with the code:

```
  ...
  def evaluate(e : Node) : Double = {
    e match {
      case Number(x) => x
      case UnaryOp("-", x) => -(evaluate(x))
      case BinaryOp("+", x1, x2) => (evaluate(x1) + evaluate(x2))
      case BinaryOp("-", x1, x2) => (evaluate(x1) - evaluate(x2))
      case BinaryOp("*", x1, x2) => (evaluate(x1) * evaluate(x2))
      case BinaryOp("/", x1, x2) => (evaluate(x1) / evaluate(x2))
    }
  }

  object FormulaParser extends JavaTokenParsers {

    val identifier: Parser[String] = ident
```

```scala
    val relative_period: Parser[RelativePeriod] = """([N|P|\+|\-]
[0-9]+|CURRENT)""".r ^^ RelativePeriod
    val number_of_periods: Parser[NumberOfPeriods] = """\d+""".r ^^ (i
=> NumberOfPeriods(i.toInt))
    val account_name: Parser[String] = """[A-Za-z0-9_]+""".r

    def account: Parser[Account] = "#" ~> account_name <~ "#" ^^ {
Account(_) }

    def function: Parser[Function] =
      identifier~"("~account~","~relative_period~","~number_of_
periods~")" ^^ {
        case f~"("~acc~","~rp~","~nbp~")" =>
Function(f,List(acc,rp,nbp))
      } |
      identifier~"("~account~","~relative_period~")" ^^ {
        case f~"("~acc~","~rp~")" => Function(f,List(acc,rp))
      }

    def node: Parser[Node] =
        (term ~ "+" ~ term) ^^ { case lhs~plus~rhs => BinaryOp("+",
lhs, rhs) } |
        (term ~ "-" ~ term) ^^ { case lhs~minus~rhs => BinaryOp("-",
lhs, rhs) } |
        term

    def term: Parser[Node] =
        (factor ~ "*" ~ factor) ^^ { case lhs~times~rhs =>
BinaryOp("*", lhs, rhs) } |
        (factor ~ "/" ~ factor) ^^ { case lhs~div~rhs => BinaryOp("/",
lhs, rhs) } |
        (factor ~ "^" ~ factor) ^^ { case lhs~exp~rhs => BinaryOp("^",
lhs, rhs) } |
        factor

    def factor : Parser[Node] =
        "(" ~> node <~ ")" |
        floatingPointNumber ^^ {x => Number(x.toFloat) } |
        account |
        function

    def parse(text : String) =
```

```
                parseAll(node, text)
    }


    // Parses 3 formula that make computations on accounts
    def main(args: Array[String]) {

        val formulaList = List("3*#ACCOUNT1#","#ACCOUNT1#-
#ACCOUNT2#","AVERAGE_UNDER_PERIOD(#ACCOUNT4#,+1,12)")

        formulaList.foreach { formula =>
            val unspacedFormula = formula.replaceAll("[ ]+","")
            println(s"Parsing of $formula gives result:\n
${FormulaParser.parse(unspacedFormula)}")
        }
    }
}
```

If we execute this parser combinator code into Eclipse by simply right-clicking on the `FormulaCalculator` class and navigating to **Run As | Scala Application**, we should obtain the following output in the Eclipse console:

```
Parsing of 3*#ACCOUNT1# gives result:
  [1.13] parsed: BinaryOp(*,Number(3.0),Account(ACCOUNT1))
Parsing of #ACCOUNT1#- #ACCOUNT2# gives result:
  [1.22] parsed: BinaryOp(-,Account(ACCOUNT1),Account(ACCOUNT2))
Parsing of AVERAGE_UNDER_PERIOD(#ACCOUNT4#,+1,12) gives result:
  [1.39] parsed: AVERAGE_UNDER_PERIOD(Account(ACCOUNT4),+1,12)
```

This output shows that the three formulae were parsed correctly and converted into classes. The final evaluation is left out from this exercise but could be set up with some actual transactions defined on the two accounts.

Introducing Scala.js

Where Java is a compelling choice to run server-side code due to its robust JVM that can be run anywhere, JavaScript is increasingly becoming the dominant choice on the client side due to its flexibility and light runtime-embedded environment as well as its growing set of tools already available in the browsers. Despite its popularity, JavaScript being a dynamic language does not offer the type of safety that languages such as Java or Scala provide. The experimental but fast-growing Scala.js initiative aims at compiling Scala to JavaScript and in my view offers a really good alternative for those who want to benefit from the power of the Scala type system all the way to the browser.

Setting up a project demonstrating the usage of Scala.js can be done in a couple of minutes and is explained in the sample "getting started" project available at `https://github.com/sjrd/scala-js-example-app`.

The example consists of a small HTML page containing a `playground` `<div>` element as illustrated in the following HTML code:

```
<!DOCTYPE html>
<html>
<head>
  <title>Example Scala.js application</title>
  <meta http-equiv="Content-Type" content="text/html; charset=UTF-8"/>
</head>
<body>

<h1>Example Scala.js application - development version</h1>

<p>After having compiled and packaged properly the code for the
application
(using `sbt packageJS`), you should see "It works" here below.
See README.md for detailed explanations.</p>

<div id="playground">
</div>

<script type="text/javascript" src="./target/scala-2.10/
example-extdeps.js"></script>
<script type="text/javascript" src="./target/scala-2.10/
example-intdeps.js"></script>
<script type="text/javascript" src="./target/scala-2.10/
example.js"></script>

</body>
</html>
```

The `div` element will be dynamically populated as:

```
<p>
  <strong>It works!</strong>
</p>
```

The tiny snippet of code written in Scala and compiled to Javascript to achieve this is given in the following `main` method:

```
package example

import scala.scalajs.js
import js.Dynamic.{ global => g }

object ScalaJSExample {
  def main(): Unit = {
    val paragraph = g.document.createElement("p")
    paragraph.innerHTML = "<strong>It works!</strong>"
    g.document.getElementById("playground").appendChild(paragraph)
  }

  /** Computes the square of an integer.
   *  This demonstrates unit testing.
   */
  def square(x: Int): Int = x*x
}
```

Once we have the access to the DOM of the HTML page through the `js.Dynamic.global` object, this simple Scala `main` method constructs a new paragraph node and adds it to the existing `"playground"` node.

The additional `square` method is used to illustrate a unit test written against the Jasmine JavaScript test framework.

The execution of the `main` method is triggered by the one line added to the `js/startup.js` file:

```
ScalaJS.modules.example_ScalaJSExample().main();
```

The generated code produced by default by Scala.js can be quite big because of dependencies to Scala libraries. Scala.js offers an optimization through Google's closure compiler that reduces the size and optimizes the JavaScript code execution when targeted for production environments.

What is the next step now? Well, we can refer interested readers to a couple of more projects that we find interesting with regard to this book:

- A project called `play-with-scalajs-example` and available at `https://github.com/vmunier/play-with-scalajs-example` deals with a simple integration sample of Scala.js and the Play Framework that we have covered in the previous chapters.

- A very interesting and more advanced usage of Scala.js is `TodoMVC` and this is a part of the `workbench-example-app` project available at `https://github.com/lihaoyi/workbench-example-app/`. It demonstrates a sample web app for making To Do Lists, a reference app specified to compare different implementations done in various languages, but has the innovative approach of being reactive in addition to being written in Scala compiled to JavaScript. A direct link to the resulting reactive web app is available at `http://lihaoyi.github.io/workbench-example-app/todo.html` and is rendered in a browser, as shown in the following screenshot:

There are already a number of projects around Scala.js listed on its home page at `http://www.scala-js.org/`. As Scala.js is maturing quickly, many more projects should be soon available.

Final tips

The following sections enlist a few final tips and tricks that you might find handy while working with the REPL.

Copying and pasting in the REPL

As a reminder, this feature introduced in *Chapter 8, Essential Properties of Modern Applications – Asynchrony and Concurrency*, makes it easy to execute a full code snippet at once in the REPL. For instance, the following lines of command illustrate how the copy and paste feature in REPL helps the easy execution of code:

```
scala> :paste
// Entering paste mode (ctrl-D to finish)

[Copy a code block from somewhere with ctrl-C/ctrl-V]

  case class Person(name:String)

  val me = Person("Thomas")
  val you = Person("Current Reader")


  val we = List(you,me).map(_.name).reduceLeft(_+" & "+_)
  val status = s"$we have fun with Scala"


[Once you are done with pasting the code block, press ctrl-D]

// Exiting paste mode, now interpreting.

defined class Person
me: Person = Person(Thomas)
you: Person = Person(Current Reader)
we: String = Current Reader & Thomas
status: String = Current Reader & Thomas have fun with Scala
```

Timing code execution in the REPL

The REPL has been a very helpful tool throughout this book to discover and
experiment with the various features of Scala. Together with the Scala worksheets
introduced in *Chapter 3, Understanding the Scala Ecosystem,* they enhance our
productivity by providing continuous feedback and make our development,
therefore, more agile. Sometimes, it is convenient to measure the time it takes to
execute statements or code snippets in the REPL. This is why we have given one
way of achieving this.

First, we define a `help` function called `using` that takes two parameters, first a `param`
argument of the type A and second, a function argument f that transforms
the type of an argument from A into B:

```
scala> def using[A <: {def close(): Unit},B](param: A)(f: A=>B): B =
  try { f(param) } finally { param.close() }
using: [A <: AnyRef{def close(): Unit}, B](param: A)(f: A => B)B
```

What `using` does is to invoke the `f(param)` function, wrapping it into a `try {}` `finally{}` block. As the idea behind this function is to apply it on an I/O resource such as `FileWriter` or `PrintWriter`, we want to guarantee that we can close the resource no matter what. This is why you can see a `param.close` call in the `finally` block. That means the `param` argument cannot just be of any type `A`; it must have the additional requirement to have a `close` method. This is exactly what is declared at the beginning of the definition of the generic `using` method (that is, `[A <: {def close(): Unit}, B]`); the `param` argument should be a subtype of `A` that contains a method with the given signature.

In general, dealing with generic types is out of the scope of this book, and you don't need to really understand the previous definition to benefit from the `using` function. The example illustrates, however, how powerful the use of generic types in Scala can be. The type system of Scala is extremely powerful and the compiler will help you very much when writing generic code, unlike the use of generics in Java.

Let's now include the `using` function into an `appendToFile` function that will be responsible for logging the evaluation of the code we write in the REPL:

```scala
scala> def appendToFile(fileName:String, textData:String) =
  using (new java.io.FileWriter(fileName, true)){
    fileWriter => using (new java.io.PrintWriter(fileWriter)) {
      printWriter => printWriter.println(textData)
    }
  }
appendToFile: (fileName: String, textData: String)Unit
```

Finally, the following `timeAndLogged` function is declared to wrap a body snippet entered in the REPL with both the logging and timing functionalities:

```scala
scala> def timedAndLogged[T](body: => T): T = {
    val start = System.nanoTime
    try {
        val result = body
        appendToFile("/tmp/repl.log",result.toString)
        result
    }
    finally println(" "+(System.nanoTime - start) + " nanos elapsed.
")
}
timedAndLogged: [T](body: => T)T
```

Until Scala 2.10.0, you could use the :wrap method of the REPL power mode (accessible from the REPL via the > :power command) to be able to execute all the console statements without further involvement of the timedAndLogged function. The :wrap feature has recently been removed from the Scala release, so you will have to explicitly wrap the code that you want timing or logging for in the timedAndLogged method and therefore, do not need to involve the power mode of the REPL for that.

For instance, you can execute the following command:

```
scala> timedAndLogged{ val input = 2014 ; println(input) ; Thread.
sleep(2000) ; input }

2014
 2004778000 nanos elapsed.
res0: Int = 2014
```

The /tmp/repl.log file we specified in the timedAndLogged function should, of course, contain the logged result, that is, 2014.

Summary

As we now reach the end of this book, we would like to emphasize some key aspects on the numerous topics and concepts we have approached during this journey with Scala.

The concise and expressive syntax of the Scala language should make your code not only more readable but also more maintainable for yourself and other developers. You don't have to give up any of the libraries of the very large and mature Java ecosystem as all the APIs can be reused directly within Scala. Moreover, you benefit from many additional great Scala-specific libraries. Our recommendation is to take a piece of Java code from a domain you understand well, maybe because you wrote it in the first place one or several times before. Then, try to convert it to Scala code and refactor it to get rid of the boilerplate and to make it in a more functional style.

The Play Framework is not just another web framework; it breaks the conventional approach of long-cycle development following servlet and EJB containers where each redeploy can take a significant time. Moreover, it is built on top of rock solid and scalable technologies such as Akka, which should make you feel confident for future heavy loads and constraining availability requirements. Finally, our personal experience with it has been very enjoyable as the Scala compiler behind it has, most of the time, given very clear feedback on what the problems are when mistakes are made, all the way to the templates and routes specifications. As both Play and Akka are exposing Java APIs as well, they can make your transition easier.

We believe the future of web development is reactive, dealing with large streams of data, as it is already happening in many areas such as social media sites involving content distribution and real-time financial/analytics services.

We have only scratched the surface of what is possible to do with Scala. As you go along and dive more deeply into individual technologies, you will discover new features and endless possibilities. Our recommendation is to take one step at a time looking for achievable goals. For instance, first get used to the Scala collections, especially as they can help you to better master Java lambdas and functional programming, then write code with pattern matching, traits, for comprehensions, then move to more advanced topics such as implicits, generics and so on.

Finally, as inspiration, there is already a tremendous number of open source projects done with Scala, many books on the individual subjects we have covered, many forums contributed by a very active Scala community, as well as several years of extremely useful online videos coming from user groups and international conferences such as Scaladays (`www.scaladays.org`), Scala eXchange (`www.skillsmatter.com/conferences/1948-scala-exchange-2014`), NEScala (`www.nescala.org`), Jfokus (`www.jfokus.se`), Scala.io (`www.scala.io`), flatMap (`www.flatmap.no`), Ping (`www.ping-conf.com`), and Scalapeño (`www.scalapeno.underscore.co.il`), to only name a few. A whole calendar site of Scala events is available at `http://www.scala2014.org`.

With that in mind, I hope you enjoyed the book enough to continue exploring Scala, writing awesome code, and having fun as much as we did!

Index

require assertion 200
REST API
  creating, from existing database 35
  JPA entities, creating 37, 38
  Maven project, setting up 37
  project, running 38, 39
  project, testing 38
  REST web service, creating 37, 38
  sample database 36
REST web service
  creating 37, 38
ResultSet object 137
run method 215

S

SBT
  about 44, 60
  code, formatting with Scalariform 68
  Eclipse project, importing 62
  IntelliJ 62
  sample project, creating 61
  single .jar archive building, sbt-assembly
      used 67
  web application, creating 64-67
sbt-assembly
  using, to build single .jar archive 67, 68
sbteclipse plugin 62, 88, 157
sbt-idea plugin 63
Scala
  DSLs 245
  JPA availability 128-135
  learning, through REPL 14
  setting up, within Java Maven project
      41, 43
  test, adding 40, 41
  XML data, binding 156-159
Scala and Java collaboration
  about 44
  collection types 44, 45
  companion objects 50
  enhanced Java interfaces 48, 50
  exceptions, handling 51-53
  JavaBean-style properties 45
  object orientation 46-48
  objects, declaring 50

ScalaCheck
  testing with 101-104
Scaladays 256
Scala dispatch library
  URL 70
Scala events 256
Scala eXchange 256
Scala for Java projects
  advantages 9-14
Scala Improvement Process (SIP) 188
Scala.io 256
Scala.js 249-252
ScalaMock
  mocking with 96-101
  URL 96
Scala REPL (Read-Eval-Print-Loop)
  about 14
  case classes 18-24
  classes, defining 16-18
  val variables, declaring 14-16
  var variables, declaring 14-16
Scalariform
  code, formatting with 68
ScalaTest
  about 88
  BDD-style testing 91-94
  functional testing 94, 96
  URL 87
ScalaTest class 88
scala.util.Try class 54
Scala Worksheets 68-70
scalaxb
  running, from SOAP web service 160-163
scalaxb library 156
Selenium tool
  URL 94
Server Side Events (SSE) 223
Simple Build Tool. See SBT
single .jar archive
  building, sbt-assembly used 67, 68
singleOpt method 137
Slick framework
  about 140-144
  benefits 139
SOAP web service
  scalaxb, running from 160-163

social security number (ssn) 15
Spark 245
Specs2
  URL 87
Spring
  URL 128
square method 251
static keyword 50
StockActor 222
streams
  handling 212
String Interpolation 32
StringSpecification test 102
SummingBird 245
system.actorOf method 198

T

TAB completion 17
test
  adding 40, 41
testing
  BDD-style testing 91
  functional testing 94
  tools 87
test-only command 90
timeAndLogged function 254
timedAndLogged function 255
timedAndLogged method 255
timing code execution, REPL 253-255
TravelAgent object 201
tuples 28
Type Inference 15
Typesafe Activator
  about 79, 111
  application creating, based on activator
    templates 80-83
Typesafe page
  URL 12

U

unit test
  adding, in Java 40
using function 254
using method 254

V

view, Play application
  rendering 119-121
VIPCustomer class 49

W

web application
  creating 64-67
web services
  calling, from Play 176-184
Web Services Description Language
    (WSDL) 160
WebSocket.async[JsValue] method 224
WebSockets 218-221
with keyword 49
Worksheets. *See* Scala Worksheets

X

XML
  manipulating 164-166
  Play requests, handling with 172, 173
XML data
  binding 155-159

Thank you for buying
Scala for Java Developers

About Packt Publishing

Packt, pronounced 'packed', published its first book "*Mastering phpMyAdmin for Effective MySQL Management*" in April 2004 and subsequently continued to specialize in publishing highly focused books on specific technologies and solutions.

Our books and publications share the experiences of your fellow IT professionals in adapting and customizing today's systems, applications, and frameworks. Our solution based books give you the knowledge and power to customize the software and technologies you're using to get the job done. Packt books are more specific and less general than the IT books you have seen in the past. Our unique business model allows us to bring you more focused information, giving you more of what you need to know, and less of what you don't.

Packt is a modern, yet unique publishing company, which focuses on producing quality, cutting-edge books for communities of developers, administrators, and newbies alike. For more information, please visit our website: www.packtpub.com.

About Packt Open Source

In 2010, Packt launched two new brands, Packt Open Source and Packt Enterprise, in order to continue its focus on specialization. This book is part of the Packt Open Source brand, home to books published on software built around Open Source licences, and offering information to anybody from advanced developers to budding web designers. The Open Source brand also runs Packt's Open Source Royalty Scheme, by which Packt gives a royalty to each Open Source project about whose software a book is sold.

Writing for Packt

We welcome all inquiries from people who are interested in authoring. Book proposals should be sent to author@packtpub.com. If your book idea is still at an early stage and you would like to discuss it first before writing a formal book proposal, contact us; one of our commissioning editors will get in touch with you.

We're not just looking for published authors; if you have strong technical skills but no writing experience, our experienced editors can help you develop a writing career, or simply get some additional reward for your expertise.

Learning Play! Framework 2

ISBN: 978-1-78216-012-0   Paperback: 290 pages

Start developing awesome web applications with this friendly, practical guide to the Play! Framework

1. While driving in Java, tasks are also presented in Scala – a great way to be introduced to this amazing language.

2. Create a fully-fledged, collaborative web application – starting from ground zero; all layers are presented in a pragmatic way.

3. Gain the advantages associated with developing a fully integrated web framework.

Java EE 7 Developer Handbook

ISBN: 978-1-84968-794-2   Paperback: 634 pages

Develop professional applications in Java EE 7 with this essential reference guide

1. Learn about local and remote service endpoints, containers, architecture, synchronous and asynchronous invocations, and remote communications in a concise reference.

2. Understand the architecture of the Java EE platform and then apply the new Java EE 7 enhancements to benefit your own business-critical applications.

3. Learn about integration test development on Java EE with Arquillian Framework and the Gradle build system.

Please check **www.PacktPub.com** for information on our titles

Printed in Great Britain
by Amazon